Monastic Perspectives on Temporality

Riitta Hujanen

Monastic Perspectives on Temporality

Time is a Mirage

Riitta Hujanen
Helsinki, Finland

ISBN 978-3-031-34807-5   ISBN 978-3-031-34808-2   (eBook)
https://doi.org/10.1007/978-3-031-34808-2

This Palgrave Macmillan imprint is published by the registered company Springer Nature Switzerland AG.
The registered company address is: Gewerbestrasse 11, 6330 Cham, Switzerland

ACKNOWLEDGEMENTS

This book is based on my PhD dissertation 'Cloistered Journeys Through Time: Paradoxical Dynamics of Enclosed Contemplative Traditions'. It was approved by Liverpool Hope University in the UK in late 2022. At the end of the *viva voce* examination, the examiners Dr. Ashley Cocksworth and Revd Dr. Michael Cullinan and the Chair Dr. William Blazek encouraged me to seek publication of this research. Senior Editor Philp Getz at Palgrave Macmillan took the challenge and helped me to take the project to the next level. By turning the doctoral dissertation into a monograph we aim to share this academic survey to wider audiences. We invite the reader to join an exploratory research journey into monastic perspectives on temporality through centuries of contemplative traditions.

As for the PhD research, I am extremely grateful to my Director of Studies Professor Mary Mills and my Research Supervisor Dr. Catherine Knowles for their insights, guidance and unfailing support. Their faith in this project, from the very beginning to the end, was invaluable. I would also like to extend my gratitude to the three Doctors who accompanied me, each through their unique contributions, at various stages of the research journey: Dr. Harry Schnitker, Dr. Cyprian Blamires, and Abbot Geoffrey Scott, OSB, of Douai Abbey.

In addition, I wish to express my gratitude to the staff at Maryvale Institute, especially Dr. Birute Briliute. I would also like to thank my fellow doctoral students at Maryvale for their shared wisdom along the way, with special thanks to Dr. Tamra Hull Fromm and Dr. Marcelo Navarro for proofreading and checking my work at various stages. The Dominican libraries in Helsinki, Finland, and Nice, France, as well as

Maryvale Institute library in Birmingham, UK, gave me access to monastic sources and other relevant literature, for which I am grateful.

My appreciation goes out to the many Bridgettines, Carmelites, Carthusians, Dominicans, Augustinians, Benedictines, Cistercians, Ursulines, Missionaries of Charity and Sisters of St. Andrew who I have crossed paths with. Your way of life remains a timeless inspiration.

CONTENTS

ABBREVIATIONS

IHM	Sisters, Servants of the Immaculate Heart of Mary
O.Carm.	Order of the Brothers of the Blessed Virgin Mary of Mount Carmel
O.Cart.	The Order of Carthusians
OCD	Order of the Discalced Carmelites of the Blessed Virgin Mary of Mount Carmel
OCSO	The Order of Cistercians of the Strict Observance (Trappists)
OP	The Order of Preachers, The Dominican Order
OSA	The Order of Saint Augustine, The Augustinian Order
OSB	The Order of Saint Benedict, The Benedictine Order
RB	The Rule of Saint Benedict
SC	Sisters of Charity
SGS	Sisters of the Good Samaritan of the Order of St Benedict
SJ	Society of Jesus
SNDdeN	Sisters of Notre Dame de Namur

LIST OF FIGURES

LIST OF TABLES

CHAPTER 1

Introduction

Why explore the concept of time among enclosed contemplatives?

It appears that despite the centuries-long history and the variety of enclosed contemplative traditions within Catholic monasticism, the concept of time has not previously been explored in the academic research.[1] There are understandable practical reasons for this. The concept of enclosure itself implies a desire for withdrawal and hiddenness. Yet, despite their enclosed way of life which embraces silence and solitude, members of contemplative religious orders can express meanings and experiences which are relevant to the external world. I believe that enclosed contemplatives have unique perspectives to share which 'the world needs to hear'.[2]

In order to reduce this gap of knowledge, the current study analysed monastic sources by exploring past and present monastic journeys travelled in Catholic contemplative cloisters through the lens of time. The

---

[1] The topic of contemplative spirituality, overall, appears under-researched. See, for example, Alison Woolley, in *Women Choosing Silence: Relationality and Transformation in Spiritual Practice* (Oxon: Routledge, 2019), 6, on lack of sustained exploration of practices of silence in practical theologians' studies.

[2] Gregg Levoy in 'Sacrifice: The Shadow in the Calling' in David Bryce Yaden, Theo D. McCall and J. Harold Ellens, eds., *Being Called: Scientific, Secular, and Sacred Perspectives* (Santa Barbara, CA: Praeger, 2015), 215–224: 217–218, on a counsel a rabbi gave to him about writing: 'it's not about you ... It's about something you need to say that you believe the world needs to hear ...'.

R. Hujanen, *Monastic Perspectives on Temporality*, https://doi.org/10.1007/978-3-031-34808-2_1

1

following was the primary research question: What do enclosed contemplatives think about time? The original idea was to investigate this broad question through interviews and other relevant sources that would reflect the perceptions and lived traditions of members of enclosed contemplative communities. In reality, it proved difficult to access enclosed communities through direct contacts and communication. Therefore, modifications of the research design were necessary. This required the adaptation of the original 'ideal' question from 'What do enclosed contemplatives think about time?' into a more 'answerable' form: 'What, on the basis of literature and other sources, can be said about what enclosed contemplatives might think about time?'

A modified approach to the research material was also necessary. Instead of interviews, a broader array of primary and secondary sources was chosen. This included published texts (books, homilies, letters, poems, and diaries written by enclosed contemplatives), some of which are not currently available in English translations; interviews of enclosed contemplatives found in published secondary sources; written and verbal descriptions by priests who had stayed in enclosed contemplative communities and shared this way of life for a period of time; and documentary films of enclosed contemplatives. Additionally, permissioned access was gained to two new original primary sources. The first relates to email correspondence with a cloistered contemplative (indicated as 'Mel', not the real name) during years 2012–2022. The second original primary source is a significant collection of unpublished poems and other writings by a Carthusian monk-poet (from the 1960s to 2022).[3]

The task was complex. The concept of time itself has many dimensions: time flows dynamically but—on the other hand—eternity indicates stability. Perceptions of time can change as well—with age and life experiences at the personal level, as well as with the development of monastic traditions over centuries. The availability and nature of sources can influence research results, especially when relying primarily on literary sources. What can be said, definitely, about even a single writer's perception of time? Here, the literary works of Thomas Merton could provide an example. Firstly, as indicated, a person's views may change significantly over time, as seems evident in Merton's case. Secondly, Merton's writings cover a broad

---

[3] For previous research on the Carthusian's poems, see Anna Maksjan, *The Mystical Dimension of the Poetry of John Bradburne and the Carthusian* (Salzburg: Institut für Anglistik und Amerikanistik, Universität Salzburg, 2007).

set of literary genres: poetry, scholarly and other publications, essays as well as personal diaries. He also used various literary styles, ranging from poetic to polemical. It might, therefore, be difficult to discern with conviction: What did Merton *really* think about time at various periods of his life? Yet, Merton left various traces of his thoughts, and we can at least conclude that the subject of 'time' was of enduring interest for him.

The initial research question stimulated additional questions. It is worth noting that the additional questions, derived from the primary question, were subject to the same modifications to make them more 'answerable'. Therefore, based on literature and other sources, what can be said about what enclosed contemplatives might think about these topics:

1. **Beginning of the Journey**. What makes a young person decide to dedicate their life inside a cloister? Do contemplatives have a preference for eternity over temporal time? To what extent did their perception of time influence the motivation and decision to spend a lifetime in an enclosed contemplative monastery?
2. **Time in Monastery**. How does the enclosed contemplative life impact one's concept of time? Is the enclosed monastic life experienced as monotonous? What is learned about relationship with God during a lifetime in a contemplative cloister?
3. **End of the Journey.** How is time perceived towards the end of one's monastic journey? What is seen when looking back to the years in the enclosed contemplative life? What is experienced at the hour of death?

The enquiry was mainly led by these three broad, fundamental research questions. It required persistent critical questioning and analysis: What does this text tell us about the concept of time as perceived by enclosed contemplative traditions? What is the context? What is the meaning of this writing from the monastic perspective?

1.1   Previous Research

It appears that this specific thematic question—the concept of time among enclosed contemplative traditions—has generated little academic research attention. While 'time' is a subject of a broad range of academic research approaches, this study focuses on monastic and non-monastic sources in order to explore the topic in the context of contemplative enclosed life within Catholic monastic traditions.

A few scholars, however, have written at least on some aspects of monasticism and time. Their key publications are briefly introduced here.

The most directly relevant study on the concept of time in monasticism is by Donato Ogliari, OSB, whose article 'Tempus Monasticum: Reflections on the Architecture of Time in the Rule of Saint Benedict' was published in the *American Benedictine Review* in 2008.[4] This article, while limiting its focus on the Rule of Saint Benedict, explores several aspects of 'monastic time'. This academic article on monastic time was interesting also because it was written by a Benedictine monk who leads a monastic life himself.

Katja Ritari's main field of research is in Celtic studies; within this discipline, she has previously published several articles and books on Irish monasticism in the early medieval period.[5] Her monograph on eschatology and monastic spirituality in early medieval Ireland was published in 2016,[6] with hagiographies and sermons from this period used as material to map out the Irish monastic allegory of lifelong pilgrimage as a journey to the afterlife. Ritari's work and observations contributed through the thematic links of monasticism, liminality, pilgrimage, and eschatology.

Carmel Bendon Davis's medieval literature study on 'space, spatiality and mysticism' can be described as a distant cousin to this current study on 'time, temporality and monasticism'. Davis's research focuses on space and spatiality in the works of three medieval mystics—Richard Rolle, *The Cloud of Unknowing* author, and Julian of Norwich. One relevant common touchpoint can be found in the simultaneous experience of immanence and transcendence that relates to both time and space. Regarding

---

[4] Donato Ogliari, 'Tempus Monasticum: Reflections of the Architecture of Time in the Rule of Saint Benedict' in *American Benedictine Review*, Vol. 59, no. 1 (March 2008), 35–52. For a related article from the perspective of the Rule of Saint Benedict, see also Russell L. Huizing, 'Benedictine Times: The Flow of Life in the Holy Rule', in *The Downside Review*, Vol. 131, no. 465 (October 2013), 171–183.

[5] Katja Ritari, 'Librán as Monastic Archetype', in John Carey, Kevin Murray, and Caitríona Ó Dochartaigh, eds., *Sacred Histories: A Festschrift for Máire Herbert* (Dublin: Four Courts Press, 2015), 391–400; '"Pilgrims in the World": Monastic Life as a Quest for Heaven in Early Medieval Ireland', in Riku Hämäläinen, Heikki Pesonen, Mari Rahkala and Tuula Sakaranaho, eds., *Pilgrimage of Life: Studies in Honour of Professor René Gothóni* (Helsinki: Maahenki, 2010), 333–45; 'Holy Souls and a Holy Community: The Meaning of Monastic Life in Adomnán's Vita Columbae', in *Journal of Medieval Religious Cultures*, Vol. 37, No. 2 (2011), 129–146.

[6] Katja Ritari, *Pilgrimage to Heaven: Eschatology and Monastic Spirituality in Early Medieval Ireland* (Turnhout: Brepols Publishers, 2016).

time, Davis suggests that mystical experience is unmediated by time and is, therefore, a transcendent experience even though the expression of that experience is immanent and reflective of contemporary social mores. Similarly, she claims, mystical space is also transcendent and immanent, absorbing and reflecting physical, social, textual, and spiritual dimensions simultaneously.[7] Davis's original idea of exploring medieval contemplative writings from the perspective of 'space' not only contributes to the aspect of enclosure but additionally offers the opportunity to complement our shared interest in spatiotemporal approaches with the perspective of 'time' in the enclosed contemplative life. Another connection is found in the theme of liminal experience, which Davis also identifies in her study.[8]

Australian theologian Jane Foulcher's study *Reclaiming Humility* can be considered another distant cousin to this current project.[9] Her approach, similarly, is thematic across various monastic traditions, from the Desert Fathers to the modern-day Trappists. In Foulcher's work, monastic tradition and spirituality is studied through the lens of 'humility'. Foulcher presents four separate sections in which she studies the virtue of humility in different monastic contexts: (1) humility and self in Desert Monasticism; (2) humility and community in the Rule of Saint Benedict; (3) humility and public life in Bernard of Clairvaux; (4) humility and the other in Christian de Chergé and the Monks of Tibhirine.

Theologian Alison Woolley has recently published a study on silence as a spiritual practice among lay and religious Christian women. Woolley identifies relationality and transformation as conceptual frameworks to explore the subject of silence. Grounded in the fields of feminist and practical theologies, she incorporates social science research methodologies in her interviews with contemplative women. She discovered that, irrespective of their initial reasons for exploring practices of silence, the research subjects of her study value these practices for facilitating transformation in their relationships with God, their temporally multiple selves, and with others.[10]

---

[7] Carmel Bendon Davis, *Mysticism and Space: Space and Spirituality in the Works of Richard Rolle, The Cloud of Unknowing Author, and Julian of Norwich* (Washington, D.C.: The Catholic University of America Press, 2008), 249.

[8] Davis, *Mysticism and Space*, 87–99.

[9] Jane Foulcher, *Reclaiming Humility: Four Studies in the Monastic Tradition* (Collegeville, MN: Liturgical Press, 2015).

[10] Woolley, *Women Choosing Silence*, 246–247.

1.1.1   Empirical Studies

For their survey on contemporary Catholic Sisters, Mary Johnson, S.N.D. de N., Patricia Wittberg, SC, and Mary L. Gautier, analysed two major national studies of female religious, conducted ten years apart (1999 and 2009) in the US.[11] These surveys were based on mailed questionnaires to members of Catholic religious institutes. The approach of this socio-logical study was to systematically examine how the new generations of sisters (post-Vatican II entrants) differ from previous ones regarding ministry, identity, prayer, spirituality, the vows, and community. They found that in previous historical periods, new religious institutes were youth movements. The challenge for religious life today is one of diversity, in order to attract new generations of sisters.[12]

As a part of research on sleep deprivation, French medical scientists conducted interviews and medical examinations of members of an undisclosed enclosed contemplative religious order. It is worth quoting the examples of meditation and contemplation given to the medical scientists, as such detailed personal descriptions by contemporary enclosed contemplatives are rarely found in empirical scientific studies:

> As an example of meditation, a monk chose the sentence "the name of God gladdens the heart of men," and mentally worked on this sentence, asking himself several questions, such as "What is the name of God in all languages," imagining the answers, and then looking how men in various countries gladden when pronouncing the name of God and thinking about Him. This mental activity was perceived as energy consuming, and the monk would be tired and even sleepy after it. Contemplation is harder to explain, as this state of consciousness with full contact with God is difficult to achieve, even after years of practice, and specifically researched in the order. One monk explained contemplation as: "I sit, look in front of me, and let be flowed by the love of God." He reported that in contrast to meditation, contemplation brought about feelings of quietness, serenity, internal peace, and was energy-filling and followed by full alertness.[13]

---

[11] Mary Johnson, Patricia Wittberg and Mary L. Gautier, *New Generations of Catholic Sisters: The Challenge of Diversity* (New York, NY: Oxford University Press, 2014).

[12] Johnson, Wittberg and Gautier, *New Generations of Catholic Sisters*, 140–141.

[13] Isabelle Amulf, Agnes Brion, Michel Pottier, and Jean-Louis Golmard, 'Ring the Bell for Matins: Circadian Adaptation to Split Sleep by Cloistered Monks and Nuns', in *Chronobiology International*, Vol 28; number 10, 2011, 930–94: 932.

Another example of medical clinical studies is the article of four psychiatry researchers who published an ethnographic study conducted in the Spanish Monastery of Santa Mónica whose community consisted of ten contemplative Augustinian nuns. The focus of this study was on emotional distress. The researchers reported that the sisters' religious choice and belief helped them to see their lives with hope and trust, as well as enhanced their self-esteem.[14] The nuns' narratives exhibited three mechanisms which, according to previous psychiatric research, might promote mental health:

1. Their system of beliefs provides them with hope, comfort, and a mental attitude of obtaining something good from every adverse situation by trusting God.
2. Their religious community supports them with increased social and emotional support.
3. Their contemplative practice emphasises a focus on God and on helping others in need, transcending the self and forgetting their own difficulties.[15]

1.2   SCOPE OF THE RESEARCH PARAMETERS

The obvious challenge was how to select from and then analyse the vast amount of material and sources on monasticism accumulated through the centuries and across various expressions of Catholic religious life. Two scoping parameters were evaluated:

1. Historical scope: the choice of the research period.
2. Research subjects: the selection of Catholic monastic traditions and religious orders.

In this context, it should be noted that the scope of this book does not cover the philosophical and metaphysical questions of God's temporality, atemporality, omnitemporality, timelessness, or eternality, which remain

---

[14] Glòria Durà-Vilà, Simon Dein, Roland Littlewood, and Gerard Leavey, 'The *Dark Night of the Soul*: Causes and Resolution of Emotional Distress Among Contemplative Nuns' in *Transcultural Psychiatry*, September 2010. Vol 47(4), 548–570: 565.

[15] Durà-Vilà, Dein, Littlewood and Leavey, 'The *Dark Night of the Soul:* Causes and Resolution of Emotional Distress Among Contemplative Nuns', 565.

subjects for ongoing academic debate.[16] This furthermore excludes other related topics of interest such as quantum physics, other approaches in physics relating to spatiotemporal research, as well as other projects relating to temporality in the philosophy of religion or theology.

Rather than moving into the crossroads of physics and metaphysics and becoming distracted by the almost endless debate about 'God and Time', the key research question remains focused on the concept of time studied in the framework of monastic journeys. The scientific debate on the topic is ongoing, and, in the meantime, monastics influenced—or rather uninfluenced—by these debates in the course of history have formed, and continue to form, their views of 'time'. Carlos Eire, a historian of late medieval and early modern Europe in his study on the historical development of the concept of eternity, goes as far as to claim that 'monks were not as concerned with figuring out how God was eternal as they were with experiencing that eternity in the here and now, as much as possible'.[17] While Eire makes a rather broad generalisation, the monastic sources analysed for the current survey lend some support for a tendency to more practical, 'lived experience' expressed through an intimate relationship *with* the eternal God rather than purely theoretical speculation *about* God's eternity. At the same time, it should be added that the focus on a relationship between God and humans likely leads to some theological considerations about God's eternal nature. This is, firstly, through the recognition of the liminal ontological difference between eternal, immortal God and mortal human and, secondly, through the uniting link between the eternal God and a human soul which carries an 'awareness' of its own immortality.

---

[16] On these subjects, see, for example, *God and Time: Essays on the Divine Nature* in Gregory E. Ganssle and David M. Woodruff, eds. (New York: Oxford University Press, 2002), where Ganssle's 'Introduction', 3–18, provides an overview on the state of the debate in the philosophy of science. More recently, Sampsa Korpela in his doctoral dissertation, *God, Time, and the Concept of Potentiality in Quantum Physics* (Helsinki: Unigrafia, 2022), contributes to the research on God's timelessness and temporality. For God's temporal and spatial omnipresence in Isaac Newton's concepts of time and space, see William Lane Craig, *'The Elimination of Absolute Time by the Special Theory of Relativity'* in God and Time, ed. Gregory E. Ganssle and David M. Woodruff (New York, NY: Oxford University Press, 2002); 129–152. For historical debates on time, see, for example, Jimena Canales, *The Physicist & the Philosopher: Einstein, Bergson, and the Debate that Changed Our Understanding of Time* (Princeton, NJ: Princeton University Press, 2015). Further on the topic, see also T.R. Mullins, *The End of the Timeless God* (Oxford: Oxford University Press, 2016).

[17] Carlos Eire, *A Very Brief History of Eternity* (Princeton, NJ: Princeton University Press, 2010), 71.

1.2.1   Historical Scope

The following would be the basic question regarding the research period: Should one cover the whole span of monastic history, or would it be more beneficial to focus on one specific era? For example, should one focus on emerging monasticism,[18] the medieval period, or contemporary times? The advantage of a narrowly defined historical period would be an in-depth approach that allows more detailed analysis and broader use of sources from the selected period. The main argument for choosing to attempt a more comprehensive historical scope is that it offers an opportunity to map the thematic 'concept of time' through the history of monasticism from the earliest writers to contemporary authors and other sources.

The thematic research interest supported the choice of a broad historical spectrum, especially as the theme itself could be considered 'timeless' by nature. A narrow historical period would moreover limit the possibility to observe any potential developments relating to the theme. Time as a theme should best be observed through a historical approach. Finally, the aim for a balanced historical scope could help to limit the risk of falling either into 'passeism' or 'presentism'.[19] By choosing a broader scope of monastic history, one avoids putting too much emphasis on the past (focus on early monasticism) or the present (focus on contemporary sources).

In this context, the findings of monastic historian Marilyn Dunn on monastic literature are of interest. Dunn argues that a large part of the purpose of monastic texts is to look back to earlier days of monasticism and even to the biblical era. She found that the constant repetition of sections taken from earlier works is one of the most noticeable features of monastic writing, in which the search for perfection was always

---

[18] Emerging monasticism here refers to the pre-Benedictine period, ca. 250–500.

[19] Downey, in *Understanding Christian Spirituality* (Mahwah, NJ: Paulist Press, 1997), 126, cautions against 'presentism' as the tendency to disregard the insight, perceptions, convictions, and shortcomings of earlier epochs as old-fashioned, irrelevant, and unable to speak to our experience. On the other hand, Patrick Sbalchiero writes about 'passeism' in the context of monastic studies in *Histoire de la vie monastique* (Paris: Desclée de Brouwer, 2008), 29: 'Il s'agit d'une perception spécifique de l'histoire qui, dans une certaine mesure, valorise passé des ordres monastiques au détriment de leur présent, de leur actualité'.

accompanied by the perception of earlier wisdom and the desire to maintain orthodox tradition.[20]

Dunn's observations on monastic texts—their tendency to rely on earlier monastic traditions and the Scriptures—seemed to apply also to some of the enclosed contemplative literary sources. To test Dunn's qualitative statement, a small quantitative sub-study was conducted. Three books published by members of contemplative orders (Carthusian, Trappist, and Carmelite) were analysed to identify the historical references or sources which the writers mentioned in their texts. Generic topics with no obvious connection to a specific historical period were chosen from each writer. The selected topics were:

1. Vocation and discernment by an anonymous Carthusian novice master[21];
2. Contemplative prayer by Thomas Merton, a Trappist monk[22];
3. Eternity and time by Wilfrid Stinissen, OCD, a Carmelite friar.[23]

The sub-study disclosed two main findings:

Firstly, in line with the observations of Marilyn Dunn, the Scriptures as well as earlier monastic writers were the most frequent reference points for the contemplative writers of this sub-study. The Carthusian and the Carmelite authors quote the Scriptures extensively, while Merton's main references are found in the first millennium and the following two centuries (41% and 17%, respectively). The Carthusian writer rarely refers to sources beyond the eleventh century; fewer than 5% of his references are to sources after the year 1200. The Carmelite favours Scripture quotations (64%), but compared to the other two authors, he has relatively more

---

[20] Marilyn Dunn, *The Emergence of Monasticism: From the Desert Fathers to the Early Middle Ages* (Oxford: Blackwell Publishing, 2007), vi-vii. Similarly, Benedicta Ward, the translator of *The Desert Fathers: Sayings of the Early Christian Monks* (London: Penguin Books, 2003; trans. B. Ward), xxi, in her introduction notes that it is 'astonishing' how this literature, over fifteen centuries old, has had a continuing influence beyond the world in which it was created. This is also exemplified by stories which are adapted and told in medieval or modern settings using different protagonists.

[21] A Carthusian, *The Call of Silent Love* (London: Darton, Longman and Todd, 1995; trans. Anglican solitary).

[22] Thomas Merton, *Contemplative Prayer* (London: Darton, Longman and Todd, 2005).

[23] Wilfrid Stinissen, *L'Éternité au cœur du temps* (Toulouse: Éditions du Carmel, 2013; trans. M-N Talle).

Table 1.1 Historical source references and mentions by contemporary monastic writers

	A Carthusian:		Merton:		Stinissen:		
	The Call of Silent Love (198 pages)		Contemplative Prayer (144 pages)		L'éternité au cœur du temps (199 pages)		Total
	Carthusian		Trappist		Carmelite		
Scriptures	338	62%	16	8%	227	64%	53%
Rules and other texts	65	12%	4	2%	2	1%	6%
BC	1	0%	2	1%	4	1%	1%
0–1000	62	11%	86	41%	11	3%	14%
1000–1200	55	10%	35	17%	0	0%	8%
1200–1500	3	1%	14	7%	8	2%	2%
1500–1700	12	2%	36	17%	35	10%	8%
1700–1900	1	0%	1	0%	18	5%	2%
1900–	8	1%	15	7%	47	13%	6%
Total	545	100%	209	100%	352	100%	100%

reference points in modern times and in the period 1500–1700. The prevalence of the latter period is explained by his thirty-five references to the two important Carmelite authors of the period, John of the Cross and Teresa of Ávila (Table 1.1).[24]

The second finding shows the degree of commonality which was found in sources used by the three contemplative monastic writers. All three mentioned Augustine and John of the Cross. The list of sources mentioned by two of the three writers gives further evidence of the broad historical scope that these contemporary writers covered: Plato, Athanasius, Desert Fathers, Evagrius, Cassian, Isaac of Nineveh, Basil of Caesarea, Gregory of Nyssa, Pope Gregory I, Bernard of Clairvaux, Francis of Assisi, Thomas Aquinas, Meister Eckhart, Johannes Tauler, Ignatius of Loyola, Teresa of Ávila, Martin Heidegger, Albert Camus, Dom John Chapman, Gabriel Marcel, Friedrich Nietzsche. This list of sources is grouped by the historical period in Table 1.2, showing the biggest concentration in sources from the first millennium.

---

[24]While it was not the aim of this sub-study, another finding was that all three monastic writers showed preference to using texts generated within their own monastic tradition along with references to the Scriptures and early monastic sources such as Desert Fathers.

Table 1.2 Sources mentioned by at least two authors

BC	*Plato*
0–1000	Augustine, Athanasius, Desert Fathers, Evagrius, Cassian, Isaac of Nineveh, Basil of Caesarea, Gregory of Nyssa, Pope Gregory I
1000–1200	Bernard of Clairvaux
1200–1500	Francis of Assisi, Thomas Aquinas, Meister Eckhart, Johannes Tauler
1500–1700	John of the Cross, Ignatius of Loyola, Teresa of Ávila
1700–1900	–
1900–	Martin Heidegger, Albert Camus, Dom John Chapman, Gabriel Marcel, Friedrich Nietzsche

Conclusions

The tendency to adhere to ancient monastic traditions and constant referencing to early monastic sources is especially evident among enclosed contemplative orders which trace their spiritual heritage—if not their direct historical origins—to the period of the Desert Fathers.

This 'self-referential' nature of monastic writing and adherence to earlier traditions poses challenges and opportunities with regard to historical scoping. As an example, researchers intending to limit their historical scope to contemporary monastics might nevertheless find it necessary to extend their perspective back to the fourth or even earlier centuries. This is because, as indicated by previous research and the above sub-study, contemporary monastic writers read and quote literature across various historical periods. This long reach would pose a scoping challenge.

There is also a positive aspect, an opportunity arising from the 'self-referential' nature. It can be suggested that the recurring turning to early contemplative traditions, when viewed in the light of historical developments and contemporary interpretations, provides a rich field for the scoping of thematic topics such as the concept of time.

However, the 'self-referential' tendency of the traditional enclosed contemplative orders is not limited to literary references only. It can be seen in other elements of their monastic way of life. For example, Francisco Rafael de Pascual, OCSO, suggests that if a Pachomian, Syrian, Provincial, or ancient British monk were to walk into a modern village or city today, they would feel rather lost. But inside the walls of a monastery, they would feel 'comfortable like a fish in the water' when it comes to clothing, order of the day, liturgical prayers, or other aspects of religious life.[25] This historian-monk's observation lends further support for choosing to attempt a broader historical scope for the current study.[26]

In conclusion, this sub-study does not claim that contemplative religious traditions have remained unchanged through the centuries. To understand that this is not the case, one only needs to compare the world of Pachomian Rules with, for example, contemplative orders maintaining websites today to allow people to submit their requests for intercession or for Mass intentions. Societies have evolved, and monasticism has adjusted with it. Equally, many contemplative orders themselves have evolved through internal reforms over the centuries. To reflect the gradual developments in monasticism, Chap. 3 presents an idea of some possible shifts in the approach of monastic withdrawal. Yet, despite changes in some aspects, the remarkable stability of spiritual tradition is observable through analytical reading of monastic sources. This is why a conscious attempt to cover a wide range of references and material, from different eras, has been made when presenting the findings of this research. This conclusion is in line with the overall paradoxical nature of monasticism as a dynamic journey that evolves over time and simultaneously stands as a beacon of stability, a spiritual tradition that endures time.

1.2.2 Research Subjects

The second question for the research parameter was the selection of monastic traditions and religious orders within the Catholic Church. Here, the decision was to choose a relatively narrow focus by limiting the scope to enclosed contemplatives, a subgroup of regulated religious life. This scoping decision follows partly from the research lens, that of 'time' and partly from the personal journey of the researcher. The practical, scoping-related reasoning is given first, followed by the personal aspect.

---

[25] Francisco Rafael de Pascual, '"El hábito no hace al monje": formas y simbolismos de los hábitos monasticos', in José Ángel García de Cortázar and Ramón Teja (eds.) *El ritmo cotidiano de la vida en el monasterio medieval* (Fundación Santa María la Real, Centro de Estudios del Románico: Aguilar de Campoo Palencia, 2015), 11–31: 25–30.

[26] A Carthusian in *The Way of Silent Love: Carthusian Novice Conferences* (London: Darton, Longman and Todd, 1993), 68, goes further claiming that 'Human beings do not change essentially, at least monastic human beings don't' in the context that—in contrast to new forms of religious life—monastic life, particularly Carthusian life, preserves the structure and goals of perennial contemplation, remaining faithful to the ancient tradition.

For simplicity, religious orders can be categorised as either active or contemplative,[27] although semi-contemplative approaches also exist. In addition, some active and semi-contemplative orders and religious congregations such as the Missionaries of Charity, founded by Mother Teresa of Calcutta, encompass two approaches: an active branch and a contemplative branch which aid and complement each other, in a shared purpose.[28] Similarly, there are cloistered contemplative branches or houses within traditional mendicant orders such as Franciscan, Dominicans, and Augustinians. Typically, men (friars) in these traditions follow apostolic vocations as preachers and priests, while there are contemplative female branches (nuns) and active branches (sisters). For example, the Carmelite family includes both enclosed nuns and sisters who are 'apostolic', which means that they are involved in active service in the world. Rather than living in enclosed monasteries that have limited contact with the outside world, these members serve in a wide range of apostolates. The sisters are often referred to as nuns, and nuns are referred to by the title of 'sister'. Strictly speaking, a nun is enclosed in a monastery, whereas an apostolic sister is active 'in the world'.[29] Within the Carmelite traditions, for example, Discalced Carmelite nuns follow the cloistered, enclosed monastic tradition.

This means that some contemplative traditions are 'strictly' monastic in the sense that their members adhere to the monastic enclosure—either in monastic buildings or hermitages within the cloister, often in remote areas—while some contemplatives live in communities in or close to cities and combine contemplative lives with some active apostolic service. To expand the scoping question further, some contemplative religious traditions additionally have secular (lay) members who take similar promises to friars and nuns but related to their lives as laypeople.

The earliest forms of monasticism followed the eremitic (hermit) approach, but the communal cenobitic way of life soon became the

---

[27] On the distinction between contemplative and active orders, see, for example, Patricia Wittberg, *The Rise and Fall of Catholic Religious Orders: A Social Movement Perspective* (Albany, NY: State University of New York Press, 1994), 46–48; on contemplative and ministerial forms of religious life in Sandra M. Schneiders, *Selling All: Commitment, Consecrated Celibacy, and Community in Catholic Religious Life* (Mahwah, NJ: Paulist Press, 2001), 308–316.

[28] https://www.motherteresa.org/missionaries-of-charity.html,   accessed   on   31 October 2020.

[29] http://www.carmelite.org/family/sisters, accessed 3 November 2020.

prevalent form of monastic life. However, various combinations of these approaches exist today. For example, the Carthusians spend most of their time in individual cells within their Charterhouses, combining the two approaches which they characterise as 'semi-eremitic form of monastic life'.[30]

The Order of Carmelites website explains the historical evolution of friars (mendicant monks) from their eremitic origin, according to the Carmelite tradition:

> The hermits were forced to leave their home on Mount Carmel and settle in Europe. There they changed their style of life from hermits to friars. The major difference is that friars are called to serve the People of God in some active apostolate. Some Religious Congregations were founded for a specific work but the Carmelite Order tries simply to respond to the needs of the Church and the world which differ according to time and place, and so, many friars work in parishes, schools, universities, retreat centres, prisons, hospitals, etc.[31]

To summarise, enclosure and the contemplative way of life were identified as an ideal combination for research. Enclosed contemplatives represent, among Catholic religious orders, the historically longest continuing tradition which combines two distinct elements: (1) separation from the world in the monastic enclosure and (2) focus on the contemplative life.

These two elements contrast with, or at least, distinguish their way of life from the daily activities, time schedules, and interpersonal interactions experienced in secular life. In comparison, members of active orders, through their work in schools, prisons, parishes, or hospitals, for example, engage more directly with the secular—or the non-monastic—way of life. In doing so, they are more likely to have to adjust to the time schedules and circumstances of the secular society in which they live and whom they serve through their apostolate.[32] Enclosed contemplative monasticism, therefore, provides a more narrowly defined scope for this study.

---

[30] http://www.chartreux.org/en/houses/transfiguration/cart-2.pdf, accessed 31 October 2020.

[31] http://ocarm.org/en/content/ocarm/charism, accessed 31 October 2020.

[32] On the impact that historical changes in relations with the environing economic and political milieus had on Religious Orders, see Victor Turner and Edith Turner, *Image and Pilgrimage in Christian Culture* (New York, NY: Columbia University Press, 2011), 4.

Importantly, the selection of enclosed contemplatives as research subjects is aligned with the first decision on choosing the full monastic history as the scope of this study. This is because, in the development path of monasticism, enclosed contemplative orders are typically older than the active orders and non-monastic religious congregations. The Missionaries of Charity—founded by Mother Teresa in 1950—can be mentioned as an example of the more recent development of such active religious congregations.

It is worth noting, at this point, that a contemplative approach to life, in the broadest sense of spirituality, can be experienced by individuals of all religions, or none, in their secular settings. At the same time, dedicated monastic ways of life have emerged among people who 'engage in the search for the Absolute'[33] with many similar practices concerning the way of life, asceticism, and methods of meditation found in the monastic life of different religions.[34] Catholic enclosed contemplative traditions, therefore, form a narrow segment in the broader contexts of the contemplative way of life and monastic way of life, as illustrated in Fig. 1.1.

In practice, this selected combination of enclosed contemplatives then narrows the focus down to the Carthusians, Benedictines, Cistercians, and

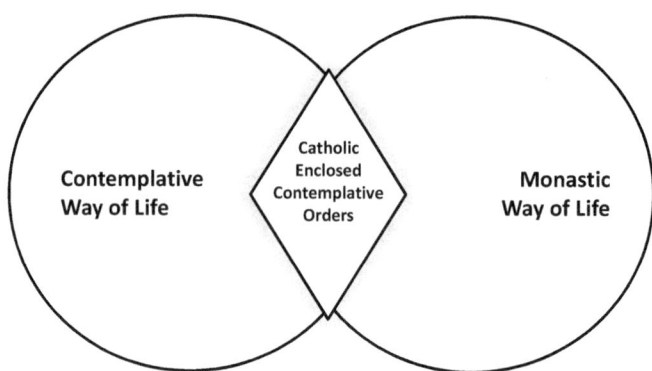

Fig. 1.1   Catholic enclosed contemplative orders in broader context

[33] Mayeul de Dreuille, OSB, *From East to West: A History of Monasticism* (Herefordshire: Gracewing, 1999), vii.

[34] See, for example, de Dreuille, *From East to West*, vii-3, who dates the first Hindu hermits to 2500–1500 B.C.

Table 1.3 Major traditional contemplative monastic orders: monasteries and members globally in 2015

	Male		Female		Total
	Monasteries	Members	Monasteries	Members	Members
Carthusians (O. Cart.)	17	296	4	36	332
Benedictines (OSB)	353	7079	809	10,362	17,441
Cistercians (OCS)	77	1733	91	1256	2989
Trappists (OCSO)	96	1963	68	1513	3476
Carmelites (O. Carm.)	382	2030	1710	12,136	14,166
Discalced Carmelites (OCD)	632	3995	826	10,694	14,689
Total	1557	17,096	3508	35,997	53,093

Cistercians of Strict Observance (also known as Trappists) and Carmelites. In addition, there are, or have been, other smaller enclosed contemplative orders, but in terms of historical and current perspective, the Benedictines, the Carthusians, the Carmelites, and the Cistercians could be considered the main representatives of enclosed contemplatives. The current membership statistics of the major traditional contemplative enclosed orders are shown in Table 1.3[35]:

While contemplative enclosed monastic traditions offer the longest historical perspective among Catholic monasticism, the traditional enclosed contemplative religious orders have experienced declining membership trends in the recent decades.[36] Table 1.3 indicates that there are currently over 50,000 members in the major traditional contemplative orders. An observation by a contemporary enclosed contemplative touches upon recent changes in monastic life, revealing a mixed picture with regard to long-held traditions:

> Religious Life today, unfortunately, is not what it once was. Many orders have abandoned the habit, the veil, the original work of their founders, and sometimes even their own Rule and Constitutions. There are many reasons for that, but despite it all, there are still many fervent Religious Communities that adhere to the traditions of Religious Life.[37]

[35] *Annuario Pontificio 2015: Pontifical Yearbook 2015 Catholic Church Directory* (Vatican: Libreria Editrice Vaticana), 1411–1674.
[36] Wittberg, *The Rise and Fall of Catholic Religious Orders*, 1–3.
[37] Email from 'Mel', a cloistered contemplative 17/08/2016.

The enclosed contemplative way of life has been a target of some criticism among the researchers of spirituality in recent years. Philip Sheldrake, for example, voices a concern that a hierarchy of values, associated with ascent, gives way to a hierarchy of lifestyles whereby professionally spiritual people have a greater share of God's being.[38] Members of monastic orders have also been regarded as 'religious virtuosi' within the Church, called by God to perfection, or they have been viewed as possessing a tendency towards elitism.[39]

A methodological question related to the scope of the current study could be as follows: instead of choosing enclosed contemplatives as the primary research subject—given that they encompass a large number of individuals and different orders over several centuries—could this project have been conducted by focusing on a limited number of individual writers instead? The answer is a partial 'yes'. This kind of approach has been used, for example, by Carmel Becton Davis in her study on space and spatiality in the works of three medieval contemporaries, Richard Rolle, the anonymous author of *The Cloud of Unknowing*, and Julian of Norwich.[40] The answer is also a partial 'no'. The aim of the current study was to study the concept of time within contemplative traditions across centuries. By focusing on a pre-defined era in history, the rich lineage of monastic tradition from the Early Desert Fathers to contemporary enclosed contemplatives could have been compromised: the historical setting would have dominated the research approach.

In summary, the choice of these particular strands of Western monasticism relates to a specific 'intersection' in the spatial-temporal scoping. 'Enclosed contemplative' traditions as a term refers to (1) spatial enclosure that relates to the idea of a journey or, rather, a non-journey; (2) temporal 'verticality' of time that, through contemplation, seeks to ascend towards God's 'eternal Now'. In this book, the research subject scoping is addressed through various levels: when appropriate, a direct reference to the specific religious Order has been made (for example, 'a Carmelite'). Alternatively, a broader term 'enclosed (or cloistered) contemplatives' has been used in

---

[38] Philip Sheldrake, *Spirituality and History: Questions of Interpretation and Method* (London: SPCK, 1985), 189.

[39] See, for example, Wittberg, *The Rise and Fall of Catholic Religious Orders*, 110–117 and Sandra M. Schneiders, *Finding the Treasure: Locating Catholic Religious Life in a New Ecclesial and Cultural Context* (Mahwah, NJ: Paulist Press 2000), 10.

[40] Davis, *Mysticism and Space: Space and Spirituality in the Works of Richard Rolle, The Cloud of Unknowing Author, and Julian of Norwich.*

more general references to these traditions. In addition, 'monastic' has been applied as a yet broader generic definition, when it has been used by secondary sources or when it was not possible or necessary to distinguish the research subject more specifically.

Finally, there are two additional personal aspects that influenced the decisions related to scope on the selection of research subjects. The first comes from having crossed paths with members of active, semi-contemplative, and contemplative religious traditions over a number of years. Conversations and correspondence about religious life and God have opened up perspectives to various forms of monasticism. It is this understanding of and respect for the variety of expressions of religious life within the Catholic Church that helped to position enclosed contemplative traditions in the wider context and thus informed the scope in this study.

The second personal aspect relates to a pilgrimage to Santiago de Compostela, a transformative experience in many ways. On the way to Compostela, conversations with an Augustinian friar gave insights into the mendicant spiritual tradition and his introduction to the spirituality of Thérèse of Lisieux through her autobiography *L'histoire d'une ame* proved invaluable.[41] Thérèse was a Discalced Carmelite nun, who lived in 1873–1897 yet, at the same time, her personal 'story of a soul' represents a trajectory along the long journey of enclosed contemplative traditions. Years later, the themes of journey/pilgrimage and enclosed contemplative life meet again and form the structure of the current study. What can one say? The relationships and influences we encounter along the way can prove transformative. Time and the paths that we follow will change us.

1.3   RESEARCH METHODS

Donato Ogliari, OSB, presents two important aspects—one which refers directly to the aim of the current topic (time and eternity), and another one which refers to the research subjects (monastics)—in his analysis of the term *saeculum:*

---

[41] The inscription written on the book 'Toujours en communion sur le Chemin, qui a Visage de Jésus. En souvenir d'un bout de chemin partagé sur le Camino de Compostela ...' speaks of the communion among the pilgrims who share part of the Way which represents the 'Face of Jesus'. The reference to the 'Way which has Face of Jesus' can be understood, firstly, Jesus as the Way, and, secondly, referring to the monastic name of *Thérèse de l'Enfant Jésus et de la Sainte Face,* the writer of the autobiography.

On one hand it is used to describe the mortal and earthly life in contrast with true life, the one beyond the earth. On the other hand it describes, with the rise of monasticism, the pagan life and then the Christian life itself as a way of life different and distinct from the *monastic way of living*.[42]

Here, Ogliari, a monastic writer, emphasises the rise of monasticism as a factor that led to the '*monastic way of living*' being considered 'different and distinct' not only from pagan life but even from the Christian life itself. Ogliari's observations of the term *saeculum*, 'which in the Christian tradition has become almost synonymous with the "world"',[43] indicate two distinctions:

1. Mortal and earthly life contrasted with true life beyond the earth;
2. Secular life contrasted with the monastic way of living.

To expand on what Ogliari refers to as 'true life' beyond the earth, a third dimension could be added: that is, God's life. This would define, or give a name to, the 'true life' that is beyond both the monastic way of living and secular life. These three distinct ways of life could then be presented in Fig. 1.2. This introduces the element of crossroads, or liminality, of monastic way of living as 'different way of life' in-between God's life and secular life.

From the research perspective, however, enclosed contemplative monasticism presents a particular challenge. It appears that, when leaving the secular society, enclosed monastics tend to turn their attention to life hidden from the world, rarely engaging in secular academic debates. One could argue that the relative scarcity of academic studies on enclosed contemplatives reflects, in a way, the hidden and withdrawn nature of the research subjects themselves. But this also provides an opportunity: the concept of time in monastic spirituality is a relatively under-researched area leaving wide space to explore. And in terms of time, there is a long history—nearly 2000 years—of monastic sources available to study.

In conclusion, an interdisciplinary approach is required to explore the monastic spiritual traditions. This implies an open, inquisitive, and analytical pursuit towards an understanding of monastic journeys and time. A systematic way of description, critical analysis, and constructive

---

[42] Ogliari, 'Tempus Monasticum', 35.
[43] Ogliari, 'Tempus Monasticum', 35.

Fig. 1.2 Three
ways of life

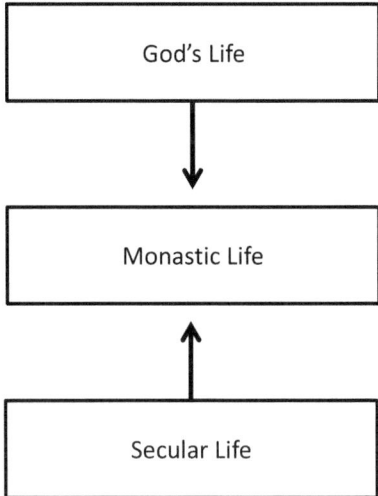

interpretation of sources and previous research seems appropriate. Accordingly, the main method here is systematic thematic analysis. Two kinds of materials were used for this analysis:

1. Primary sources such as monastic rules and other written or documentary material produced by monastic and non-monastic authors.
2. Secondary sources, namely previous academic and other research.

Systematic description and interpretation of literary and other sources and critical analysis were used to construct the themes and categories that form part of this work. In practice, regarding the primary sources, this meant systematic reading of the materials while persistently asking the questions: (1) What does this text say about 'time'? (2) What is the context of the temporal reference in this text?'

This 'thematic' method, when applied systematically to a broad and varied selection of primary sources (ranging from *Sayings* of the early desert dwellers to recent documentary films or emails from a cloistered contemplative), differs from the detailed study of a limited number of sources that may be more widely used in the research of spirituality. The systematic method is especially suitable for 'covering a lot of ground' due to its application of a specific thematic lens. The disadvantage is that it is rather labour-intensive and may lead to reading through several sources that yield few major insights from the thematic perspective. However, the systematic approach helps in establishing 'clusters' of ideas and categories that build towards the discoveries. This means that even if not all the relevant quotations from all the reviewed sources could be referenced, the systematic approach supported the conviction that the selected quotations represent broader thematic categories. It refers to the 'self-referential' tendency that can reinforce certain themes. In this study, thematic systematic (textual and contextual) analysis combined with constructive interpretation of the sources was conducted by three steps:

1. Textual thematic analysis: initial systematic identification of passages that relate to temporality.
2. Contextual thematic analysis: emergence of clusters that led to discovering 'categories' of temporality (liminality, relationship, eschatology).
3. Constructive interpretation: application of categories as conduits within the journey framework.

On two occasions, additional quantitative sub-studies were applied to a small sample of sources with the aim of testing specific ideas related to the main systematic thematic analysis. This was a useful exercise in the sense that both sub-studies—using limited material—seemed to produce similar findings compared to the analysis and conclusions derived from the broader scope of materials. The sub-studies, therefore, seemed to support the ideas of the wider arguments. However, there is a major difference between pure *textual or quantitative* analysis derived from a narrow set of sources and the *contextual analytical reading* that is required to understand more fully the ideas or meanings behind the singular words or expressions. A purely quantitative textual approach alone would likely fall short in grasping some of the complex and even paradoxical themes that emerge from the study of monastic spirituality.

An additional method to complement the existing research and primary source analysis could have been the collection of new material by, for example, interviewing members of the enclosed monastic orders. After considering the difficulties in obtaining permissions to gain access to enter enclosed contemporary monasteries, it became clear that such an approach would not be feasible. While some limited correspondence could be exchanged with members of monasteries of enclosed orders, the gates generally remain closed to a broader and deeper interaction with monasteries. From the researcher's perspective, the desire to respect the explicit choice of the enclosed monastics, who wish to limit their contacts with the secular world, contributed to the decision to follow a 'less intrusive' approach. However, it was possible to gain access to some recently published material, such as documentaries and interviews of contemporary members of contemplative religious orders. Taking into account the broader historical scope, the main method, nevertheless, had to rely on literature analysis.

1.4   SOURCES

The main sources can be divided into two categories: (1) monastic sources which have been created by members of religious orders, and (2) other relevant sources, produced by non-monastic authors, which regulate, document, or describe monastic traditions or spirituality. Additionally, to take into account the historical scope, it is necessary to expand the use of sources beyond the existing contemplative religious orders. There are two reasons for this:

1. The very earliest forms of the eremitic contemplative life (e.g., the Desert Fathers or pre-Benedictine monastic religious orders) no longer exist. However, they have left relevant documents which inform about their thinking and practical approach to monasticism.
2. Some existing contemplative orders, such as Carmelites, either trace their historical origins to the early (undated) period of eremitic tradition or at least refer to the ancient historical traditions through frequent use of earlier monastic sources such as Cassian or the Desert Fathers.

This means that the definition of monastic sources, here, will additionally cover periods and traditions which pre-date the existing forms of the enclosed contemplative life. However, the purpose here is not to compare differences across various enclosed contemplative traditions or orders. Instead, the aim is to study the concept of time as perceived and experienced by enclosed contemplatives during their monastic journeys, through history.

1.4.1   Monastic Sources

A source is considered monastic if it has been created by a member of a monastic religious order, or by an individual who led contemplative life as a hermit or as a member of a Christian community during the early period of monasticism. These sources cover a range of materials, from the *Sayings of the Desert Fathers* and early monastic rules to current works by contemporary monastic authors.

It would be incorrect to classify the Scriptures as a monastic source. However, starting from the earliest monastic texts, such as the *Life of Anthony*, the Old and New Testament texts are constantly present through multiple references. From the historical perspective, monasteries played a major part in the distribution and study of the Bibles; before the invention of printing techniques, many monasteries were occupied in the manual copying of the Scriptures. Monks and nuns live and breathe the Scriptures through their daily prayers of the Psalms, in the Holy Mass as well as in their practice of *Lectio Divina*, the quotidian reading and meditating of the Word. As a result, it could be argued, the Scriptures penetrate the daily lives of those in religious orders through reading, praying, and working.

Monastic Rules
The main monastic rules used in the current study are the Rules of Pachomius, the Rules of St. Basil, the Rule of Saint Benedict, the Rule of St. Augustine, the Carmelite Rule, and the Statutes of the Carthusian Order. These provide the historical background and traditions for monasticism. With the exception of the Rules of Pachomius, which has only historical value, these rules represent regulations which are still applied by existing religious traditions today.

Monastic Literature
Monastic literature is sourced in the form of books, published diaries and letters, articles, sermons, and teaching materials used in novice formation as well as prayers and poems[44] by monastic writers.

---

[44] Poetry seems to have been an important medium for contemplatives to share their inner religious experiences throughout centuries. David Foster, in *Contemplative Prayer* (London: Bloomsbury, 2015), for example, argues for the need of creative thinking to provide a threshold in experience where explanation stops and notes that 'poetry has been a regular companion for those trying to respond to liminal experience', 136–137.

Early Monastic Literature

Some of the earliest monastic sources are hagiographies, such as the classic *Life of Anthony* written by Athanasius.[45] Another hagiography is the *Life of Saint Honoratus* (d. 430), the founder of the Lérins island monastery; it was written by Hilary of Arles and dates probably from 431.[46]

John Cassian's (c. 360–c. 435) *Conferences*[47] and *The Monastic Institutes*[48] are important sources not only because they describe the early years of monasticism but also due to their long-standing use in monasteries in the East and the West. His contribution is still frequently referenced in the works of monastic writers. Writing at the same time, in the tradition of the desert monks, Evagrius Ponticus (345–399) produced two significant texts: *The Praktikos* and *Chapters on Prayer*.[49] Their contemporary, Palladius of Galatia, a monk himself, travelled to live among the Desert Fathers and, in 419–420, completed his writings about the encounters in *The Lausiac History*.[50] In a similar approach, a group of seven monks visited the Egyptian deserts in 394, and their journey produced the description of the lives of the early Christian ascetics, known as *The Historia Monachorum in Aegypto*.[51] *The Apophthegmata Patrum*[52] consists of stories and sayings attributed to the Desert Fathers and Desert Mothers, dating from approximately the fifth century. The main sources from Augustine of Hippo (354–430) have been his rules and his autobiography *Confessions* (Table 1.4).[53]

The monastic writings of the twelfth-century Cistercians are represented by Bernard of Clairvaux (1090–1153) and William of Saint-Thierry

---

[45] Athanasius, *Life of Anthony* (Pickerington, OH: Beloved Publishing, 2014).

[46] Hilary of Arles's text is included in Mireille Labrousse, *Saint Honorat* (Bégrolles-en-Mauges: Abbaye de Bellefontaine, Vie Monastique, no. 31, 1995). The monastery of Lérins, founded by Honoratus, is today occupied by a community of Trappist monks.

[47] John Cassian, *Conferences* (Brookfield, WI: First Rate Publishers, 2016).

[48] John Cassian, *The Monastic Institutes* (London: The Saint Austin Press, 1999; trans. J. Bertram).

[49] Evagrius Ponticus, *The Praktikos and Chapters on Prayer* (Trappist, KY: Cistercian Publications, 1972; trans. J. E. Bamberger).

[50] Palladius of Galatia, *The Lausiac History* (Great Britain: Aeterna Press, 2014; trans. W.K.L. Clarke).

[51] *The Lives of the Desert Fathers: The Historia Monachorum in Aegypto* (Collegeville, MN: Liturgical Press, 1980; trans. N. Russell).

[52] *The Desert Fathers: Sayings of the Early Christian Monks* (London: Penguin Books, 2003; trans. B. Ward). From here-on *Sayings*.

[53] Augustine, *Confessions* (Harmondsworth: Penguin Books, 1975; trans. R.S. Pine-Coffin).

Table 1.4   Early monastic sources

		Main sources
c. 235–460	Desert Fathers	Apophthegmata Patrum, Historia Monachorum in Aegypto
251–356	Anthony	Life of Anthony (by Athanasius)
292–348	Pachomius	Rules of Pachomius
c. 330–379	Basil of Caesarea	Longer and Shorter Rules, Letters
345–399	Evagrius Ponticus	The Praktikos, Chapters on Prayer
c. 348–465	Shenoute of Atripe	Monastic Rules
354–430	Augustine of Hippo	Confessions, Rule of St. Augustine
c. 360–435	John Cassian	Institutes, Conferences
c. 363–431	Palladius	The Lausiac History
c. 350–429	Honoratus	Life of St. Honoratus (by Hilary of Arles)
c. 579–649	John Climacus	The Ladder of Divine Ascent

(c. 1075/85–1148). The Franciscan Friar and Bishop Bonaventure's (c. 1217–1274) *The Soul's Journey into God*[54] is thematically relevant to this study. *The Cloud of Unknowing*[55] written in the fourteenth century by an unknown author, thought to be a Carthusian monk, provides a central source that has been an influential reading for monastic and other audiences. *The Imitation of Christ*,[56] published first in 1418, is equal in importance as a widely read classic among the religious.

The classic Carmelite monastic sources include the selected works of Teresa of Ávila (1515–1582)[57] and her contemporary John of the Cross (1542–1591).[58] In addition, a more comprehensive list of monastic 'ascent literature' covering the classic contemplative texts is found separately in Chap. 4. From the period between the classic Carmelites and the nineteenth century, widely read relevant work is by Eusebius Nieremberg, SJ

---

[54] Bonaventure, *The Soul's Journey into God* (London: SPCK, 1978; trans. E. Cousins).

[55] *The Cloud of Unknowing and Other Works* (London: Penguin Books, 2001; trans. A. C. Spearing).

[56] Thomas à Kempis, *The Imitation of Christ* (Mineola, NY: Dover Publications, 2003; trans. A. Croft and H. Bolton).

[57] Teresa of Ávila, *The Way of Perfection* (Mineola, NY: Dover Publications, 2012; trans. E. A. Peers) and *Interior Castle* (Mineola, NY: Dover Publications, 2008; trans. E. A. Peers).

[58] John of the Cross, *A Spiritual Canticle of the Soul and the Bridegroom Christ* (Great Britain: reprint of 1889, trans. D. Lewis); *Ascent of Mount Carmel* (Bottom of the Hill Publishing, 2010; trans. E. A. Peers); *Dark Night of the Soul* (Mineola, NY: Dover Publications, 2003; trans. E. A. Peers).

(1595–1658), *A Treatise on the Difference Between Temporal and Eternal*,[59] which was originally published in Spanish in 1640. Approaching current times, the main monastic source is Carmelite nun Thérèse of Lisieux (1873–1897) whose letters[60] and autobiography[61] reflect experiences of her monastic journey.

Contemporary Monastic Literature

The most relevant monograph for the concept of time from a monastic perspective is the recent publication of Carmelite sister Lucie Rivière[62] who has written on Saint Teresa of Ávila's perception of time, integrating the framework of *chronos* and *kairos* through various aspects of Teresian Carmelite spirituality. Another relevant book is the thematic study of Wilfrid Stinissen, OCD, which discusses the present moment and the eternity of God in the light of the Carmelite spiritual tradition.[63] Carmelite Sister Kinga of the Transfiguration[64] (1973–2009) wrote a diary that was published after her death, an autobiographical source for her monastic journey.

Among the main sources of contemporary monastic literature on enclosed contemplatives is the published series of Carthusian Novice Conferences.[65] The writer of these conferences is identified as a 'novice master', but according to the tradition of the order, the names of living writers are not disclosed. Other contemporary Carthusian published sources include poems, sermons, and collections of monastic writings.[66]

---

[59] Eusebius Nieremberg, *A Treatise on the Difference between Temporal and Eternal* (Philadelphia, PA: Eugene Cumminskey, 1833; reprinted by Kessinger Publishing).

[60] Thérèse of Lisieux, *Letters: General Correspondence 1877–1890* (Washington, D.C.: ICS Publications, 1982; trans. J. Clarke).

[61] Thérèse of Lisieux, *Story of a Soul* (Washington, D.C.: ICS Publications, 2016; trans. J. Clarke).

[62] Lucie Rivière, *Un temps supérieur à l'espace: La vie cloîtrée selon Thérèse d'Avila* (Toulouse: Éditions du Carmel, 2018).

[63] Stinissen, *L'Éternité au cœur du temps*.

[64] Kinga de la Transfiguration, *Je ne me suis pas dérobée …* (Toulouse: Éditions du Carmel, trans. Carmelites of Magyarszék, 2017).

[65] The Carthusian Novice Conference titles used in this study were: *Interior Prayer* (1996); *The Call of Silent Love* (1995); *The Way of Silent Love* (1993), published by Darton, Longman & Todd in London.

[66] See for example: *They Speak by Silences* (Herefordshire: Gracewing, 2006); *Where Silence is Praise* (1997; trans. A Monk of Parkminster) and *The Wound of Love* (1994) published by Darton, Longman, & Todd (London); *In Praise of Silence: poems and images* (2009) published by St Hughs Press (Horsham).

This study further draws from a unique new source, a collection of unpublished poems and other texts written by a Carthusian monk.

Monasticism, contemplation, and time were among the recurring topics of the broad literary production of Thomas Merton (1915–1968), who comes from the Trappist contemplative tradition. The evolution of Merton's thinking, reflected in his writing, serves as evidence of how a person's attitudes and perceptions can change throughout their monastic journey. As Patrick Hart, the editor of a collection of Merton's articles on monasticism, notes: 'Reading these pages in preparation for publication, I am amazed at the evolution in Merton's thinking on the monastic life in the Church'.[67] Without going further into Merton's personal and monastic journey, his literary works provide an array of perspectives related to the concept of time.[68]

In addition, there are several quotes sourced from email correspondence with a cloistered contemplative (indicated as 'Mel', not the real name) during years 2012–2021.

[67] Thomas Merton, in Patrick Hart, ed., *The Monastic Journey*, (London: Sheldon Press, 1977), ix.

[68] Thomas Merton, *The Seven Storey Mountain* (London: SPCK, 2015); *The Sign of Jonas* (London: Burns & Oates, 1961).

CHAPTER 2

Research Elements and Structure

The key research elements are:

- Subject: Enclosed contemplative life
- Analytical lens: Time
- Framework: Journey

The metaphor of journey is related to the flow of time, and, as a sequential concept, it provides a suitable framework to explore temporality. These key elements are shown in Fig. 2.1.

2.1 Lens: Concept of Time

Analytical reading was chosen as the method to explore the sources through the specific lens of 'time'. It is therefore important to consider some aspects of this lens to understand how enclosed contemplatives perceive this topic in general and in their daily lives. What does the concept of time actually mean? How is it employed and experienced in the context of monastic journeys?

This introductory examination is divided between (1) God's time—the eternity of the Eternal and (2) monastic time. Monastic time is established as a conduit which aims to connect human temporal time with God's time. Monastic life represents a bridge and an intersection where two

© The Author(s), under exclusive license to Springer Nature   29
Switzerland AG 2023
R. Hujanen, *Monastic Perspectives on Temporality*,
https://doi.org/10.1007/978-3-031-34808-2_2

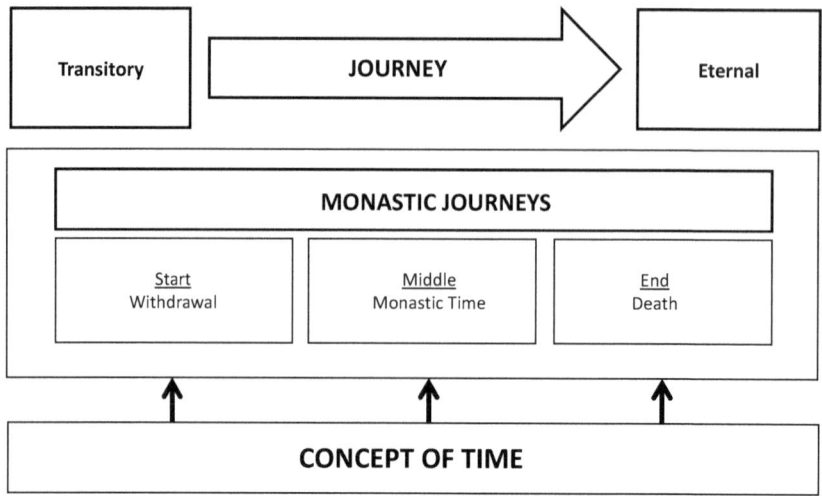

Fig. 2.1 Monastic journeys from transitory to eternal through the lens of time

dimensions and persons (vertical and horizontal, God and human) can meet. This means that monastic time incorporates aspects of liminality, relationship, and eschatology, which negotiate between the purely secular temporal concept of time and God's time. In line with the previous reasoning, where monastic life was situated in an intermediary position between God's life and secular life, monastic time can be positioned between God's divine and human secular times (Fig. 2.2).

In order to understand the lens applied to time, the following subsections will focus mainly on two dimensions of time: God's time and monastic time. However, the use of the analytical lens allows for observations across the relationships and interactions between divine, secular, and monastic times.

2.1.1   God's Time: The Eternity of the Eternal

It can be argued that God's temporal and spatial omnipresence defines eternity. For example, Isaac Newton argued that the idea of universal time was coupled with that of God because God endures forever and is everywhere present; and by existing always and everywhere, he constitutes

Fig. 2.2 Monastic time in relation with God's divine time and human secular time

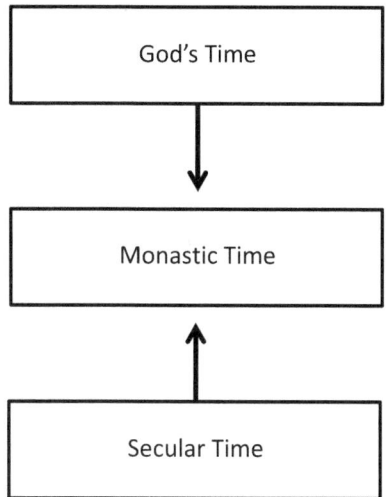

duration and space.[1] Classical Christian theology holds, as summarised by John Peter Kenney, that God created space and time and finitude, but his being is eternal and immaterial and infinite.[2] This indicates the distinction between God's ontological being and God's creative action. The Eternal, in his divine omnipotence, has chosen to create time. From this follows that, paradoxically, God's immutability combines with ceaseless dynamic action and his eternity with the present. A reflection from a Carthusian monk defines the divine eternity as a 'changeless present' in which the 'divine generation' is the *eternal and unending divine act which is indistinguishable from the divine Being*:

> The divine eternity is a changeless present, wherein the Father begets the Son, and both breathe forth the Holy Spirit ... The divine generation did not take place at the beginning of time, once and for all. It is a divine act, or rather it is the divine act, eternal and unending, which never ceases and is never interrupted, any more than is the divine Being from whom, in reality, it cannot be distinguished. Now—at every moment of time—this act is

[1] See Jimena Canales, *The Physicist & the Philosopher: Einstein, Bergson, and the Debate that Changed Our Understanding of Time*, 226–227.

[2] John Peter Kenney, *Contemplation and Classical Christianity: A Study in Augustine* (Oxford: Oxford University Press, 2013), 169.

being accomplished: the Son is born of the Father. *Ego hodie genui te*—this day have I begotten thee. (Psalm ii, 7)[3]

James Gordon states in his article on divine spatiality that, in philosophical terms, for God to be omnipresent means God must be *wholly* present at any and all regions at the same time.[4] Further, according to the scholastic theological tradition, God exists immaterially and completely fills all places resplendently; God's essence has no boundaries.[5] Gordon identifies four essential aspects of God's omnipresence from the biblical perspective. In the Old Testament, the divine omnipresence relates to God's liturgical encounter with the people of Israel, and with the cosmos as a whole, through his dwelling place in the temple. First, he observes that God's presence to the created order in general is distinct from God's special dwelling presence in the tabernacle and the temple. For Israel, there was no place in the created realm in which one could flee from God's presence, yet the temple represented a special instance of God's dwelling. Second, the 'elusive' nature of God's presence, especially with reference to the temple, is emphasised, making room for the possibility of God's absence—the idea of presence therefore entails also the possibility of absence. Divine omnipresence does not make God's presence a 'given' but rather a 'gift'. Thirdly, there is always a personal dimension—*a being related to*—in the experience of God's presence. Finally, God's presence in the tabernacle and temple is a decidedly spatial presence; but God is not only there, as if the boundaries of a physical space could contain God. God is present in persons and places in specific ways even though there is no place in creation that could escape God's presence.[6]

The idea about divine omnipresence, therefore, assumes that God himself is immaterial, infinite, transcendent, and eternal but, simultaneously, through his immanence God can relate to creatures whose existence is defined within temporal and spatial limits.

The concepts of time/eternity carry various meanings within the monastic context. They can refer to 'God's Eternal Now', his eternal

[3] A Carthusian, 'The Blessed Trinity and the Supernatural Life', http://transfiguration. chartreux.org accessed on 20 July 2019.

[4] James R. Gordon, 'Rethinking Divine Spatiality: Divine Omnipresence in Philosophical and Theological Perspective' in *The Heythrop Journal*, May 2018, Vol. 59, No. 3; 534–543: 535.

[5] Gordon, 'Rethinking Divine Spatiality', 536.

[6] Gordon, 'Rethinking Divine Spatiality', 538.

existence as well as the significance of the present moment. The contrast between the human concept of time, with its various tenses, and God's eternal perspective is displayed in the interview of a Carthusian monk in the documentary *Into Great Silence*, filmed at the Grande Chartreuse:

> The past, the present, these are human. In God, there is no past. Solely the present prevails. And when God sees us, He always sees our entire life. And because He is an infinitely good being, He eternally seeks our well-being. [7]

The contemporary Carthusian echoes Philo's (ca. 20 BC–40 AD) thinking of time, as both conclude that in God's eternity there is only the present. More precisely, Philo writes in *Deus 31*:

> Thus with God there is no future, since he has brought the boundaries of the ages under his own power. For God's life is not a time, but eternity, the archetype and pattern of time; and in eternity there is neither past nor future, but only present existence.[8]

Augustine writes at length on the concept of time in Book XI of *Confessions*, recognising that God is outside time in eternity. People may try to savour the taste of eternity, but their thoughts still twist upon the ebb and flow of things in past and future—'if only their minds could be seized and held steady, they could be still for a while and, for that short moment, they would glimpse the splendour of eternity which is for ever still'.[9] He believes that people would then contrast eternity with time which is never still and see that it is not comparable. They would understand that in eternity all is present; and how eternity, in which there is neither past nor future, determines both past and future time.[10] Following Augustine's train of thought, it could be argued that humans need a sequential, horizontal concept of time as they travel through their earthly existence. Time is what stops everything happening at once. Yet, another

---

[7] *Into Great Silence*, directed by Philip Gröning, original title: *Die große Stille*, Germany, 2005.

[8] Philo of Alexandria: *The Contemplative Life, Giants and Selections* (Mahwah, NJ: Paulist Press, 1981; trans. D. Winston), 108.

[9] Augustine, *Confessions*, XI.11.

[10] Augustine, *Confessions*, XI.11.

vertical dimension of time (eternity) can be glimpsed at least intermittently in moments of staying still, in silence and contemplation.[11]

The writer of *Ecclesiastes* describes the difficulty that humans experience in the face of temporality and God: 'he has put a sense of past and future into their minds, yet they cannot find out what God has done from the beginning to the end'.[12] Augustine, likewise, struggles to fully understand the concept of time: 'I confess to you, Lord, that I still do not know what time is'.[13] But in the midst of the changeable human condition, Augustine fixes on eternity and on the hope of a total union with God:

> You, my Father, are eternal. But I am divided between time gone by and time to come, and its course is a mystery to me. My thoughts, the intimate life of my soul, are torn this way and that in the havoc of change. And so it will be until I am purified and melted by the fire of your love and fused into one with you.[14]

Following Augustine's idea of relationship and union with God, Adalbert de Vogüé, a Benedictine scholar, underlined the importance of understanding that 'eternal life is not something, but someone'. With reference to the Gospel and Epistles of John, he identifies 'life' and 'eternal life' as proper names of Christ, which leads to the conclusion: 'Consequently, to desire eternal life is to desire Christ'.[15] This means that the monastic hope, according to de Vogüé, is less of a dream of one's own future, than the expectation of a meeting with a *divine person, who is living in the present as well as in the future*.[16] In other words, the monastic journey, rather than aiming for a distant 'spatial' destination, becomes a pilgrimage towards Another, the divine Person who is Eternal Being and lives eternally, in the present as well as in the future. This means that God's omnipresence, his capacity to be present in all places and times, enables

---

[11] See Kenney, *Contemplation and Classical Christianity* on analysis of Augustine's unmediated contemplation experience in Ostia, described as 'a marker of the soul's momentary spiritual association with eternal Wisdom', 133.

[12] Eccl 3:11 (NRSV).

[13] Augustine, *Confessions*, XI.25.

[14] Augustine, *Confessions*, XI.29.

[15] Adalbert de Vogüé, *To Desire Eternal Life: Hope Yesterday and Today* (Petersham: St. Bede's Publications, 1998; trans. J. B. Hasbrouck, 17.

[16] de Vogüé, *To Desire Eternal Life*, 18. Italics mine.

relationships with humans who are each on their individual journeys within specific times and places.

For those, like Guigo I, the fifth prior of the Grande Chartreuse in the early twelfth century, who are captured by the quest 'to seek a happiness which cannot be made but which is eternal',[17] a lifelong paradoxical journey of 'approaching infinity' opens up towards loving and knowing the eternity and immensity of God:

> God is eternal and immense. He is so great that he should be loved as much. Hence he who loves him is eternal and immense. However, no one can love him in the manner and as much as he ought to except one who knows him absolutely and perfectly, and how great he is. Yet no one can do so except he himself. Therefore true eternity and true immensity lie in him alone. God has commanded man to love that which he cannot ever love too much.[18]

The question therefore becomes the following: How to bridge this gap between humans and the eternity and immensity of God?

As argued above, Christ was identified as both 'life' and 'eternal life', yet Jesus is also identified as the Way to life, a gate to the Father. The Word was made flesh, God became a man in Christ, and his *kenosis* forms the bridge, between God and humankind as well as between eternity and temporality. In his Apostolic letter *Tertio Millennio Adveniente*, Pope John Paul II points towards the Incarnation as a culmination in the history of

---

[17] Guigo I, in Robin Bruce Lockhart, ed., *Listening to Silence: An Anthology of Carthusian Writings* (London: Darton, Longman and Todd, 1997), 18–19.

[18] Guigo I, in *Listening to Silence*, 19. This dilemma of knowing and loving God is expressed also in *The Cloud of Unknowing*, Ch. 6: 'But now you ask me, "How am I to think of God himself, and what is he?" And to this I can only answer, "I do not know".... By grace it is possible to have full knowledge of all other created things and their works, and indeed of the works of God himself, and to think clearly about them, but of God himself no one can think. And so I wish to give up everything that I can think, and choose as my love the one thing that I cannot think. For he can well be loved, but he cannot be thought ... and beat on that thick cloud of unknowing with a sharp dart of longing love, and do not give up, whatever happens', 27–28. The same topic—the interaction between knowing and loving—was addressed by Walter Hilton in *The Scale (or Ladder) of Perfection* (Great Britain, 1901), Book 3, Ch. IV, 245, where he explains why a soul should covet nothing else but only the love of God. According to Hilton, love comes out of knowing; and the more God is known, the better He is loved. Therefore, one must covet love because love is the cause why a soul comes to knowing and to the love that comes out of it. The relationship between loving and knowing thus forms a 'self-reinforcing loop'.

salvation and writes that *'time has a fundamental importance'*[19] in Christianity; in other words, time has become a dimension of God who is himself eternal:

> Within the dimension of time the world was created; within it the history of salvation unfolds, finding its culmination in the "fullness of time" of the Incarnation, and its goal in the glorious return of the Son of God at the end of time. In Jesus Christ, the Word made flesh, time becomes a dimension of God, who is himself eternal ... From this relationship of God with time there arises *the duty to sanctify time*.[20]

John Paul II here links 'time' with creation, the Incarnation and the eschatological glorious return of the Son of God at the end of time. Time is relational to God. From this follows that time can be used by humans as a means of building a relationship with God by sanctifying their use of time. It is, indeed, their duty. How monastic time responds to this consideration is the topic of the following subsection.

2.1.2   Monastic Time

The first consideration relates to a distinction between secular time and monastic time. How do they differ? An argument for the *monastic way of living* being 'different and distinct' from the secular way of life was presented previously. This then leads to the suggestion that monastic studies can also be considered as a 'different and distinct' academic field which, when exploring monastic spirituality, employs interdisciplinary methods.

The need for an interdisciplinary research approach arises from the nature of monasticism which has a role of a conduit between the temporal human and the eternal God, the horizontal (secular) approach to life and the vertical (related to divinity). Therefore, when exploring monastic journeys, we are dealing with crossroads between anthropology (and other human sciences) and theology. Similarly, enclosed contemplative life can be identified as 'liminal' positioning, a facilitator for a personal relationship

---

[19] Jean Paul II, *Tertio Millennio Adveniente*, (Vatican City: Libreria Editrice Vaticana, 1994), 10.
[20] John Paul II, *Tertio Millennio Adveniente*, 10.

between human and God. This fundamental relationship is also reflected in the distinction of time between 'temporal and eternal'. The idea of 'monastic time', similarly, can be identified as a conduit that connects the divine/eternal and human secular/temporal times.

The second consideration relates to the existence of different, but not necessarily separate, dimensions of divine and human time which is found in the second letter of St. Peter: 'But do not ignore this one fact, beloved, that with the Lord one day is like a thousand years, and a thousand years are like one day'.[21] This relates to the proposition that monastic journeys—from the beginning to the end—are, at least for some, associated with a heightened awareness of these different dimensions of time: that of the human temporary perspective and that of God's eternal perspective. From this follows that the enclosed monastic way of life can provide an environment that facilitates a partial convergence of these dimensions within monastic time.

Time Preferences

It has been said that a monk is 'a lover of eternal life'.[22] Considering the monastic journeys of enclosed contemplatives, some of the first research questions were: Do contemplatives have a preference for eternity over temporal time? To what extent did their perception of time influence the motivation and decision to spend a lifetime in enclosure and contemplative monastic life?

The idea of a 'time preference' is discussed by Eric Rowe and Jerome Neyrey with reference to an anthropological study published in 2000 by John J. Pilch[23] who identified three dominant time orientations among peoples: 'future-oriented', 'present-oriented', and 'past-oriented'. While no culture seems ever to have been exclusively one of these, according to his research argument, a culture has a dominant preference for one with a secondary but minor orientation for another.[24] Pilch summarises the characteristics of these orientations: (1) present-oriented people pay little

---

[21] 2 Pet 3:8 (NRSV).

[22] de Vogüé, *To Desire Eternal Life*, 11.

[23] John J. Pilch, *Healing in the New Testament: Insights from Medical and Mediterranean Anthropology* (Minneapolis, MN: Fortress Press, 2000).

[24] Eric Rowe and Jerome J. Neyrey, 'Christ and Time – Part Three: "Telling Time" in the Fourth Gospel', in *Biblical Theology Bulletin*, 40, 2, (2010), 79–92: 86.

attention to what happened in the past and regard the future as both vague and unpredictable; (2) past-oriented people include those who revere or worship their ancestors as well as those who have high regard for tradition; (3) future-oriented people place an emphasis upon the future which is anticipated to be 'bigger and better'.[25] This preference for a dominant (and a secondary) time-orientation, identified by Pilch, applied to both cultures and peoples in his study.

From the perspective of 'concept of time among enclosed contemplatives', it could be relevant to ask if there are present-oriented, past-oriented, and future-oriented preferences among monastic individuals as well. If so, what would be their dominant preferences? This question introduces an opportunity for a dialogue between anthropological and theological perspectives.

A quote from the *address* of John Paul II to cloistered nuns in Bologna, in 1997, provides a theological contribution to the question of time preferences. In his speech, Pope John Paul II emphasised the monastic enclosure as a proclamation of the primacy of God, and the pre-eminence the eternal:

> Your life, with its separation from the world expressed concretely and effectively, proclaims the primacy of God and is a constant reminder of the pre-eminence of contemplation over action, of the eternal over the transitory.[26]

If the eternal in the monastic approach has pre-eminence over the transitory and temporal, then it may be beside the point to try to investigate the time-orientation preference if the reference to time is limited only to the transitory temporality. The main question should then focus on 'transitory versus eternal' rather than positioning the problem within a

---

[25] Rowe and Neyrey, 'Christ and Time – Part Three', 86.

[26] Congregation for Institutes of Consecrated Life and Societies of Apostolic Life, *Verbi Sponsa: Instruction on the Contemplative Life and on the Enclosure of Nuns* (Vatican City: Libreria Editrice Vaticana, 1999). From here on, '*Verbi Sponsa*', footnote 60. This theme is found also in footnote 54 of the same document: Cf. John Paul II Address at the Plenary Meeting of the Sacred Congregation for Religious and Secular Institutes on 7 March 1980: 'The abandonment of enclosure would mean loss of what is specific in one of the forms of religious life, with which the Church manifests to the world the pre-eminence of contemplation over action, of what is eternal over what is temporal'.

framework that presents the 'transitory' temporal categories of 'past, present and future' as the only reference points. This is an important qualification to make.

Jean-Philippe Houdret, OCD, indeed argues for a distinction between the French expressions of *futur* (future) which denotes a limited tense of temporality and *avenir* (eternity) which is unlimited and beyond temporality. He argues that the future belongs only in the temporal domain, as a part of the sequence in the flow of time when we refer to the past, the present, and the future. Eternity, in contrast, is of a totally different order: it is the happening of eternity, its 'advent', which we can experience in time under a 'double register': as 'already' and as 'not yet'. Eternity is not merely 'beyond time', but it happens and is already present in the temporality.[27] This double-registered definition of eternity, it could be suggested, extends further beyond linguistics; it can refer to the liminal and eschatological existential experiences of 'being' (already) and 'becoming' (not yet) along transformative contemplative monastic journeys. Eternity presents itself simultaneously as stable and dynamic.

Sub-study of Time Preferences
In order to explore the question of monastic time preferences, a sub-study was conducted. A collection of homilies held in a Carthusian monastery and published by the title *The Spirit of Place*[28] was selected for textual analysis. The rationales for choosing this particular book relate to its origin and genre. The book covers the liturgical cycle over several years, indicating that this is a collection of actual homilies held in the monastery, likely not originally intended for external publication. The publication process would have involved some selection, but individually, these homilies appear to represent a genuine expression of the Carthusian tradition and life. These homilies were addressed to 'brothers', an exclusively monastic audience. This reflects an authentic feel of a 'monk-speaking-to-another-monk' and can therefore provide insights into what is said within an enclosed contemplative community. The quantitative results are shown in Table 2.1.

---

[27] Jean-Philippe Houdret, 'Le temps et l'éternité' In *Carmel: Au seuil de l'éternité: Le temps et la vie spirituelle*, Éditions du Carmel, Dec 2000, No 98, 7–14: 12.
[28] A Carthusian, *The Spirit of Place: Carthusian Reflections* (London: Darton, Longman and Todd, 1998). These homilies are attributed to a single anonymous writer, 'A Carthusian'.

Table 2.1 References to time in *The Spirit of Place*

Temporality	References	%
Past	14	
History	31	
Specific reference in the past	27	
Past total	**72**	**19.0%**
Today	18	
Now	26	
Already now	9	
Daily	53	
Current times	21	
Liturgical time	34	
Present total	**161**	**42.6%**
Future temporal	**36**	**9.5%**
Eternal	**57**	**15.1%**
Time (general)	**52**	**13.8%**
Total references	**378**	**100%**

Based on this sub-study, a few conclusions can be made:

1. Present-oriented references represent ca. 43% of the total, followed by 19% of references to past, 15% to eternal, and nearly 10% to future. In addition to tensed temporal categories, ca. 14% of references were made to general 'neutral' time.
2. It would be incorrect to draw any broader conclusions about monastic time preferences based on the limited material of this single sub-study. A broader study would be required to make any substantive claims about time preferences among enclosed contemplatives. Nevertheless, within this analysis, it is worth noting that apart from a certain concentration on various expressions of the 'present', references are fairly evenly distributed across the other temporal, neutral, and eternal categories. The preponderance for the 'present' in this sub-study may partially relate to the decision to include 'liturgical time' into the 'present' category. This, in turn, relates to the chosen genre, homilies, where frequent references are made to the feast of the present day; for example, 'Let us take advantage of today's feast to renew the consecration of ourselves to the Father'.

3. While the quantitative textual approach offers insights into how an individual Carthusian author approaches the concept of time, a contextual approach would be required for a more systematic thematic analysis of the topic.

4. Despite the limited scope of this sub-study, it is evident that the concept of time is a recurring topic in the selected monastic source with nearly 400 references to a broad scope of temporal categories. There are 104 text pages in the book; this equates to 3.6 temporal references per text page. To give an idea of the variety of references relating to the concept of time, examples taken from the sub-study are presented below.

5. Several references provide an initial indication of the themes that will be subject to more in-depth contextual analysis. For this reason, the results of this quantitative sub-study will be only briefly summarised here.[29] Despite the obvious limitations, a small sub-study of this kind may be a useful method to identify emerging themes as preparation of a broader systematic research.

Analysis of selected references by temporality:

PAST

Our going forward is also a going back to the source of all, to become what we are eternally in God.

God is our past, God is our future and we find him in Christ in our present. He is not enclosed in our time.

Some dreams are the voice of the past, our own past and that of the human race.

We must not cling on to the past, good or bad.

To seek God truly is … letting go of what is behind, not looking back.

I have never regretted it and there was no going back.

… leaving behind what is to be left behind in order to be free …

Brief Analysis

The above sample falls into two categories: (1) relationship with God who is the source of all in the past and who represents all human temporalities

---

[29] The phrases and sentences used for this quantitative sub-study are shown primarily to indicate their textual classifications into specific 'temporality categories' rather than to provide systematic thematic analysis which requires qualitative contextual reading.

without being himself enclosed to human time; (2) past as a reference to a period before entering monastic life, characteristically something that has been irrevocably left behind. These kinds of references were prevalent in this sub-study. It appears that 'past' for a Carthusian monk refers to a life that he has left behind, upon his decision to withdraw from secular society at the beginning of his monastic journey. It could be argued that these past temporalities also reflect a distinction between God's time, pre-monastic (secular) and monastic time.

PRESENT

The same grace of resurrection is at work in our community as such, here and now.

Now God wills everything that is, the real here and now, as the real of all time.

If God exists, the taking of the Carthusian habit today has sense, is even rigorously coherent.

… your simple yes to the mysterious wisdom and love of God's willing here and now.

Already we are risen in Christ: in a hidden way, the eternal realities are present.

Our hearts may be a living altar from which constantly ascends before God pure prayer …

… receiving the gift of life at each moment with wonder and gratitude …

At every moment, God's creative love sustains us and all things in being.

We can positively will everything, always and everywhere, that God wills.

We do not, we cannot always understand; we can always believe and will and give thanks.

Each morning we are born again of God's creative goodness …

Every time Christ touches us there is new life, a new beginning.

This is the most valuable contribution we can make to our troubled times.

To enter into the Charterhouse nowadays for a young man represents a sort of emigration.

Brief Analysis

References to various aspects of 'present' were the most frequent in the book. They were related to such expressions as today, now, already now, daily, current times, and liturgical time. Two main themes can be summarised in the above sample: (1) 'already here and now', and (2) 'always, constantly, each day'. The first is a recurring theme in monastic source materials. It forms a bridge between present temporality and realised eschatology. The second theme relates to the recurrent, cyclical nature of monastic time.

FUTURE
Our going forward is also a going back to the source of all, to become what we are eternally in God.

The Spirit ... would turn their minds towards the future, a future defined by God's promises.

... the Holy Spirit is our future.

This may involve a promise or a vow to God concerning his or her future years.

The shape of the future is uncertain.

We can go forward in hope, confidence and joy ...

... dares to dream great dreams and to go forward towards their realisation in the joy of hope.

... without the need to know and control everything so as to secure our future.

Whatever the future holds ... We do not know where God is leading us and we do not need to know.

Hopefully, in the end, we will yield to the light of truth, accept to be loved and to love totally.

Brief Analysis
Expressions in this sample refer to the 'temporal future' that relates to the remaining years of an individual's lifetime. Future, or what lies ahead as the religious contemplative goes forward in time, is unknown and uncertain, but it is faced by trust and hope in God.

ETERNAL
Then in all simplicity, we can adhere to that which is eternal and essential.

... into the eternal embrace of the Father's love

... nothing should be clung to but what is eternal.

Our spirit desires a plenitude of life beyond earthly limits, a conscious communion with Being.

... knowing and loving God as he is in himself ... it is without diminution or end.

The value of human time, its real value, can only be seen against the background of eternity.

... this space of uncertainty allows us to let in something of God's eternity, in his merciful pardon.

We can open and always reopen the dimension of eternity in our own lives ...

We too hope, one day, to enter into the eternal beatitude of God.

... to give us communion in his own eternal life ...

Already we are risen in Christ: in a hidden way, the eternal realities are present.

The Father has sent us his Word in order to lead us into his eternal beatitude.

Finally we believe that he will attain to the ineffable mystery of the Father's eternal love.

... for what can be seen is temporary, but what cannot be seen is eternal ...

... adhering to Christ and following in his footsteps, through death to life eternal.

... we are born into the plenitude of eternal life.

... the glory of the totally undreamed of newness of eternal life.

... reaching out in intention and in hope unto the eternity inhabited by God.

Brief Analysis

The 'eternity' and 'eternal' unfold here as enormous, limitless, with a multitude of meanings. Eternity is a concept that, in this sample, refers to (1) eternity of God and his eternal qualities such as love and merciful pardon; eternity is also referred to as a space 'inhabited by God'; (2) eternal life and beatitude that humans can hope to attain one day. 'Eternity' overlaps here with 'present' temporality in the line: 'Already we are risen in Christ: in a hidden way, the eternal realities are present'. Such overlapping references were common in this sample book, as the Carthusian author frequently and fluidly moved across temporalities.

TIME

Our time is mortal time, measured out.

It remains human time, measured more by its spiritual emotional content than by the clock.

This is monastic time.

No two times are the same. Your time is not my time.

... for we are responsible, must answer for the use of our time ...

To seek God truly ... is rare, and difficult to maintain throughout a lifetime.

... this veiled bodily presence, situated in the trajectory of time and mortal life ...

... bringing the Resurrection into contact with the ordinary human condition in time ...

... to carry the burdens of his cross as they present themselves in the vicissitudes of real life.

The transformation of our whole being will take time.

Christ has ascended into heaven and yet Christ will be with us on earth till the end of time.

Christ lives in and through us in space and time.

Our liberty is realised in time.

Brief Analysis

These are not temporal references per se. They express a neutral concept and consciousness of 'time'. Or, rather different 'times', such as mortal, human, monastic time, or simply the trajectory, and passage of time, a vehicle of transformation in human life. Time presents itself as a way to create a relationship with Christ, who is in heaven and 'with us till the end of time' and who 'lives in and through us in space and time'.

Time Preferences in Other Monastic Sources

An example of monastic preferences relating to transitory projects and eternal hopes is expressed by Adalbert de Vogüé:

> Whether it succeeds or not, a temporal and earthly project is only time and earth. The proper element of our hope is to transcend these limits. What we expect of God is God himself. Our hope for everlasting life goes beyond all history. It plunges into the impossible and the divine. The joy of our hope is that of Christ risen, the first-born of the dead, with whom we shall live forever.[30]

This is in line with a preference for a hope in God that transcends beyond the temporal and earthly endeavours. The sight is on everlasting life that plunges into the impossible and divine mysteries. The monastic

---

[30] de Vogüé, *To Desire Eternal Life*, 12.

journey points towards the eschatological eternity beyond the human conceptions of measurable times.

According to Donato Ogliari, the classical Latin meaning of *mundus* is related to the conceptual world of space and *saeculum* to that of time. Thus, *saeculum* is connected to the worldly time, and to individuals who live without eternal hopes, in contrast with the destiny of Christian salvation.[31]

> The saying "To become strangers in the ways of the world" thus faces the monk with the choice of entering a lifestyle and a time that is "different" from the worldly ... It is a "different" life and a "different" time because it lived in a form that is qualitatively new, or as a gift ordered to salvation. Thanks to this gift, the monk can advance on the way of seeking God, a way that ends only with the end of one's earthly life.[32]

Ogliari describes the monastic journey as qualitatively different in terms of 'way of life' and in terms of 'concept of time'. It is also viewed as a dynamic journey. The monk can 'advance' in a way which ends only at the end of one's earthly life. The purpose of this journey is to 'seek God'.[33]

Time Belongs to God

The entry to a monastery marks a reset in many ways compared to the previous life in the world. In the secular setting, one may perceive to be in control of one's usage of time, at least to some extent. With the entry to monastic life, this is likely to change as, like with other 'possessions', monastic life calls for handing over the control of one's daily timetable in obedience and poverty. Upon the entry to a monastery, a person adopts not only a new monastic name and clothing but also a distinct monastic time.

It appears that the concept of time is part of a hierarchy where ultimately time belongs to God. And as part of the monastic schedule, time is regimented to serve God. This 'ownership of time' is linked to obedience to the clock or obedience to the call of a superior to give time to whatever is required.

---

[31] Ogliari, 'Tempus Monasticum', 37.

[32] Ogliari, 'Tempus Monasticum', 37.

[33] See also John Skinner, *Hear Our Silence: A Portrait of the Carthusians* (London: Harper Collins Publishers, 1995), 74: according to Dom Cyril, Carthusian monks consider as the only possible sense of their life 'to seek him who has found them'.

Sister Angela Thérèse, a Carmelite nun interviewed by Mary Loudon, found that the most difficult adjustment at the beginning of religious life was that 'one's time is not one's own':

> To be here in Carmel is to be completely open to what He asks of you, and not trying to manipulate things to how you would like them to be … Even silly little things like when the bell rings and you're in the middle of doing something … you respond to the bell because it's the Lord calling you to the choir … I think those things in the early days are the hardest to come to grips with: the fact that one's time is not one's own. In fact, the day isn't one's own from the beginning to end.[34]

Monastic life typically follows a more or less detailed legislation on use of time. Russell Huizing, in his study of time in the Benedictine Rule, makes the following observations:

1. A monk's whole life revolved around rest, prayer, study, and work with appropriate breaks for eating. Benedict recognised these as more than simply routine activity. They represented the very journey of life itself, which is why they are repeated every day.
2. In general, the day was broken up into seven times of prayer:

   - Lauds at the time of waking (sometime between midnight and 2 am)
   - Prime at 6 am
   - Terce at 9 am
   - Sext at noon
   - None at 3 pm
   - Vespers at 6 pm
   - Compline before going to sleep

3. The sevenfold time of prayers accomplished a daily message sent to the monk that there was no part of the day in which God should not and could not be worshipped. The whole day was covered with the praises of God.[35]

---

[34] Mary Loudon, *Unveiled: Nuns Talking* (London: Chatto & Windus, 1992), 22–23.
[35] Huizing, 'Benedictine Times', 176.

Another way to assess 'how monastic time belongs to God' is to calculate hours spent on prayer and other activities. A group of medical researchers who monitored sleep patterns in two enclosed contemplative monasteries found that the members of the religious order slept on average 6.5 hours per day (+/-0.6 h).[36] The monks followed a regular regimen of prayers for a total of six hours per day (ordinary days) or seven hours per day (twice a week). In addition, they did meditation or contemplative prayer and read and studied religious books for another two to three hours per day. Each member also had a duty for the community (e.g., budget, liturgy, formation of new candidates, library, alcoholic beverage manufacture, distribution of food, and secretarial work).[37]

While externally it is possible to measure hours dedicated to various activities, the monastic reality likely is a more holistic experience of time. A poem by a Carthusian monk gives a vivid image of a situation where six monks are waiting for an old Toshiba printer to be replaced with a new printer:

The Old Toshiba[38]
It served its day and something gleaming takes.
   Its place. The expert in modern science seeks
   To integrate the new for hours on end.
   He pulled every trick without success
   While six of us just hung around. I felt
   Impatient, what a waste of precious time.
   But happily the thought of God arose
   And peace (not such as the world can give) restored
   My calm. God's creating me for this:
   To grow in patience awaiting the hour to pass.
   He allows it. His will is all that counts.
   My waiting pleases him. My work gives him praise.
   My time in choir gives honour. What more can man
   So humble do? His will is Love, his Love
   Is all our peace. However sharply we taste
   Futility, in Love no second's waste.

---

[36] Amulf, Brion, Pottier, and Golmard, 'Ring the Bell for Matins', 930.
[37] Amulf, Brion, Pottier, and Golmard, 'Ring the Bell for Matins', 932.
[38] A Carthusian, *The Old Toshiba*, an unpublished poem, May 2021.

The poem captures the dynamic of moving from impatience ('what a waste of precious time') to the patient acceptance of waiting. This comes from the realisation that the monk can think about God in any situation. God's will is love, and in love no second is wasted. What appears to be idle time becomes an opportunity to encounter God, and a learning experience to grow in patience through waiting. The humble monk regains peace and calm. All monastic time belongs to God.

Perceptions of Time
Patrick Leigh Fermor wrote about his observations in a French Cistercian monastery and concluded that time passes in a monastery with disconcerting speed. Except for the great feasts of the Church, there were no landmarks to divide time up other than the cycle of seasons. Days and soon weeks were passing almost unperceived: 'The speed of this temporal lapse is a phenomenon that every monk notices: six months, a year, fifteen years, a lifetime, are soon over: and as I found it easier to talk to them, the only regret I heard was that they had delayed so long in the world before coming to the Abbey'.[39] A similar observation about time was made by Thomas Merton, OCSO, who reflected on his enclosed life in the Gethsemani five years after his entry to the Trappist Order. Merton described how his five years in the tranquillity of the monastery had gone by like five weeks[40]:

> God has put me in a place where I can spend hour after hour, each day, in occupations that are always on the borderline of prayer ... I get plenty of time alone before the Blessed Sacrament. I have got into the habit of walking ... along the wall of the cemetery in the presence of God ... He has disposed everything in my life in order to draw me inward, where I can see Him and rest in Him.[41]

According to the Carthusian monk, Francis de Sales Pollien (1853–1936), life in a Carthusian monastery is so full of interest and animation that time passes unnoticed: 'The religious, engaged in prayer and penance, scarcely perceives the lapse of time, and when at length he quits his cell for heaven, he will be far from feeling that the way thither has

---

[39] Patrick Leigh Fermor, *A Time to Keep Silence* (London: John Murray Publishers, 2004), 38.
[40] Thomas Merton, *The Sign of Jonas*, 15.
[41] Merton, *The Sign of Jonas*, 20.

been tedious'.[42] This is echoed in the response of a cloistered contemplative to my written question: *'I read a text by a Carthusian monk who stated that in a monastery time passes very quickly ... that he barely notices the passage of time. Do you agree?'* The reply was:

> If we can add our "two cents" to this subject we would have to say that time in the cloister does indeed pass quickly. So often people have the misconception that [we] are bored praying all day, but on the contrary, our lives are immersed in our Divine Spouse! Cloistered life is an extension or can we even say a continuation of the Liturgy of the Church. Our Faith teaches us that time stands still when the Holy Mass is offered because when we have Christ on the altar we are transported to the foot of the Cross on Calvary – we are outside of space and time.[43]

The contemplative religious continued by explaining that despite the earthly realities of daily duties and works, the lives of the cloistered contemplatives are so immersed in the Divine that time in a way has no meaning for them:

> We live on the vertical plane, not on the horizontal. Our lives are like one long prayer, going from one moment to the next, giving, sacrificing, living our lives only for the One thing that matters – God. If one lives on such a deep, supernatural order, then yes, time passes by so quickly. What may seem a moment in contemplative prayer is in reality an hour, but for those who are captivated by the Beloved, time is of no importance. We are living our Heaven on earth ... there is no time in Heaven, only unending bliss and union with the Blessed Trinity.[44]

According to Ogliari, the Benedictine Rule gives time value by rescuing it from external fleetingness and from economic functionality. Time offers an internal architecture where the contemplatives can live it as a reality which pertains to their spiritual dimension. In God, time becomes a receptacle of salvation capable of rescuing the religious from the grip of the fleeting and the material.[45] In other words, time belongs to God and his eternal salvific plan, and the monastic environment, in a certain way,

[42] *Listening to Silence*, R. B. Lockhart, ed., 84.

[43] Email from 'Mel', a cloistered contemplative, 11/01/2016. Original gendered term replaced by [we].

[44] Email from 'Mel', a cloistered contemplative, 11/01/2016.

[45] Ogliari, 'Tempus Monasticum', 51.

liberates the use of time from human temporal and material consider-ations. It can be argued that, in this respect, the monastic lives at the crossroads: in the present instant of the 'horizontal' temporal time and simultaneously in 'God's Eternal Now'. Monastic enclosure offers a con-nection point where the verticality of God's eternity intersects with the human present moment. As Ogliari puts it, time, in some sense, is the capacity to acquire and accept God's reign on the part of the monk and the monastic community.[46]

In the context of the temporal, transitory time, there is a sense of unique value and urgency in the use of present time. The value of eternal time and the preciousness of the presence of the temporal time can be recognised simultaneously. The two concepts of time (transitory and eternal) do not cancel each other out. The present moment is not something to be ignored, wasted, or lost. The fleeting and perishable nature of time makes it precious, more valuable than any material possession one might own. In the words of an early Christian desert hermit: 'if gold or silver are lost, you can always find something as good as you lost. But the man who loses time can never make up what he has lost'.[47]

The Threefold Monastic Time

Referring to the previous work of Donato Ogliari, who, according to Russel Huizing, identified two measures of time in the Rule of Saint Benedict—the external chronological passage of time and the internal maturation of the individual into a purified, sanctified worshipper of God—Huizing adds a third measure of time, the sacral.[48] This sacral time, according to Huizing, can be identified with the solemn festivals of the Christian calendar—Christmas, Easter, Epiphany, Pentecost, Thursday/Friday/Saturday of Holy Week, and the Ascension were considered days of special worship in the monastery. In addition, Sunday differs from the

---

[46] Ogliari, 'Tempus Monasticum', 50.

[47] *Sayings*, 126.

[48] Huizing, 'Benedictine Times', 173. In the reference article, Ogliari appears to identify two types of time: the 'cosmic or astronomic or natural time', which he associates with exter-nal time, and, behind it, the 'monastic time', which is cyclic and repetitive in nature owing to the interior rhythms of Daily Office and the liturgical year. Therefore, one could argue that the third, 'sacral', measure of time suggested by Huizing is already integrated within the concept of 'monastic time' as presented by Ogliari. See Ogliari, 'Tempus Monasticum', 38–46. It could be further inferred that it is the 'sacral', repetitive 'monastic' time that puri-fies the individual into a worshipper of God.

other days in its liturgy.[49] Benedict made the holy days of the Christian calendar 'the gravitational center of his Rule'.[50] According to Huizing,

> As the individual regulates time, they deepen in self-discipline. As the individual deepens in self-discipline, they are confronted with the presence of God as He revealed Himself in Jesus. As this happens day after day, week after week, year after year, the individual begins to be transformed.[51]

Huizing identifies the element of *recurrence*, expressed as 'day after day', 'year after year', as a characteristic of monastic life. Within the progressive, linear nature of chronological time, a cyclical movement likewise exists. The recurrence is observed in the daily liturgical hours, regular attendance at the celebration of the Eucharist, and through the experience of participating in the cycle of the liturgical year.

Donato Ogliari argues that the spatial dimension, visibly incarnated by the monastery as a place of spiritual edification, can be understood in a new temporal dimension. He goes on to argue that it is in this sense that we can speak of *monastic time*, a time that is driven by the search for God, on both the objective and subjective planes. Such was the main occupation, according to Ogliari, when Benedict legislated the true and proper 'law of time' and in carefully planning its distribution along the course of the day. Very little time is left to the monk's own choice. Ogliari concludes that monastic time seems to flow according to a 'double reference of an objective nature': independent and not subject to that diversification which an individual use of time would inevitably involve.[52]

In his analysis of monastic time in the Rule of Saint Benedict, Ogliari notes that the daily *horarium* remains always the same; on the other hand, it continually changes. The rule is sensible to the rhythm and duration of daylight and of darkness. It regulates the daily time of the community in such a way that the framework of the day remains the same, but it permits variation and harmonious coordination in accordance with the movement of the seasons. The Liturgy of the Hours, for example, preserves intact its structure throughout the year but follows the principle that the Morning Office always begins at sunrise—just as every activity ceases at sundown.[53]

---

[49] Huizing, 'Benedictine Times', 179.
[50] Huizing, 'Benedictine Times', 180.
[51] Huizing, 'Benedictine Times', 180.
[52] Ogliari, 'Tempus Monasticum', 38.
[53] Ogliari, 'Tempus Monasticum', 39–40.

James Clark, a medieval and early modern historian, further notes that the medieval Benedictine tradition observed the transition from night to daytime by the formal change of clothes and shoes as well as by a daybreak meal; these practices were generally unknown in the wider secular society for much of the Middle Ages.[54]

The Rule of Saint Benedict introduces a 'triple perspective' which influences the Divine Office, meal times, as well as the division of time between *Lectio Divina*, work, and rest in the life of a monk. But although the monastic year follows the division across three different schemas, there is a recurring constant, a 'cardinal point' around which monastic time in all its components revolves: the celebration of Easter.[55] In this respect, Lent has a role in the anticipatory sense of the monastic journey towards the fulfilment of Easter:

> Just as the monk "desires eternal life" beyond the present existence, so he "looks forward to holy Easter" beyond Lent … Lent is a reduced model of the whole of life. Looking forward to Easter during these forty days is also a miniature image of the great desire of eternal life which runs through the whole of our lives. Each year during the Lent … the monk revives and deepens his desire for the Easter which shall never pass away.[56]

This preparatory nature of the annual Lenten time, therefore, can be understood metaphorically as a lifelong preparation for Passover and resurrection from an eschatological perspective.

Ogliari further proposes a dual function for monastic time where all time belongs to God, and time itself finds its meaning as a vehicle for salvation:

> It is the Liturgical Year that confers value on monastic time, raising it visibly above the flat and grey neutrality of cosmic time and conferring on it a salvific value. In its cycle and at regular intervals, it reminds the monk that

[54] James Clark, *The Benedictines in the Middle Ages* (Woodbridge: The Boydell Press, 2014), 125.

[55] Ogliari, 'Tempus Monasticum', 44–45.

[56] de Vogüé, *To Desire Eternal Life*, 52.

all time belongs to God, but it also reminds him that time itself is the vehicle for the quest for God.[57]

As a conclusion, a threefold approach to time can be proposed: (1) cosmic/chronological; (2) cyclical/sacral/liturgical; (3) divine/eternal. These measures of time find a reference point in creation. The eternal and immortal God created both the temporal time and the mortal beings. The cosmic time offers a sacral/liturgical space for the mortal beings to search and find the eternal God, and in him, salvation and immortality. This indicates that the central monastic question related to time is not so much about one's *mortality* but about the *immortality* of one's soul.

The early Benedictine considerations of 'time that belongs to God' set the framework for monastic life for the following centuries. Moving forward in history, it is worth noting two further developments relating to time in medieval Christianity. Firstly, as argued by Carlos Eire, medieval piety was characterised by a rhythmic quality, an endless oscillation between (1) ordinary undifferentiated time; (2) sacred recurring time which was the conjunction of *here* and *now* with *there* and *then*. According to Eire, this sacred recurring time represented a 'higher' kind of time which intersected with ordinary time and was indeed a *liminal* entryway connecting ordinary time with eternity. The Passion of Christ had an eternal, timeless quality to it because it was made present with every celebration of the Eucharist but also because it was relived and re-enacted every year during Holy Week.[58] The same was true of other major feasts, as Eire indicates:

> The cyclical nature of all feasts lent them an aura of eternity, both within and outside of time. Time did not have a straight, one-directional horizontal flow ... Instead, time was layered on various tracks and studded with vertical doorways and all sorts of thresholds to eternity, where one could find oneself transported to higher realities and eternal moments, if one paid attention.[59]

---

[57] Ogliari, 'Tempus Monasticum', 40. See also André Louf, *In the School of Contemplation* (Collegeville, MN: Liturgical Press, 2015; trans. P. Rowe), 148–149, on how the daily prayer of Psalms marks the passage of time; how relays of prayer are spontaneously created throughout days and nights as the religious endeavour to transcend the passage of time and pass over into God's eternal present; and how this causes them to enter into the divine rhythm of God.

[58] Eire, *A Very Brief History of Eternity*, 91.

[59] Eire, *A Very Brief History of Eternity*, 92.

Eire raises two central themes on medieval piety. First, he speaks of the concept of 'higher' religious time which opens a liminal doorway from the one-directional horizontal time through a vertical threshold to eternity. Second, the Passion of Christ provides a timeless and eternal quality to ordinary life through the recurring daily and annual celebration of the Paschal mystery.

More specifically relating to religious life during the Middle Ages, the monastic framework provided the liturgical calendar, the regnal year of the superior, and the personal term of profession as parallel points of reference for marking time. For example, monks' obituaries in this period generally closed with a reference to the years since their profession into the order (i.e., '*vixit in habitu monachiali*'). Therefore, as observed by James Clark, the monastic concept of time was 'self-consciously' separated from the chronological framework which became increasingly familiar for the secular world.[60]

2.2   FRAMEWORK: JOURNEY

This study uses the 'journey' as a framework to organise what is discovered when looking at the sources through the lens of time. There are three supporting perspectives for this choice of framework. First, temporality (time) is frequently experienced or described as a journey by the enclosed contemplatives. Second, journey represents the dynamism that covers an individual's lifetime and potential changes in their understanding of temporality along the way. Time moves even if one stays still, enclosed in a monastery. Time is, then, the movement that constitutes the journey. Third, this framework allows the consideration of the dual dimensions: (1) horizontal journey in temporal time in this world; (2) vertical journey in relationship with the eternal God with the hope of an eternal existence beyond this time in heaven.

Three monastic sources are used as an introduction for the structural framework of journey. First, John Binns, a scholar of early monasticism, presents the dynamic interconnectedness of the monastic movement—as a physical and interior spiritual journey within time—in his work on Christian monasteries of Palestine in 314–631:

---

[60] Clark, *The Benedictines in the Middle Ages*, 126.

Desert spirituality has at its root movement. It involves a physical journey from the city to the desert, even if, for many of the saints, this is by way of the intermediate stage of the coenobium. This movement is mirrored in the interior life of the soul as the saint becomes closer to God, more sensitive to his leading, and more able to approach him. He leaves earth and enters heaven through his asceticism. As a result the moment of death, for the saint, loses its abrupt quality of discontinuity and, instead, becomes a deepening of an already achieved status.[61]

The key monastic terms in this text are movement, journey, asceticism, interior life, earth, heaven, and relationship with God. The central concept is movement, which can be expressed on different levels. Using the terminology of horizontal and vertical, these movements can be classified as follows:

(1) Horizontal: a physical withdrawal from the city to the monastery, and eventually further into the desert. This exterior journey is mirrored in the monk's interior life.

(2) Vertical: in the monastery the soul moves closer to God, more able to approach him. In his interior life, the saint (monk) begins the transition from earth towards heaven. Physical death, eventually, proposes an existential threat. But for the monk, the 'final journey' denotes a passage towards a deepening of an already established relationship with God.

The second source presents a traditional approach of a threefold trajectory for spiritual journeys, mapped out by John of the Cross in *Ascent of Mount Carmel*. His journey of ascent to God contains three stages:

1. Start of the journey by detachment from this world (beginning of night, as things begin to fade from sight).
2. The road of faith which the soul travels (midnight, total darkness).
3. Goal of the journey: the incomprehensible and intimate God who remains obscure for the soul during this life (close of night, near the light of day).[62]

---

[61] John Binns, *Ascetics and Ambassadors of Christ: The Monasteries of Palestine 314–631* (Oxford: Oxford University Press, 1996), 239.

[62] John of the Cross, *Ascent of Mount Carmel* (USA: Bottom Hill Publishing, 2010; trans. E. A. Peers), Book 1, Ch. 2.

These stages during the earthly journey are characterised by darkness. They are compared to a night that must be passed in this life in order to eventually attain to divine union with God:

> The journey of the soul to the divine union is called night for three reasons. The first is derived from the point from which the soul sets out, the privation of the desire of all pleasures in all the things of this world, by detachment. This is night for every desire and sense of a person. The second, from the road it travels; that is faith, for faith is obscure, like night, to the understanding. The third is from the goal to which it tends, God, incomprehensible and infinite, who in this life is as night to the soul. We must pass through these three nights if we are to attain to divine union with God.[63]

The start of the journey, according to John of the Cross, is 'this world', and the goal is to attain 'divine union with God'. It is worth noting that the destination refers to a specific state, 'divine union', which can be attained in heaven after this life. But ultimately, it can also refer to God himself.

The third introductory quote is from the Carthusian Statutes, which present the monastic cell as a kind of 'holy ground' where earth is joined to heaven, as well as the divine to the human, during a long journey to attain the land of promise:

> Our principal endeavour and goal is to devote ourselves to the silence and solitude of the cell. This is holy ground, a place where, as a man with his friend, the Lord and his servant often speak together; there is the faithful soul frequently united with the Word of God; there is the bride made one with her spouse; there is earth joined to heaven, the divine to the human. The journey, however, is long, and the way dry and barren, that must be travelled to attain the fount of water, the land of promise.[64]

Taking the elements from these texts and other similar sources, it is possible to construct a general framework for a monastic journey. The journey begins with withdrawal, as the individual leaves the secular world

---

[63] John of the Cross, *Ascent of Mount Carmel*, Book 1, Ch. 2. The translation of this text is taken from Bernard McGinn, ed., *The Essential Writings of Christian Mysticism* (New York, NY: Modern Library, 2006).

[64] Carthusian Statutes, Book 1, Ch. 4.1. Retrieved from http://transfiguration.chartreux. org/statuts-en-1.htm on 14/12/2021.

and enters the monastery. The monastery represents a place 'set apart' for consecrated life, where the mortal human and the eternal God can meet, and where the individual expects to stay for the rest of his or her transitory temporal life. In the intersection between the horizontal and vertical movements, the monastery becomes a vehicle for a journey from the world to heaven.

The initial withdrawal is counterbalanced by 'contribution', through various forms of interaction, between the monastery and the world. In the context of enclosed contemplative life, this contribution can be communicated through writings, music, produced goods, hospitality, teaching, masses, and prayers offered for the fellow humans 'in the world'. It can also function as a paradoxical 'non-communication' where contemplative enclosed life raises a silent sign of an eschatological message: pointing towards the verticality of the salvific time, as a reminder about the finitude of the earthly life and about transitory nature of this world.

2.2.1   The Horizontal and the Vertical

The concepts of the horizontal and the vertical are considered first, as they form the central structure of the journey. It is worth noting that there is nothing specifically monastic in these concepts. The transitory life on earth in this world (below) and the eternal life in heaven (above) are frequently contrasted in the Scriptures: 'Set your minds on things that are above, not on things that are on earth'.[65] And, 'Those who love their life lose it, and those who hate their life in this world will keep it for eternal life'.[66]

In summary, Christian journeys can be viewed as two-dimensional movements in time and space:

(1) Horizontally, as exterior movement within the earthly perimeter (spatial) and as a progression in the human transitory life from birth to death (temporal).

(2) Vertically, as an interior ascent towards God and as an aspiring journey from world to heaven (spatial) and from transitory to eternal (temporal). While some 'foretaste' of these aspirations can be experienced during this transitory life, this movement can be only completed after physical death.

[65] Col 3:2 (NSRV).
[66] Jn 12:25 (NSRV).

A parallel of horizontal and vertical journeys is found in Italian literature. Sante Matteo compares two major Italian works of literature, Marco Polo's *Travels* and Dante Alighieri's *Divina Commedia*, arguing that despite historical similarities and connections, the two texts and the two journeys these depict are radically different. Marco's *Travels* describes a horizontal journey, a superficial exploration of this world, with no attempt to access a metaphysical realm, while Dante's *Comedy* presents a vertical journey, eventually leading up to a transcendent realm above the earth.[67] As Matteo expands:

> While Marco Polo's text might be considered an early example of a travelogue, based on an ostensibly real journey, during which he visited existing places, Dante's text, in contrast, is a fictional poem about an imagined journey. Furthermore, as opposed to Marco's travels along the surface of the world, Dante's is a vertical journey away from the surface of the earth, first down through Inferno and then up through Purgatorio to Paradiso.[68]

The purpose of the vertical path depicted by Dante relates to the journey of a soul which travels beyond the immanent physical world towards a spiritual beatitude in the transcendent seventh heaven. For Dante, the pilgrim must train his gaze to see beyond the immanent and evanescent physical world of the body and focus on the metaphysical realm of the divine, the transcendent Empyrean realm where, according to Christian belief, the eternal soul dwells.[69]

Dante Alighieri describes the Empyrean vision which was granted to him, at the end of his vertical journey: to gaze at the brightness of the Divine Majesty as eternal light. In contemplation of God, as the summation of all that is good, complete understanding of past, present, and future is gained:

> Wondering I gazed; and admiration still
> Was kindled, as I gazed. It may not be,
> That one who looks upon that light, can turn

---

[67] Sante Matteo, 'Horizontal and Vertical Journeys in the Italian Imagination: Marco Polo and Garibaldi versus Dante and Victor Emanuel II', in *MLN 129 Supplement* 2014 (Johns Hopkins University Press, 2014), SS7–S20: S8.

[68] Matteo, 'Horizontal and Vertical Journeys in the Italian Imagination', S12.

[69] Matteo, 'Horizontal and Vertical Journeys in the Italian Imagination', S12.

To other object, willingly, his view.
For all the good, that will may covet, there
Is summed; and all, elsewhere defective found,
Complete.

Oh eternal light!
Sole in thyself that dwell'st; and of thyself

Sole understood, past, present, or to come ....[70]

Similar metaphors between horizontal and vertical journeys are found in the autobiographical *Story of a Soul*. Thérèse of Lisieux knew at age fifteen that she wanted to become a cloistered contemplative nun.[71] During a train journey to Rome, where she would ask the Pope's permission to enter religious life, her thoughts contrast a journey in the world with one inside the cloister walls. Contemplating the Swiss landscape, she describes the sights seen through the train windows, much like Marco Polo could have written about his 'horizontal' journeys:

First, there was Switzerland with its mountains whose summits were lost in the clouds, its graceful waterfalls gushing forth in a thousand different ways, its deep valleys.[72]

These summits, however, lifted Thérèse's soul to higher, Dantesque 'vertical' planes:

... how much good these beauties of nature, poured out *in such profusion*, did to my soul. They raised it to heaven which was pleased to scatter such masterpieces on a place of exile destined to last only a day.[73]

While she appreciates the natural beauty on earth—which she calls a place of exile—it is considered merely transitory, 'destined to last only a day'. On her return trip to France, Thérèse again describes, first, the earthly, horizontal beauty around her before lifting her eyes upward:

[70] Dante Alighieri, *The Divine Comedy* (London: Wordsworth Editions, 2009; trans. H. F. Cary), 433–434.
[71] Thérèse of Lisieux, *Story of a Soul*, 205.
[72] Thérèse of Lisieux, *Story of a Soul*, 194.
[73] Thérèse of Lisieux, *Story of a Soul*, 194.

On the return trip the scenery was magnificent. We travelled at times along the side of the sea and the railroad was so close to it that it seemed the waves were going to come right up to us … We passed through fields of orange trees laden with ripe fruit, green olive trees with their light foliage, and graceful palm trees. It was getting dark and we could see many small seaports lighted up by many lights, while in the skies the first stars were beginning to sparkle.[74]

Thérèse anticipated that should her wish to enter to Carmel come true, this would be the last scenic trip in her life.

Ah! what poetry flooded my soul at the sight of all these things I was seeing for the first and last time in my life! It was without regret I saw them disappear, for my heart longed for other marvels. It had contemplated *earthly beauties* long enough; *those of heaven* were the object of its desires and to win them for *souls* I was willing to become a *prisoner!*[75]

Thérèse prepares to exchange the earthly sceneries into the marvels of heaven. At the same time, she associates her entry to an enclosed contemplative cloister with voluntary imprisonment in order to win souls to heaven. She thus anticipates the contribution that her withdrawal to monastic life would extend to others.

The monastic use of the word *saeculum* can also be identified with the horizontal approach of life. Ogliari notes that Paul's expression in 2 Tim 2:4 'business affairs of life'[76] (*negotii saeculares*) and the expression 'ways of the world'[77] (*saeculi actus*) used in the Benedictine monastic rule both consider the *saeculum* (translated by 'world') as the reality in which human life unrolls in its concreteness along the coordinates of space and time.[78] This is the tangible, concrete, visible, and temporal approach to life. The vertical ascent metaphor used in this context refers primarily to the vertical interior journey: 'as one ascends, one leaves mundane realities to be closer to God'.[79]

---

[74] Thérèse of Lisieux, *Story of a Soul*, 212.

[75] Thérèse of Lisieux, *Story of a Soul*, 212–213.

[76] 2 Tim 2:4 (NSRV): 'To satisfy the one who recruited him, a soldier does not become entangled in the business affairs of life'.

[77] See RB 4.20: 'To become strangers to the ways of the world'.

[78] Ogliari, 'Tempus Monasticum', 35.

[79] Lawrence Cunningham and Keith Egan, *Christian Spirituality: Themes from the Tradition* (Mahwah, NJ: Paulist Press, 1996), 53.

In simple terms, regarding the horizontal and vertical aspects, there are extreme configurations at both ends. On one extreme end, there are people who limit their entire focus to the horizontal, earthly level of life, denying the existence of God and of the vertical aspect altogether. At the other end, there are individuals who take the vertical consideration to its very extreme. This latter approach is found in Nancy Klein Maguire's account of the Carthusians in the 1960s, where she refers to the monks' singular and simple logics of the faith: 'If there is a God, they thought that a reasonable person would seek a relationship with Him and only pay attention to Him'.[80] Or, as suggested by Christiana Piccardo, OCSO, 'the monastic vocation corresponds to man's natural tension toward the absolute, a tension that finds fulfilment only in God'.[81] And in between these two extremes, the majority of people in the world navigate their way with varying levels of attention towards the horizontal and vertical over the span of their lives.

2.2.2   Monastery as a Journey

The horizontal/vertical movements within the world and to heaven would apply as general directions in Christianity as well as in many other religions. What, then, differentiates enclosed contemplative monastic journeys?

The requirement for an extreme radical commitment is described by Henri J. M. Nouwen, a Catholic priest, as he considers his observations about monastic stability and leaving everything behind to follow Jesus with 'no return'. Nouwen shares the story of a Trappist monk, John. John explained that while he was studying in the university and serving in the Navy, he could always count on being able to leave these institutions, if he found situations or the life disagreeable. But during his novitiate with the Trappists, John understood that commitment to enclosed contemplative life was different: there was not such a way out—it was 'for keeps'.[82]

The vertical monastic journey can be understood both through spatial and temporal aspects. While the vertical 'ascent' addresses the spatial

---

[80] Nancy Klein Maguire, *An Infinity of Little Hours: Five Young Men and their Trial of Faith in the Western World's Most Austere Monastic Order* (New York, NY: PublicAffairs, 2006), 207.

[81] Christiana Piccardo, *Living Wisdom: The Mission and Transmission of Monasticism* (Collegeville, MN: Liturgical Press, 2014; trans. E. Warden), 121.

[82] Henri J. M. Nouwen, *The Genesee Diary: Report from a Trappist Monastery* (London: Darton, Longman and Todd, 1995), 63.

movement from world to heaven, 'time' is related to the temporal journey from transitory to eternal.[83] In the spatial sense, for the enclosed monastics, the horizontal journey is usually confined to a limited perimeter within the monastery's walls. This, in turn, could facilitate a nearly unlimited focus on the spiritual vertical dimension. As Carmel Bendon Davis posits, the diminishing of the outer physical space (in the assumption of a contemplative or solitary abode) offered a possibly inexhaustible expansive internal space in which the individual's relationship with God could be explored and secured.[84]

Among the Desert Fathers, Anthony advocated a 'journey inwards'. He advises his fellow monks not to look far for virtue, but suggests 'it is within us, and is easy if only we are willing. That they may get knowledge, the Greeks live abroad and cross the sea, but we have no need to depart from home for the sake of the kingdom of heaven, nor to cross the sea for the sake of virtue'.[85] The Carthusian Statutes display similar aversion to travelling the world in search of the divine: 'Having left the world forever in order to stand continually before the divine majesty, and being mindful of this our special task, we view with horror the thought of going out and traveling about through town and country'.[86] This suggests that upon entering monastic life, the world, along with the desire to travel around the world, has been left 'forever'. The restless movement of the past life has been replaced by the stability of the cell, by standing 'continually' before the divine majesty. This ideal of stability in the Carthusian Statutes extends even to the wandering of the mind: 'We should not allow our minds to wander through the world in search of news and gossip; on the contrary, our part is to remain hidden in the shelter of the Lord's presence'.[87]

John Climacus (c. 579–649), in his *Ladder of Divine Ascent*, likewise warned monks against wandering from place to place and suggested instead to 'let the monastery be for you a tomb before the tomb'.[88] Similarly, a letter attributed to Russian Orthodox *starets* Nil Sorskij

[83] Cf. Eire, *A Very Brief History of Eternity*, 231–232, where 'Infinity' refers to space and time, while 'Eternity' is associated only with time.

[84] Davis, *Mysticism and Space*, 94.

[85] Athanasius, *Life of Anthony*, 20.

[86] Carthusian Statutes, Book 2, Ch. 13.1.

[87] Carthusian Statutes, Book 1, Ch. 6.4.

[88] John Climacus, *The Ladder of Divine Ascent* (Mahwah, NJ: Paulist Press, 1982; trans. C. Luibheid and N. Russell), 113.

(1433–1508) advises a fellow monk: 'Never leave your cell but stay there like in your coffin'.[89] Commitment to obedience, stability, and contemplation was also insisted upon by monastic writers in the eleventh and twelfth centuries. As noted by medieval historian Diana Webb, the spiritual man was to be alienated from the world, a *peregrinus*, a stranger in relation to it, but not a vagrant.[90] Relating to monastic stability and pilgrimage, she writes:

> It was not merely possible, but tempting, to interpret life itself, that ineluctable process from the cradle to the grave, as a pilgrimage from an earthly to a heavenly birth. The monk had chosen the perfect environment to enact this pilgrimage.[91]

Here, pilgrimage and monastic enclosure converge again as a paradoxical vessel that carries one's journey from birth to death, from earth to heaven.

Donato Ogliari notes that stability has considerable influence on the perception of time, by the profound interaction that always exists between space and time.[92] *Stabilitas*, with reference to monastic vows in the Benedictine tradition, points to a time offered and occupied by the condition of a life assumed forever in the heart of a precise community, under a rule and an abbot and in an attitude of gratitude. This is viewed in the light of 'monastic offering of self' which, according to Benedict, means that the monk must renounce self-will and his own desires so that time will not be encumbered with personal projects. Combining these considerations, Ogliari concludes that *stabilitas* in the 'physical-local' sense and in the 'interior-spiritual' sense are called to complement one another in a fruitful interaction.[93] In other words, monastic stability encompasses both space (staying in a precise monastery) and time (regulated and vowed forever).

Ogliari argues that the same symbol of the 'way' (via) as applied by Benedict to the monastic life indicates both the spatial dimension and the temporal; therefore, one can claim that the Rule of Saint Benedict can

---

[89] George Maloney, *La spiritualité de Nil Sorskij: L'hésychasme russe* (Bègrolles-en-Mauges: Abbaye de Bellefontaine, 1978), 342. Translation mine.

[90] Diana Webb, *Medieval European Pilgrimage, c. 700–c. 1500* (Hampshire: Palgrave, 2002), 84.

[91] Webb, *Medieval European Pilgrimage, c. 700–c. 1500*, 84.

[92] Ogliari, 'Tempus Monasticum', 46.

[93] Ogliari, 'Tempus Monasticum', 47–48.

describe the life of the monk as consisting in a 'beginning' and in a 'goal' to be reached.[94] It could be inferred that the Benedictine use of 'way' to describe monastic life is aligned with the framework of monastic journeys used in the current study, where the dual concepts of travelling through time (transitory/eternal) and space (world/heaven) are identified, in addition to the reference of Christ himself as the Way.

We conclude with a brief summary of five aspects which relate to the monastery as a journey.

First, enclosed monastic life represents an intermediary and liminal state in which the religious has withdrawn from the world, but has not yet arrived at the destination. Therefore, the enclosed religious is situated somewhere in-between, half-way between the world and heaven. Following this reasoning, monastic literature has given cloisters such denotations as 'Edenic garden', 'earthly paradise', and 'heaven on earth', with direct reference to the intermediary positioning of monasteries between the transitory and eternal.[95] However, the broad range of metaphors identified throughout this study provides an indication of a more multifaceted liminal nature of enclosed contemplative life. These expressions range from outright morbid 'coffin', 'tomb', 'purgatory', 'death' to negative 'exile' and 'prison' through neutral 'intersection', 'intermediary', 'threshold', 'crossroads' to heavenly 'angelic', 'paradise', and 'Edenic garden'. It is possible to view this range of expressions and metaphors as different ways of experiencing the monastic journey, which may seem 'long and arduous', as the Carthusian Statutes describe it. It is also thinkable that there can be a progression during the journey: starting with the *negative* connotation of renunciation (death to the world) through the *neutral* 'intermediary' stage in the monastery and finally approaching the end with the *positive* prospect of entering the 'true life' in the desired destination in heaven.

Second, the monastic journey has been compared to a pilgrimage where the religious does not travel horizontally 'to places' but progresses instead in other directions. These directions can be identified as vertical (towards the Divine), exterior (the religious community, broader society), and interior (towards self-knowledge, meeting with God in the interior spiritual life). Similarly, the metaphor of exile is frequently used in monastic

---

[94] Ogliari, 'Tempus Monasticum', 37.

[95] See for example Lawrence S. Cunningham, *Thomas Merton and the Monastic Vision* (Grand Rapids, MI: William B. Eerdmans Publishing Company, 1999), 27.

literature when describing the longing for the heavenly homeland. While the exile has not actually been imposed by a worldly authority, in an allegorical sense, there can be an internally experienced exile. If one regards oneself as separated and exiled from one's true homeland (heaven), what difference does it make, on earth, where one dwells on a temporary basis? Similar to pilgrimage, the idea of exile points towards the transitory nature of the journey. The travellers recognise the temporary status in which they find themselves. Being exiled means being kept away from one's own native country. Pilgrimage and exile therefore can be seen as two expressions of the transitory and intermediary status of the monastic traveller.

Third, monastic literature makes occasional references to purgatory, which can be equally viewed as a liminal or intermediary state where a person, after death, has left the world but not yet entered heaven. In monastic terminology, it could be understood in an allegorical sense that the religious have chosen to experience a 'self-imposed pre-mortem penance'[96] before their physical death. This can also be interpreted as a sequence, in which entry to an enclosed cloister marks the point of death and a tomb (allegorically) and what follows is purgatory (metaphorically) in the form of monastic life, with its aim as a preparation for everlasting blessedness in heaven.

The fourth aspect takes into account the direction of the journey. Movement in the vertical dimension can be expressed as a series of descents and ascents and experienced as participation in Christ's life. This includes periods of transitioning: between suffering and loving, sacrifice and happiness, and from humility to glory, death to resurrection. While the aim is for vertical ascent, the soul seems to go first through descent, humility, and suffering. In the words of a contemporary cloistered contemplative:

> Suffering is a part of the Christian life, and much more so for the Religious Christian life, since we all seek to be more like Christ Crucified … Goodness and love is diffusive … it has to give, and suffering is just another avenue of the complete generous gift of oneself.[97]

---

[96] Cf. Joshua R. Brotherton, 'Hope and Hell in Balthasar' in *The Thomist*, Vol. 81, No.1, (January 2017), 75–105: 101. Brotherton defines 'purgatory' as 'imposed postmortem penance'. Similarly, a self-imposed pre-mortem penance could associate the monastery as *metaphorical* purgatory before physical death.

[97] Email from 'Mel', a cloistered contemplative, 17/08/2016.

Fifth, monastic journeys are essentially 'non-journeys': the religious are on the move towards their desired destination, even if, paradoxically, this happens in enclosure. The main movement takes place within the interior life, while simultaneously the horizontal passage of time naturally flows towards the end of one's life journey.

2.3   Categories: Liminality, Relationship, and Eschatology

In the previous subsection, monastic life was considered within a framework of a two-dimensional horizontal/vertical journey. The horizontal monastic journey is presented as one's 'seventy or eighty years' timeline in this transitory world as a pilgrim or an exile. The vertical journey referred to one's interior spiritual path from transitory to eternal. This trajectory to be travelled addresses what Colleen McDannell and Bernard Lang describe as 'the main problem of religion: how to bridge the gap between the human and the divine'.[98]

How to bridge the temporal gap between the human and the divine? Three categories that relate to a transitional monastic journey can be identified:

The category of relationship is associated with the idea of monastic journeys in time and space on earth where relationships with the Eternal can be built 'Already Here and Now', while still on the way. The category of eschatology points towards the eternal beyond this current temporality and beyond the transitory nature of this world as understood in Christian eschatology. This is the idea of 'There and Then', the destination of the journey. There is a parallel between the 'smaller eschatology' in the microcosm of the individual's journey towards a new body and the newness of the eternal mode of being in heaven and between the 'grand eschatology' of the macrocosm of the created universe which is travelling towards the recreation of the new heaven and new earth. The tension of between the 'Already Here and Now' and 'There and Then', between the transitory and the eternal, is experienced as a state of liminality: that of waiting and of being on a journey, at the crossroads, in the intersection, or even in a purgatory waiting for a transformation.

---

[98] Colleen McDannell and Bernhard Lang, *Heaven: A History* (New Haven, CT: Yale University Press, 2001), 54.

2.3.1   Liminality of the Monastic Journey

Liminality is a term reintroduced into the academic discussion in the 1960s by Victor Turner, an anthropologist researching in the fields of theology and sociology. He applied liminality initially in his research on initiation rites of tribal societies. The concept of liminality was first developed by French folklorist and ethnographer Arnold de Gennep in the early twentieth century (1908).[99]

'When we first began to look for ritual analogues between "archaic", or "tribal", and "historical" religious liminality, beginning with the Catholic Christian tradition … we turned … to the ceremonies of the Roman rite. But in the liturgical ceremonies … we found nothing that replicate the scale and the complexity of liminality of the major initiation rituals of the tribal societies with which we were familiar',[100] Victor and Edith Turner wrote in their study about pilgrimage. They noted that one obvious difference was seen in the spatial location of liminality. As an example, in many tribal societies, initiands are secluded in a sacralised enclosure, clearly set apart from the villages.[101] This gave rise to their observation that in the 'historical' religions, comparable seclusion had been exemplified only in the total lifestyle of the specialised religious orders.[102]

The Turners identify contacts with the secular society as an element that corresponds with the degree of liminality.[103] This observation is relevant for the scoping question on active and enclosed orders. Monastic enclosure, due to more limited interaction with the secular society, provides a more distinct and differentiated environment from the research perspective. It could be inferred from the Turners' proposition that a stricter enclosure leads to a higher degree of liminality, as they write: 'Of course, as the history of monasticism has shown, the orders become decreasingly liminal as they enter into manifold relations with the environing economic and political milieus. That, however, is a matter of a different book'.[104]

---

[99] Turner and Turner, *Image and Pilgrimage in Christian Culture*, 2.

[100] Turner and Turner, *Image and Pilgrimage in Christian Culture*, 2–3.

[101] Turner and Turner, *Image and Pilgrimage in Christian Culture*, 3.

[102] Turner and Turner, *Image and Pilgrimage in Christian Culture*, 4.

[103] Turner and Turner, *Image and Pilgrimage in Christian Culture*, 4.

[104] Turner and Turner, *Image and Pilgrimage in Christian Culture*, 4. The current study, in a small part, attempts to explore liminality and monastic enclosure, indicated as a topic for further research ('a matter of a different book') by the Turners.

According to the Turners, all sites of pilgrimage have this in common: they are believed to be places where miracles once happened, still happen, and may happen again.[105]

> Miracles or the revivification of faith are everywhere regarded as rewards for undertaking long, not infrequently perilous, journeys and for having temporarily given up not only the cares but also the rewards of ordinary life. Behind such journeys in Christendom lies the paradigm of *via crucis*, with the added purgatorial element appropriate to fallen man.[106]

This idea of pilgrimage as a paradigm of via *crucis* and purgatory therefore applied to all Christians who left their ordinary lives to take the long and often perilous journey in order to experience miracles or a revivification of faith. Pilgrimages for lay people and seculars were, however, infrequent—maybe only once in the lifetime—opportunities for liminal external experiences. In contrast, monastic contemplatives and mystics could make daily interior salvific journeys without leaving their cloisters:

> While monastic contemplatives and mystics could daily make interior salvific journeys, those in the world had to exteriorize theirs in the infrequent adventure of pilgrimage. For the majority, pilgrimage was the great liminal experience of the religious life. If mysticism is an interior pilgrimage, pilgrimage is exteriorized mysticism.[107]

Liminality as a term has broadened from its original usage as defined by de Gennep and Turner. It has become a broad concept that can refer to people, or groups of people, who hold temporarily or permanently a status that is marginal, 'in-between', such as monastics, refugees, pilgrims, and exiles. It can refer to spaces which constitute some kind of discontinuity or threshold[108] between places, such as airport transit lounges, train stations, and harbours. In religious terms, purgatory might represent liminality. Equally, transitional states such as sleep, unconsciousness, and death could be defined as liminal. Finally, liminality can denote a gradual transition in

---

[105] Turner and Turner, *Image and Pilgrimage in Christian Culture*, 6.
[106] Turner and Turner, *Image and Pilgrimage in Christian Culture*, 6.
[107] Turner and Turner, *Image and Pilgrimage in Christian Culture*, 6–7.
[108] *Limen* (Latin) translates into 'threshold'.

time such as twilight, or a precise moment of discontinuation such as New Year's Eve.

The Turners' original definition of liminality provides a useful operative concept in the sense that it encompasses both temporal and spatial aspects. This means that it can be used to analyse both a currently experienced transition (now, here) as well as exploring the potentiality of a future status (then, there). As they write:

> It has become clear to us that liminality is not only transition but also potentiality, not only "going to be" but also "what may be," a formulable domain in which all that is not manifest in the normal day-to-day operation of social structures ... can be studied objectively, despite the often bizarre and metaphorical character of its contents.[109]

The decision to enter a monastery to spend a lifetime in enclosure and contemplative life can be viewed as a means to specifically break away from one's past in the secular world or, in general, from the passing nature of this transitory world, to a monastic vocation. In the temporal sense, liminality has its main reference point in the past. The initial break-away from the secular life can be motivated by eschatological—temporal and spatial—considerations which emphasise the priority to the eternal (heaven, infinity) over the transitory time (this life) and place (this world). It can also be motivated by the search of the Divine, the Eternal as Person, and the desire to build a deeper loving relationship with the Person—God—while still along the way.

Monastic liminality is associated with living in the crossroads, the waiting room, self-imposed pre-mortem purgatory, longing and engagement (as preparation for marriage), *vigil* and waiting, hope, in an exile in a foreign land longing for a return to one's proper homeland, on a journey or pilgrimage between one's domestic dwelling and holy shrine, 'in-between' heaven and earth. In addition, the monastery itself is perceived to stand at the crossroads between heaven and earth, a waiting room and an intersection.

In summary, there appears to be a constant dynamic in the temporal and ontological relationships between God and humans. This is reflected in the horizontal and vertical, journey and enclosure, movement and waiting, ascent and descent. The monastic life is furthermore compared to

---

[109] Turner and Turner, *Image and Pilgrimage in Christian Culture*, 3.

angelic life, purification and preparation for heaven; a progressive journey during which the religious are going through a transformation from mortal humans to immortal heavenly beings.

The condition of liminality is not limited to the start of the journey; it appears to remain a permanent and prevailing condition along the way until the very end, where another threshold is reached. Here, physical death presents another liminal experience, when it is time to leave behind what is known and familiar and to pass on to what is unknown and 'beyond' the experience of this world. However, the break-away experience at the start of the monastic journey probably characterises, in a unique way, the threshold between the past life in the secular society and the enclosed contemplative life.

2.3.2 Relationship—Already Here and Now

Relationship with God can be viewed as a motivation to embark on the monastic journey. A lifetime in the monastery is then consecrated to the building and deepening of that relationship. And dedicated time is necessary for any relationship to flourish and grow. This opportunity for a restoring of a relationship between the creatures and Creator, an individual and God, is made possible by the Incarnation of Christ, and his salvific journey on earth, in spatiality and temporality. The omnipresence of God and the sending of the Holy Spirit allow for an experience of participation and divine indwelling 'Already Here and Now'.

This relationship, while anchored in the individual's past life and looking forward into the eschatological future, in this context, can be best characterised by the present time, with the presence of the Divine and Eternal in the daily monastic life. The growth of this relationship between a religious and God is enhanced by the monastic structures: its regulated way of a life divides time in a predictable way between prayer and work as well as provides support by the monastic community and superiors. It is a matter of a personal relationship that begins on earth in faith and is expected to reach its fulfilment after death, with a hope to extend such a loving relationship, established in temporality, into 'all eternity'.

Consequences of the relationship between an individual and God can lead to participation in Christ's mission in his role of intercession and sacrifice for the benefit of others.[110] This is expressed in the contribution that contemplatives, through their liminal role, perform as intermediaries between God and the people living 'in the world'. Their dedicated time in monastic enclosure and their consecration for a lifelong relationship with God set them apart to serve their fellow humans through prayer of intercession.

In terms of an individual's vertical relationship (with God) and horizontal relationships (with others), Mayeul de Dreuille, OSB, has argued that the monastic tradition is a meeting point of two currents, horizontal and vertical, both of which carry the monk to God through complementary means. He defines the vertical current as 'the direct ascent of the soul to God, the search for the love of God, pure charity'. The horizontal current refers to 'the approach to God through the members of the spiritual family of the Brethren; their turning together towards God and a sharing of this experience'.[111]

The current study focuses primarily on the individual's vertical relationality with God. By engaging with the monastic sources primarily through a temporal lens, 'time', the focus turns on 'vertical relationality' that is *totally unique*: namely the eternity of the Eternal. In contrast, 'horizontal relationality' between humans reflects their *shared* temporality, their common condition as mortal creatures. The importance of the vertical 'God–human' relationship appears to take a precedence when temporality (instead of 'relationality') is used as the thematic lens. However, horizontal relationality—time spent with others—is obviously ever present in communal monastic traditions.

2.3.3   Eschatological Hope—There and Then

The eschatological meaning of monasticism pertains to the hope of reaching heaven and eternity, 'beyond' the temporal and spatial sense, as the true and ultimate goals of the monastic journey. Yet, the intimate relationship with God, the Eternal Person, experienced in the present moment and time, is also a key motivation for monastic journeys. The eschatological dimensions therefore do not point solely towards verticality

---

[110] Cf. Ritari, 'Librán as Monastic Archetype', 394: in medieval Irish monastic tradition, committing to monastic life could be compared to offering oneself as a 'living sacrifice to God'.

[111] de Dreuille, *From East to West*, 121–122.

Fig. 2.3 Parallel journeys of the microcosm and macrocosm

or horizontality but also towards the awareness and recognition of the Divine and transcendent 'Other'. This relationship, during the monastic journey, is perceived to be a liminal one, where contemplation and prayer can momentarily lead to an experience of transcendence 'Already Here and Now', while, on other times, the journey is conducted, not in the tangibility of seeing or touching but in hope and faith, in the obscurity of night, darkness, and unknowing.

A distinction is to be made between the smaller, personal eschatology of an individual (microcosm) and the grand, universal eschatology of humankind (macrocosm). From this perspective, the monastic eschatological message touches upon the destiny of the individual (from birth, life journey, and death to resurrection) as well as the destiny of this world and humankind (from creation, duration of the history, the end of time, and the creation of new heavens and new earth). The parallel journeys of the microcosm and macrocosm are determined by God's eternal plans (Fig. 2.3).

Enclosed contemplatives are seen as images and witnesses of the eschatological message for the world. Through their detachment from what is passing and transitory, they remind the secular society about the value of what is eternal and lasting. The monastic journey places them into a liminal position, which is recognisable for others, while they themselves seek hiddenness and enclosure. It can be claimed that this subtle monastic way of 'non-communication', in a paradoxical way, has communicated the message about the prominence of God, and the priority of the eternal over the transitory, through centuries.

2.3.4   Monastic Archetypes

How do these three categories relate to other findings in monastic studies? Patrick Sbalchiero, a French historian, has identified twelve 'archetypes' of

Christian monasticism: imitation of Christ, nostalgic of the first Christian community, supplement of or preparation for martyrdom, fight against the forces of evil, exodus, angelic life, return to the original innocence, anticipation of *Parousia*, the 'true philosophy', folly for Christ, cult of the rule, and primitivism.[112]

Nine of Sbalchiero's twelve 'archetypes' of monasticism can be mapped against the categories identified in the current study:

Liminality: Exodus, identification with the first Christian community, fight against evil.

Relationship: Imitation of Christ, martyrdom, folly for Christ.[113]

Eschatology: Anticipation of *Parousia*, angelic life, return to original innocence.

However, three of Sbalchiero's 'archetypes' cannot be directly associated with the categories of the current study. These are cult of the rule, primitivism, and the 'true philosophy'. It could be argued that these elements might not represent primary 'religious' motivations for monastic life in the same way as the other nine 'archetypes' do. Instead, they could rather be considered as secondary, derived expressions that describe various ancient philosophical or religious ways of life.

2.3.5   Kaleidoscope—Categories Overlapping

The basic substance and meaning of each of the three categories was outlined individually in previous subsections. As it turns out, the picture is not simple and one-dimensional. Instead, the scenery observed through the analytical lens of time resembles more of a kaleidoscopic view than a singular telescopic discovery. The main categories have overlapping areas which are shown in Fig. 2.4. Each category overlaps with other ones, as follows:

The experience of liminality can be expressed as the ontological difference between the Creator and the creature, God and human. This 'liminal relationship' can be explored in, and through, contemplative prayer.

---

[112] Sbalchiero, *Histoire de la vie monastique*, 19–29. Translations mine.

[113] An example of 'Folly for Christ' might be Carthusian Dom Jacques Dupont's explanation of monastic life: 'Indeed, we waste our lives for Jesus because we love him. But whoever has fallen in love, knows that love is capable of the greatest foolishness!' quoted in Tim Peeters, *When Silence Speaks: The Spiritual Way of the Carthusian Order* (London: Darton, Longman and Todd, 2015), 113.

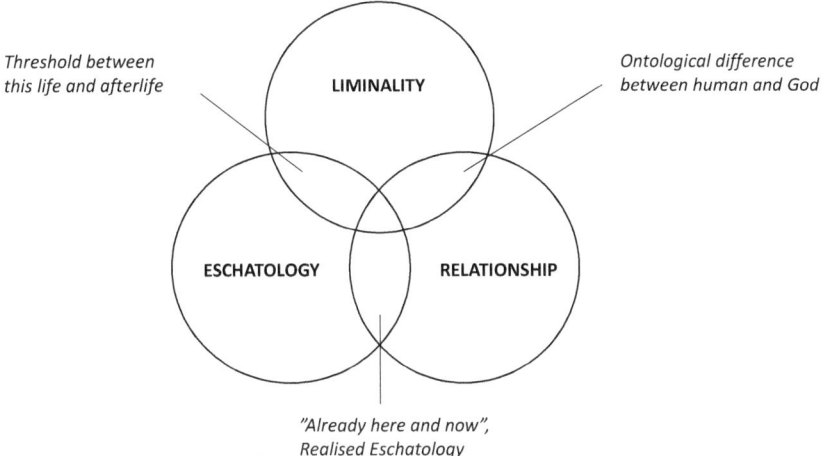

Threshold between this life and afterlife

Ontological difference between human and God

LIMINALITY

ESCHATOLOGY

RELATIONSHIP

"Already here and now", Realised Eschatology

Fig. 2.4 Categories: liminality, relationship, and eschatology

The experience of relationship can be expressed through the concept of 'realised eschatology' which brings forward the eschatological hope in the realisation of a deepening relationship with God that begins during life's journey, already here and now, and grows for all eternity.

At the end of the journey, another threshold is encountered in the reality of physical death. A completely new liminal eschatological threshold presents itself in the crossing of the border between this familiar material temporal world and an unknown spiritual afterlife in eternal heaven. This can be described as 'future eschatology' to differentiate from 'realised eschatology' and could be associated with deification and union with God, when the relationship is realised face to face (Fig. 2.4).

However, every lens has its limits, always and especially when approaching matters relating to knowledge of God. The kaleidoscope may have blind spots. But what has been seen during the research journey cannot become unseen.

2.3.6   *Categories Within the Monastic Journey Framework*

So far, the findings consist of three categories related to temporality in enclosed contemplative life. These categories overlap with each other by forming a kaleidoscopic view of monastic life. In this subsection, the

Table 2.2   Thematic expressions of categories along monastic journeys

	LIMINALITY	RELATIONSHIP	ESCHATOLOGY
START	Break-away from world	Falling in love with God	Monastery as a means
MIDDLE	Ontological difference with God	Participation in Christ's journey	God's omnipresence: Already here and now
END	Threshold: From this life to afterlife	From engagement to wedding feast	Eschatological hope: There and then

categories are mapped against the framework of monastic journey. This sets the categories into a matrix structure (Table 2.2).

This matrix offers two dimensions and two ways of answering some of the broad initial research questions about the concept of time along monastic journeys. It provides a structure to study the relationship between the three categories in the context of the progression of the monastic journey.

Starting by category (labelled at the top row), different expressions of, for example, liminality, during the progression of monastic journeys can be studied. At the start, liminality may be experienced as a radical break-away from the secular society (the world). During the time in the monastery, the religious likely encounter and deal with the ontological liminal difference between themselves and God in the environment of contemplative enclosure. Finally, liminality presents itself through another new threshold as the religious prepare to pass from this life to the afterlife as their journey approaches the end.

Starting by stage of journey (labelled on the left columns), one can investigate how different categories are present along the stages of monastic journeys. As an example of this approach, Chap. 3 contains a sub-study of different motivations to enter religious life at the start of the monastic journey. These are related to the above categories, where the motivations to enter a monastery can be associated with a desire for a clear break-away from the world, or with 'falling in love with God', or as a means to prepare for eternal life.

This is not to claim that the above matrix represents an exhaustive mapping of all the expressions that are possible within this category/ framework structure. The purpose is rather to exemplify and conceptualise some experiences related to monastic journeys and temporality.

2.4   APPLICATION OF CATEGORIES IN ENCLOSED CONTEMPLATIVE LIFE

The main elements—concept of time as the analytical lens, journey as the framework, and categories—can be employed to explore some of the paradoxes associated with enclosed contemplative life. How can these categories be applied as conduits to understand the dynamics of enclosed contemplative life as a journey in time? This is outlined in Table 2.3.

Liminality operates as a conduit between withdrawal from the world and contribution to the world. The paradox is how the decision to leave the world can lead to various forms of contribution to the world from which the religious has withdrawn. The start of the journey takes a distinctly 'monastic' perspective because it relates to motivations for withdrawal to monastic life and the role of monasteries as intermediaries between the world and the Divine. 'Past' (or possibly breaking away from the past) is the dominant temporality at the start of the journey: at the threshold of entering monastic life, one leaves behind the past life, while the new life is only just beginning.

Relationship operates as a conduit between the incarnation (descent) and ascension (ascent). The paradox is how humility can turn into glory. The mystery is in that God became man to help humans become God-like. The middle of the monastic journey moves to consider the divine perspective, the chain of salvific divine mysteries. These are perpetually contemplated during the monastic life, the dedicated period of journey for cultivating and growing the relationship between God and the religious. 'Present' is suggested as the dominant temporality during the middle of the journey. The relationship with God is experienced in the daily lives of the religious through their participation in Christ's journey, through God's temporal and spatial omnipresence as well as through contemplation.

Eschatology operates as a conduit between death and life: the mystery of how death can turn into everlasting life. The end of the monastic

Table 2.3   Categories applied as conduits

	Perspective	Paradox/mystery	Conduit	Resolution	Temporality
START	Monastic	Withdrawal	Liminality	Contribution	Past (break-away)
MIDDLE	Divine	Incarnation	Relationship	Ascension	Present
END	Human	Death	Eschatology	Life	Future/eternity

journey incorporates the perspective of an individual who is ageing and approaches the moment of death. It is 'human' in the sense that all individuals will ultimately face this moment alone. At the same time, all humankind shares this 'human condition', as it travels towards the same eschatological destiny. This is the stage of the journey where the temporal focus is more clearly and imminently oriented towards the future (or eternity).

CHAPTER 3

Beginning of the Journey

Prayer of a Young Nun

> Your presence here in this enclosed place,
> Your presence in the looks you give me,
> Your presence just when all is beginning,
> Your presence even in Your absence.[1]

The beginning of the Way symbolises the calling to the enclosed contemplative path where a positive response to this calling leads to a liminal monastic experience of a departure, of leaving the past life behind to enter a new Way of life. The Way is a reference to Christ which indicates that by accepting the monastic path, one can enter into a dedicated, vowed relationship with God. A final point of destination is designated to this Way, where the goal of the journey is associated with eschatological hope, the kingdom of heaven.

---

[1] Prayer of an anonymous nun, lines 4–7, from a booklet included in the documentary DVD film on Carthusian nuns in *Une vie en Chartreuse* (2018) produced by The Carthusian Order, 20. This expresses the beginning of an enclosed journey of a young nun. Note the paradoxical line, 'Your presence even in Your absence'.

3.1   From Withdrawal to Contribution

The question about withdrawal to monastic life will be approached from three perspectives. The first topic is the multifaceted theme of liminality which, while prevailing throughout the monastic journey, is most prominent in the early stages of the monastic journey. At these early stages, liminality is predominantly associated with many of the life-changing aspects of monastic experience such as withdrawal from the world, renunciation of one's past life, and entry to a new way of the enclosed contemplative life. These elements present a moment of disruption, a radical liminal threshold between the old and the new in many aspects, including substantial changes in one's status, one's use of space and time—a whole new way of life. Various break-away allegories have been used throughout centuries to describe the decision of embarking on a monastic journey. The second perspective is to analyse the motivations for a positive response to a monastic calling in the context of time. The third topic explores the contributions that the religious may offer as intermediaries between the Divine and society. In short, by withdrawing from the world and by embracing their liminality, enclosed contemplatives function as intermediaries between the secular and the Divine. In a schematic form:

WITHDRAWAL   LIMINALITY   CONTRIBUTION

Withdrawal is a voluntary act that creates a liminal status for the individual who joins a monastic community. This withdrawal leads to two kinds of liminal experiences: (1) dynamic liminality that is associated with the horizontal and vertical distance to be travelled in space and time, on a journey to a symbolic holy land (pilgrimage) or homeland (exile); and (2) permanent liminality that represents an institutionalised liminal status lived in the stability of the enclosed monastery which provides an environment for building a relationship with God through internal transformation. Withdrawal is the first step to the enclosed contemplative life which, through its dynamic and permanent forms of liminality, enables the religious to become intermediaries who serve the secular society they withdrew from.

3.2   Reflections

There is an allegorical parallel between pilgrimage and monastic journeys. In this context, some comparisons between monastic approaches and pilgrimages can be made based on my personal experience. Along the over

1000-kilometre journey from Le Puy-en-Velay in France to Santiago de Compostela in Spain, three pilgrim archetypes were encountered:

1. **The renouncers**: those who single-mindedly focused on the destination, always the first to leave the *refugio* in the morning, walking the longest daily distances, enduring any physical hardship to reach Santiago as soon as possible.
2. **Pilgrimage as a means**: those who focused on the pilgrimage as a religious act; some had completed the Camino multiple times, or had made pilgrimages to other destinations.
3. **Loving the Camino**: those who were usually the last to leave the *refugio* in the morning; they progressed towards the destination, enjoying the companionship of the people they met and the beauty of nature along the way, while enduring the daily hardships and sufferings in the hope of completing their pilgrimage.

These classifications bear some similarities with the three approaches to withdrawal outlined in this chapter. It should be noted that these archetypical approaches are based on personal observations rather than on wider surveys. However, recent interdisciplinary research lends some support for the vertical/horizontal pattern and the concept of time/space of pilgrimage journeys.[2]

The theme of pilgrimage represents the individual monastic journeys where the start is often inspired and motivated by the sacred destination. However, while progressing towards the goal, the pilgrim may discover

---

[2] In recent research on contemporary pilgrimage, see Tatjana Schnell and Sarah Pali, 'Pilgrimage today: the meaning-making potential of ritual' in *Mental Health, Religion and Culture*, November 2013, Vol. 16, 887-902: 901, the researchers found that personal commitment to *vertical self-transcendence* is strongly related to religious and spiritual motives to pilgrimage, while after the journey, pilgrims also show an increased commitment to *horizontal self-transcendence, unison with nature*, and *community*. Their conclusion on pilgrimage was: 'The meaning-making potential of the ritual unfolds when individuals encounter it sincerely, putting on the pilgrim's attire inwardly and outwardly, and submitting to the hardships – and revelations – of the journey'. See also Alexandra Peat, 'Modern Pilgrimage and the Authority of Space in Forster's A Room with a View and Woolf's The Voyage Out' in *Mosaic: a journal for the interdisciplinary study of literature* (Winnipeg: University of Manitoba), December 2003, 139–153, where she argues that travel, through both space and time, offers the possibility of rupture that affords a release from the limitations of reality. The reference to rupture is connected with an individual's identification of a desire for divine transcendence.

that the holy end itself already casts some joy and meaning to the daily journey, justifying the effort and pains experienced on the road. Without a specific pilgrimage destination, on the other hand, the traveller might feel directionless. It is the hope of reaching the destination that, as the ultimate goal, provides the motivation for the journey from the start to completion. At this point, the conclusion is as follows: monastic journeys, like pilgrimages, are individual and can be approached from different perspectives, but the final destination—an earthly pilgrimage sanctuary or the Heavenly Kingdom—is the same for all those who share the path.

3.3   Liminality

Liminality is understood here in the context of withdrawal into enclosed contemplative life. In this respect, liminality is compared to other forms of transitory and transformative journeys, such as pilgrimage (voluntary) and exile (involuntary). Connotations to motion, movement, and dislocation indicate a form of dynamic liminality. Withdrawal, especially in the early ascetic traditions, could mark a disruptive break-away experience. However, following the introduction of monastic rules, entry into religious life is today an adaptive process through various stages from being an observer, an aspirant, a postulant, a novice, to taking initial and permanent vows.[3] Sustained and extended withdrawal is discussed in the second part of this subsection where permanent liminality is experienced in monastic stability, *stabilitas*.[4]

3.3.1   Dynamic Liminality: Exile and Pilgrimage

The metaphors of Christians as exiles and pilgrims on earth are frequently used in monastic traditions.[5] Exile and pilgrimage, as allegories, both involve movement. However, 'exile' carries a negative undertone of involuntary wandering and longing for homeland, while 'pilgrimage' would imply a voluntary, positive, goal-oriented expedition. Either way, both metaphors indicate a transitory, liminal state, a journey somewhere in-

---

[3] Note that stages and terms of this progression vary across monastic traditions.

[4] See Bjørn Thomassen, *Liminality and the Modern: Living Through the In-Between* (Oxfordshire: Routledge, 2018), 90-93, on monasticism as an example of 'permanent liminality' within his research framework.

[5] See, for example, Ritari, 'Pilgrims in the World', 333-45.

between.[6] In the monastic context, this is exemplified in the words of a Carthusian monk: 'This world is, and always will be, a place of exile and pilgrimage; a desert to be crossed, where for a moment we pitch our tent, soon to strike it again and continue our journey'.[7]

Cassian, in his *Conferences*, uses the metaphor of a journey to the Promised Land specifically concerning withdrawal from the world.[8] Renunciation represents a beginning, a call for departure: 'Go from your country'.[9] If one's renunciation is perfect, he may be found worthy to enter 'the land that I will show you'.[10] Cassian stresses the grace of God throughout the journey: the beginning of salvation results from the call of the Lord, and the completion of perfection and purity is the Lord's gift 'in the same way'.[11] Monastics can be compared with God's chosen people who wandered to the Promised Land through the desert from Egypt led by Moses.[12]

Monastic life, according to Katja Ritari, can be viewed as a transformative spiritual journey, a pilgrimage, which invites the religious to 'become eternal in place of mortal, wise in place of stupid, heavenly in place of earthly'; it is also as a purificatory process which prepares the pilgrim to encounter the holy.[13] Ritari argues that the connection between penance and pilgrimage becomes clear when pilgrimage is understood as exile undertaken voluntarily to expiate sins or as an ascetic practice with peni-

[6] Francis Kline, OCSO, *Lovers of the Place: Monasticism Loose in the Church* (Collegeville, MN: Liturgical Press, 2012), 100, describes this 'transformation to the Promised Land' as a hope for place that is not yet known: 'Having left the society and the spirit of the age, but not having yet arrived at the goal of the kingdom of God, the monk finds himself in a kind of limbo'. He belongs no longer 'here', but his is not yet 'there'.

[7] A Carthusian, *They Speak by Silences*, 75. See also Jean-Philippe Houdret, 'Le temps et l'éternité', 14: 'We are pilgrims, journeying in faith and hope, inserted in time, oriented towards eternity. We wait for eternity and we are already in eternity, when we already live of the life of God, even if it is in the obscurity of faith and the bareness of hope'. Translation mine.

[8] Cassian, *Conferences*, Conf. 3 Ch. X.

[9] Gen 12:1 (NRSV).

[10] Gen 12:1 (NRSV).

[11] Cassian, *Conferences*, Conf. 3 Ch. X.

[12] A monastic superior can be likened to Moses who represents an intermediary between the God's people and God and shows the way to their new homeland. See, for example, Labrousse in *Saint Honorat*, 32-33, suggesting that Honoratus, the founder of the Lérins monastic community in France (around year 400), was compared to Moses by his contemporaries as he was to open the way through the desert and deliver his brothers from slavery to the Promised Land.

[13] Ritari, 'Pilgrims in the World', 338-339. The quotation is from Columbanus.

tential overtones. In both cases, pilgrimage is more associated with leaving one's homeland and placing one's destiny into the hands of God, than pilgrimage in the sense of visiting holy shrines. The destination, rather, is in heaven than in some location on earth.[14] According to Ritari, in the typical Irish usage, pilgrimage (*peregrinatio*) is a favourite metaphor for the journey of life to heaven, especially for monastic life. This aligns with multiple examples throughout history where individuals entered the monastery to wipe out their sins, making the heavenly kingdom the goal of their purgative monastic sojourn.[15]

The theme of pilgrimage is also discussed by Carmel Bendon Davis in her study on medieval enclosed mystics, where she refers to Victor Turner's finding that 'pilgrimage can be thought of as extroverted mysticism, just as mysticism is introverted pilgrimage'. She concludes that an earthly pilgrimage implies a traversing of space, but a mystical pilgrimage is an inward journey.[16] Accordingly, historian Diana Webb suggests that from the medieval monastic perspective, the monk's (or nun's) quest for the heavenly Jerusalem was the true pilgrimage, not a second-best reflection: 'The professed religious was urged to understand and embrace this greater reality rather than to hanker after lower satisfactions of mere holy sightseeing. Jerusalem the city was, after all, only a place in a world destined to pass away'.[17] Worth highlighting here is how the notion of the earthly city of Jerusalem contrasts with the heavenly Jerusalem which will be eternal, and therefore a more highly valued destination than any place which is destined to pass away in time. However, it appears that an earthly pilgrimage was still a possibility, as historical records from the Later Middle Ages show that a dispensation to make a personal pilgrimage could be sought by a monastic.[18]

From the framework of journeys from transitory to eternal, the horizontal trajectory taken within the secular setting could be compared with wandering and travelling the world, where there is a greater risk of straying and losing the vertical way. In comparison, while the monastics travel

[14] Ritari, 'Librán as Monastic Archetype', 394. On proposed connections between monasticism, penance, and pilgrimage in early medieval period, see also C.H. Lawrence, *Medieval Monasticism: Forms of Religious Life in Western Europe in the Middle Ages* (Oxon: Routledge, 2015), 61-63.

[15] Ritari, 'Librán as Monastic Archetype', 393-394.

[16] Davis, *Mysticism and Space*, 88.

[17] Webb, *Medieval European Pilgrimage, c. 700-c. 1500*, 171.

[18] See Clark, *The Benedictines in the Middle Ages*, 272.

their horizontal journeys on earth, having left the world, their monastic way represents a road-tested 'regulated' itinerary which is designed to allocate time so that, in the enclosure and occupied with daily prayers, the vertical aspect of the journey remains a constant presence in their lives and minds. In a similar vein, Victor and Edith Turner refer to pilgrimage as 'a carefully structured, highly valued route to a liminal world where the ideal is felt to be real, where the tainted social persona may be cleansed and renewed'.[19] This is the determined approach of pilgrims who have set their sights on the sacred goal.

René Gothóni, a scholar whose research interests cover monasteries and pilgrimage, notes a further allegorical linkage between pilgrimage and soul's journey to God:

> A pilgrimage is the outer manifestation of an inner journey, often referred to as an allegory of the soul's journey to God. Thus it is cosmologically meaningful. The height of the journey is the arrival at the pilgrimage centre and the encounter with the divine. There the pilgrim perceives the gap between what he should be (according to the religious tradition) and what he really is, i.e. he suddenly realizes the discrepancy between the precept and the practice.[20]

Gothóni states that this experience is, in fact, the very essence of a pilgrimage because what has been experienced cannot become unseen, what has been realised cannot be unrealised.[21] Gothóni concludes that a pilgrimage is a journey during which the 'mundane values of the previous life-style are abandoned and replaced by values that enhance spiritual development'.[22] His description of pilgrimage aligns with the current study that regards monastic journeys as 'withdrawal from the previous life-style' and 'entering a monastic way of life that enhances spiritual development'. The pilgrim's realisation of 'discrepancy' and need for transformation and the 'gap' that Gothóni refers to when encountering the divine find a parallel in the monastic dynamic aim for transformation and in the recognition of

[19] Turner and Turner, *Image and Pilgrimage in Christian Culture*, 30.
[20] René Gothóni, 'Pilgrimage = Transformation Journey', in *The problem of ritual:* based on papers read at the Symposium on Religious Rites held at Turku, Finland, on 13–16 August 1991, 110-115: 112-113.
[21] Gothóni, 'Pilgrimage = Transformation Journey', 113.
[22] Gothóni, 'Pilgrimage = Transformation Journey', 113.

the ontological difference, the 'gap' between God and human, the eternal and the temporal.

This study analyses several poems written by a contemporary Carthusian monk. The first one describes the 'interior pilgrimage' that relates to contemplative monastic traditions. This poem was chosen to illustrate the liminal experience of a pilgrim-monk who follows the road of ancient tradition on his way to a homeland in the heavens, but who also finds the homeland interiorly in his heart. The pilgrimage unfolds gradually, in a relationship with Christ, and ends in the destination of new heaven where the Father's love encompasses all.

Pilgrim of the Interior

"The Kingdom is within you. Follow me."
My journey's well trodden ground. Where all have walked
To find him so must I go. The road is thick
With travellers, a solemn joy prevails. Yet all
Are blind: "We walk by faith not sight." We trust
The One who called to silence, who went before,
Through death and resurrection, to an unknown Land.
Our homeland is in the heavens and in the heart.
The Land is nowhere. We seek no land or place.
The Kingdom is a reign of peace; all hearts at peace
And every yearning resolved. He is our peace
Beyond the anguish of time and martial law.
He is our freedom; insidious darkness, sin,
The sting of death, plucked from the heart. A new
Creation of stars, a higher cosmos of hearts
Spin out brilliant from him. He is our hope
And our salvation. Silent we follow lost
In mystery. Our pilgrimage unfolds more
By trust than steps, desire than deeds, love
Than ancient maps. The call's unique: the Cross
Calls to the depths of God: ""There will I speak
To your heart and you shall know that I am God."
"Deep echoes deep" in the pilgrim's candid heart.
The pilgrimage descends till Christ presents
His pilgrims "clothed in parted tongues of Fire":
The Father's love's in all and all are One.[23]

---

[23] A Carthusian, in Robin Lockhart, ed., 'O Bonitas!' Hushed to Silence (Herefordshire: Gracewing, 2001), 98.

The main thematic references of the poem are identified and analysed below.

1. Title: 'Pilgrim of the Interior' indicates interior journey (pilgrimage).
2. *The Kingdom is within you* points towards interiority (Lk 17:21), but with the destination, 'Kingdom', capitalised.
3. *Follow me* refers to the call to monastic life.
4. *My journey's well trodden ground. Where all have walked to find him so must I go. The road is thick with travellers, a solemn joy prevails. Yet all are blind: 'We walk by faith not sight'.* These lines continue with the journey theme (journey, road, travellers, walking) linking it with the monastic tradition (well-trodden road, thick with travellers, all have walked).
5. *We trust the One who called to silence, who went before, through death and resurrection, to an unknown Land.* There is a sequence of: Call to monastic life (called to silence) -> participation in Christ's journey (who went before) -> descent (death) and ascent (resurrection) as a vertical journey -> destination of the journey (unknown Land, heaven).
6. *Our homeland is in the heavens and in the heart. The Land is nowhere. We seek no land or place.* The destination of the journey is found simultaneously in the heavens and in the heart. There are additional liminal expressions (the Land is nowhere, we seek no land or place). Note the differing capitalisations of 'Land/land' used in the same line to distinguish the spatial images.
7. *He is our peace beyond the anguish of time and martial law.* Relationship with God is associated with peace beyond time. 'Peace' in God is contrasted with the 'anguish' of time.
8. *He is our freedom; insidious darkness, sin, the sting of death, plucked from the heart.* Relationship with God is here associated with freedom. Freedom liberates from the darkness and sting of death.
9. *A new creation of stars, a higher cosmos of hearts spin out brilliant from him* refers to Eschatology (a new creation of stars, a higher cosmos).
10. *Our pilgrimage unfolds more by trust than steps, desire than deeds, love than ancient maps.* Pilgrimage is here used as a metaphor for the monastic journey. It appears that the contemplative way of life is compared with the active way of life (trust, desire, and love < contrasted > with steps, deeds, and maps).
11. *The call's unique: the Cross calls to the depths of God: 'There will I speak to your heart and you shall know that I am God'. 'Deep echoes deep' in*

the pilgrim's candid heart. The call to the monastic way of life is a call 'to the depths of God'. It is a call to a relationship with God in which 'I will speak to your heart' and where 'Deep echoes deep'. During this journey, the monk becomes a 'pilgrim'.

12. *The pilgrimage descends till Christ presents his pilgrims 'clothed in parted tongues of Fire':*
   the Father's love's in all and all are One. The journey metaphors continue with 'pilgrimage' and 'pilgrims'. A vertical trajectory is indicated with a descent and an ascent (pilgrimage descends <until> Christ presents pilgrims to the Father's love). This passage and the poem ends with the themes of relationship and eschatology (Father's love in all and all are One).

In conclusion, this stage represents a great paradox: as the religious *exteriorly* enters the enclosed space of the cloister, *interiorly* dynamic vertical pilgrimage is about to begin. Accordingly, Lucie Rivière, a contemporary Carmelite sister, notes that it does not take long for a nun to make a tour around the cloistered space of a Carmel where she will live confined in the same place, the same buildings, the same garden. Prayer alone will open to her the 'wide and royal way of freedom'. She suggests further that 'from meditation to meditation, according to the gradual law of temporality the Carmelite advances in her pilgrimage, in search for the Spouse'.[24]

3.3.2   Permanent Liminality: In the Intersection between Earth and Heaven

'Dynamic liminality' can be understood as embarking on the liminal monastic journey through allegories of movement and journeys, such as pilgrimage and exile. 'Permanent liminality', simultaneously, presents the enclosed contemplative life as a permanent state of monastic stability. This is experienced as a liminal space 'in-between', in an intermediary place, in the intersection between earth and heaven.

What makes the monastery an intersection on the road from the transitory to the eternal? The question is related to the spatial image of the monastery as an intermediary place between earth and heaven. Lawrence Cunningham notes that monastic literature often described the monastery as an Edenic garden (*hortus conclusus*, cloistered garden) where monks

---

[24] Rivière, *Un temps supérieur à l'espace*, 84-85.

waited to be called back to God.[25] Medieval literature frequently compared the monastery to an earthly paradise (*paradisus claustralis,* cloistered paradise) even though this paradise was only a preparation for the ascent to heaven.[26]

The idea about religious life as a liminal state between 'earthly life' and 'citizenship of heaven' can be found in the earliest monastic sources. In *Historia Monachorum in Aegypto,* Egyptian monks were described as having achieved a complete state of detachment by withdrawing to 'angelic life'.[27] Through their withdrawal, they had distanced themselves from this transitory world, and while still on earth, they lead a heavenly way of life. 'They do not busy themselves with any earthly matter or take account of anything that belongs to this transient world. But while dwelling on earth… they live as true citizens of heaven'.[28] The writer adds that many of the monks were 'astonished' when they heard what goes on in the world, for they had attained a complete forgetfulness of earthly affairs.[29] Athanasius, likewise, refers to the early monks as citizens of heaven who

---

[25] Cummingham, *Thomas Merton and the Monastic vision,* 27. For further reference to cloistered gardens, see Ana Duarte Rodrigues, 'Beyond contemplation, the real functions held at the cloisters' in Ana Duarte Rodrigues, ed. *Cloister Gardens, Courtyards and Monastic Enclosures* (Centro de História da Arte e Investigação Artística da Universidade de Évora and Centro Interuniversitário de História das Ciências e da Tecnologia, 2015), 13-35: 16-17 with the term 'cloistered garden' contributed Honorius Augustodunensis (1080–1154) who wrote *Opera exegetica,* a commentary on The Song of Songs, where an enclosed garden is compared to the purity of the Virgin. This is where the phrase *hortus conclusus* is originated. Duarte Rodrigues suggests that a correspondence between this phrase and the cloister garden was made because of both the ideas of form and monastic seclusion. The cloister garden was therefore an *hortus conclusus.* This expression was later used by Italian bishop Sicard of Cremona (1155–1215) and French bishop Guillaume Durand (c. 1230–1296).

[26] Cunningham, *Thomas Merton and the Monastic Vision,* 27. Cunningham makes a connection between Dante and Merton saying that it was 'not a rhetorical flourish for Merton to call his spiritual autobiography *The Seven Storey Mountain.* The clear allusion… was to Dante's ascent of the purgatorial mount as the seven deadly sins, beginning with pride, were burned away in anticipation of arrival in the Garden of Eden'. Cunningham further notes that Dante borrowed the imaginary of ascent from monastic literature, and that the idea of spiritual ascent had its own antecedents in the ascetical literature of antiquity, 27.

[27] *The Lives of the Desert Fathers,* Prologue, 5.

[28] *The Lives of the Desert Fathers,* Prologue 5-6.

[29] *The Lives of the Desert Fathers,* Prologue 6.

colonised the desert and enrolled themselves for citizenship in the heavens.[30] John Climacus even claims that 'a monastery is heaven on earth'.[31]

Another radical expression of an intermediary status between 'this world' and 'the next world' can be found in Desert Father Abba Poemen's explanation as to why he had not replied when he had been asked a question: 'I've no reason to do so, for already I am dead. Dead men do not speak. It is not my fault that I am still here in your company'.[32] Here, one senses the monk's slight frustration from having to live (at least temporarily) in a liminal state on earth, in community with others, when he considers himself already dead.

The idea of a monastery as a halfway house between the transitory world (with its tensed past—present—future temporalities) and the eternal heaven is illustrated in Fig. 3.1. The monastic journey points towards the transcendent divine eternity beyond the human conceptions of measured and measurable times and places.

This intermediary status of the monastery is displayed in Katja Ritari's reconstruction of monk Librán's transformative journey in sixth-century Ireland and England, where Librán's story could be reduced to two matching sets of geographical and social movement[33]:

The World –> The Monastery –> Heaven
Sinner –> Monk –> Citizen of Heaven

Ritari concluded that 'in both cases, the monastic (as a space and a status) holds the intermediary place as the liminal stage in the process of transformation from human to angelic being. The monastery as a place can thus be understood as being set apart, halfway between earth and heaven'.[34] Ritari, therefore, associates monastic liminality specifically through *space* and *status*. To complement this, a *temporal* dimension can

---

[30] Athanasius, *Life of Anthony*, 14. Cf. Peter H. Görg, *The Desert Fathers: Saint Anthony and the Beginnings of Monasticism* (San Francisco, CA: Ignatius Press, 2011; trans. M. J. Miller), 27, notes that the term 'registration' or 'enlistment' selected by Athanasius alludes to recruiting soldiers with monks seen as soldiers of Christ who travel abroad and face uncertainty, fighting the enemies of their own inclinations and drives and the temptations of the devil's army.

[31] Climacus, *The Ladder of Divine Ascent*, 111.

[32] *Sayings*, 97.

[33] Ritari, 'Librán as Monastic Archetype', 398.

[34] Ritari, 'Librán as Monastic Archetype', 398.

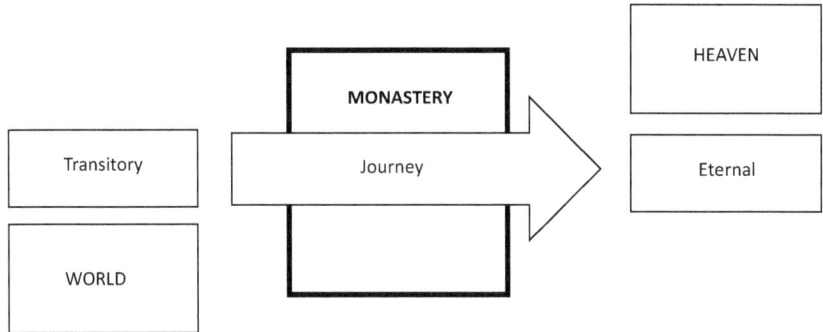

Fig. 3.1 Monastic journey from transitory to eternal

be suggested as another element of monastic liminality. Thus, monastic time is an intermediary (liminal) time between transitory and eternity:

Transitory secular time -> monastic time -> eternity

Utilising early Irish monastic sources, Ritari further compares the monastic journey to a purificatory process that prepares the pilgrim to encounter the holy.[35] The penitential attitude finds here another connection between monasticism and pilgrimage, both considered liminal states. Gothóni, indeed, points to pilgrimage as a form of ascetic practice:

> The fallen man repents his sins and asks for God's forgiveness and mercy. By going on a pilgrimage, the pilgrim narrows the gap between the life of Jesus and modern life. Through God's grace the pilgrim, the fallen man can come to Heaven, which is the ultimate goal in a Christian life.[36]

In terms of liminality, it is worth noting that both monasteries and prisons are included as examples of the spatial dimensions of liminality (relating to areas, zones, and 'closed institutions') in Danish sociologist Bjørn Thomassen's recent study.[37] To take this idea further, the difference in the spatial dimension of liminality is that enclosure within a prison is an

---

[35] Ritari, 'Pilgrims in the World', 338-339.
[36] Gothóni, 'Pilgrimage = Transformation Journey', 113.
[37] Thomassen, *Liminality and the Modern*, 91.

involuntary confinement, whereas in a monastery it is a voluntary choice.[38] Another possible similarity is that prison and monastery both represent 'a life at the margins of society'. But again, there is a difference in the voluntary/involuntary axes. It is worth noting here that monastic traditions have indeed offered an opportunity for grave sinners to enter the monastery for the atonement of crimes or sins committed,[39] or to serve some time in a paramonastic penitential community attached to a monastery.[40]

As proposed, monastic life is associated with images of an intermediary state, place, or temporal existence between earth and heaven. This calls to mind purgatory as another liminal state of existence in the Catholic tradition. Earthly purgatory could, therefore, be used as a metaphor to describe the intermediary, transformative, and purificatory nature of monastic life. The idea of a monastery as 'self-imposed pre-mortem penance' in relation to purgatory as 'imposed post-mortem penance' is shown in Fig. 3.2.

Thomas Merton, OCSO, in a concise observation, summarises what could be characterised as 'twofold liminality' of monastic life. He associates the monastery with *both* paradise *and* purgatory on earth: 'An Abbey is an earthly paradise because it is an earthly purgatory'.[41] In other words, if we interpret Merton correctly, monastic life experienced as a purgatory *'already here'* turns the monastery into a paradise *'in anticipation'*. Furthermore, monastic life as training of and anticipation for one's 'future life' can be compared to a preparatory school[42]: a transformative

---

[38] Cf. Louis J. Lekai, *The White Monks: A History of the Cistercian Order* (Okauchee, WI: Monastery of Our Lady of Spring Bank, 1953), 106, notes that according to de Rancé, the founder of the Trappist Order, monasticism was basically a form of penitential life. Monasteries were like prisons, and their inmates were considered criminals, doomed to spend their lives in severe penances. Their proper activity was to lament their sins, and the discipline of the house, the menu, and daily schedule were to be arranged accordingly.

[39] See, for example, Lawrence, *Medieval Monasticism*, 142-143. For similar stories about the desert dwellers, see, for example, Palladius, *The Lausiac History*, Ch. XIX on 'Moses the Robber' who gave himself up to a monastery to practice asceticism.

[40] Ritari, 'Librán as Monastic Archetype', 392.

[41] Thomas Merton, in Robert Inchausti, ed., *The Pocket of Thomas Merton* (Boston, MA: New Seeds, 2005), 102; from The Secular Journal of Thomas Merton (New York, NY: Farrar, Straus & Cudahy, 1959).

[42] See RB Prologue 45 which refers to the monastery as 'a school for the Lord's service'. See also Merton, *The Seven Storey Mountain*, 372: 'The monastery is a school – a school in which we learn from God how to be happy. Our happiness consists in sharing the happiness of God, the perfection of His unlimited freedom, the perfection of His love'.

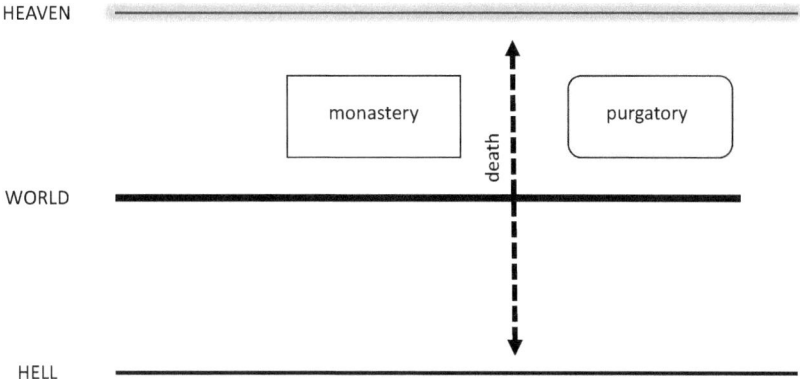

Fig. 3.2 Between world and heaven

institution that aims at perfecting and preparing the religious for an angelic life in heaven.

From a temporal perspective, regardless of the metaphor used for the monastery, whether it is compared to a school, prison, or purgatory, the liminal state is still only transitory. These metaphorical states are not indefinite or eternal. Carthusian Dom Innocent refers, in fact, both to a school and paradise as he reflects on the temporality of human existence: 'Life would be a disaster if we did not know that death would come to us one day. How could men remain indefinitely in the valley of tears? We are born to meet God… *Death is the end of school. Afterwards comes Paradise*'.[43]

These references to monastery as a purgatory or a prison—and to world, in general, as a 'valley of tears'—seem to imply strongly negative notions of time. Does monastic culture, therefore, indicate clearly negative temporal experiences? One could suggest that the repetitive daily *horarium*, lack of control over one's own time and conflicts arising from the community life, might be sources of boredom or frustration. From the spatial-temporal and social perspectives, enclosed contemplative life could potentially present itself as remarkably monotonous: a similar *horarium* every day (temporal), confinement to enclosure with virtually no prospects for individual journeys outside the walls of the monastery (spatial) and being surrounded daily by the same faces in the same community (social).

---

[43] Nicholas Diat, *A Time to Die: Monks on the Threshold of Eternal Life*, (San Francisco, CA: Ignatius Press, 2019; trans. D. le Merrer), 161. Italics mine.

Monastic life is not suitable for everyone, and indeed not all who enter a monastery end up staying. It would be a topic for a separate study to explore reasons, time-related or other, for individuals leaving the enclosed contemplative life. However, as the majority of sources used in this study relate to those who have actively chosen to stay in a monastery, the overall experience of monastic time is positive. Time is perceived as a gift of God and as such valuable and dynamic.

To summarise, liminality was introduced as a category that is associated with the enclosed contemplative life. Liminality is omnipresent throughout the enclosed contemplative life. It operates as a dynamic element, as a spatial or temporal movement, and as a permanent state that is associated with monastic stability. The aim is next to demonstrate how liminality can be viewed as a conduit and a facilitator between: (1) monastic withdrawal from the world at the beginning of the monastic journey; (2) contribution to the world. This liminal space and status allow the monastics to perform a role as intermediaries between the world and heaven.

3.4   Withdrawal and Renunciations

From the perspective of monastic journeys, the first step is renunciation of the world. In extremis, renunciation can be experienced as a form of dying.[44] Death to the world gives room to a new life, lived according to the evangelical counsels. It leads to the renunciation of self-will (obedience), worldly possessions (poverty), and intimate relationships (chastity). This is found implicitly in *Sayings*, where the Desert Fathers refer to themselves as 'already dead'. When the monk Arsenius was delivered the news about a large inheritance from his relative, he said: 'I died before he did. Now that he is dead, how can he make me his heir?' He renounced the will and accepted nothing.[45]

---

[44] The idea of death to self and the world is evident in Cassian, *The Monastic Institutes*, Book 4, Chapter 34, where Abba Pinufius, in his speech to a new brother who is about to be received in the monastery, claims: 'Self-denial is nothing other than the sign of mortification and bearing the cross. So that you may know this day that you are dead to this world and its works and desires'. It can be argued that while the entry to the monastery marked an initial death, dying becomes a daily exercise for the monk from thereon. For Cassian in *Conferences*, Conf. 18, Ch. VII, those living in monasteries constantly renew the fervour of their original act of renunciation, and 'never fulfilling their own will, they are crucified daily to this world and made living martyrs'.

[45] *Sayings*, 53.

Indeed, an early term used for monks was 'renouncers' (*'apotaktikoi'*), which referred to the choice to renounce career, status, property, marriage, and family.[46] An example of what this could mean is found in Donato Ogliari's observation regarding the transitory nature of what is being renounced; monks renounce certain aspects of life that pass away with time, such as family, status, career, and goods.[47] It could be added here, regarding eschatological theme, that not only will the 'things of this world'[48] pass away with time but that *this world itself* will pass away,[49] as will the temporal time associated with this world, at the end of time. It could be further proposed that the idea of self-denial and daily recurring (negative) *renunciations* of possessions, own will, and married status is counterbalanced by the corresponding (positive) *commitments* to poverty, obedience, and chastity in the periodic renewal of monastic vows, after the initial profession to monastic life. This is consistent with the idea of monastic journeys where the first steps, in the beginning, require major voluntary, life-changing decisions that involve 'breaking away' from the secular world and renunciation of certain aspects or options in life. But as the monastic journey progresses towards the middle and the end, it can be assumed that, if the individual remains committed to monastic life, the positives derived from ongoing dedication will outweigh the initial negations of the 'threshold' experience.

While all Christians generally believe that God provides—through work, wealth, family, and Church—monastics, who have left behind their former secular status and relations, even more radically depend on Divine Providence. They rely on God for the needs of both body and spirit,[50] and these daily needs are now fulfilled within the monastic community.[51]

---

[46] William Harmless, *Desert Christians: An Introduction to the Literature of Early Monasticism* (New York, NY: Oxford University Press, 2004), 232.

[47] Ogliari, 'Tempus Monasticum', 36.

[48] 1 Jn 2:15 (NRSV).

[49] 1 Jn 2:17 (NRSV).

[50] See Evagrius, *Chapters on Prayer*, Ch. 129: 'Trust in God for the needs of your body and then it will be clear that you are also relying upon him for the needs of your spirit'.

[51] See, for example, Bentley Layton, *The Canons of Our Fathers: Monastic Rules of Shenoute* (Oxford: Oxford University Press, 2016), 77, 83.

A distinct 'monastic reading'[52] related to leaving everything to follow Jesus can be applied to Mark's Gospel (Ch. 10) in this sequence of exchanges:

> Man: 'Good Teacher, what must I do to inherit eternal life?'[53]
>
> Jesus: '[Go], sell what you own, and give the money to the poor, and you will have treasure in heaven; then come, follow me'.[54]
>
> Peter: 'Look, we have left everything and followed you'.[55]
>
> Jesus: 'Truly I tell you, there is no one who has left house or brothers or sisters or mother or father or children or fields, for my sake and for the sake of the good news, who will not receive a hundredfold *now in this age*— houses, brothers and sisters, mothers and children, and fields, with persecutions—and *in the age to come* eternal life'.[56]

The italics added to '*now in this age*' and '*in the age to come*' could be understood pointing towards a distinct eschatological message in Jesus's promises to his followers. It appears that leaving behind the temporal earthly possessions and relations first, 'in this life', leads to consequences which, similarly, are transitory in nature (possessions, relations, and persecutions) and, subsequently, 'in the age to come', lead to eternal life as the ultimate reward. This passage could also indicate that what has been left

---

[52] The researcher acknowledges that biblical texts can have various interpretations. For this reason, the term 'monastic reading' is introduced here in recognition of a tendency for an idiosyncratic monastic interpretation of the Scriptures. This 'monastic reading' could be considered as 'radical, literal interpretation'. Regarding early monastic traditions, see, for example, Peter King, *Western Monasticism: A History of the Monastic Movement in the Latin Church* (Kalamazoo, MI: Cistercian Publications, 1999), 56-57, who claims that the monastic movement of the fourth century was 'deeply scriptural'. The current study has encountered this in several topics which formed early monastic traditions such as withdrawal, evangelical counsels, communal life, and continuous prayer. But 'monastic reading' can (paradoxically) sometimes be identified also as 'allegorical interpretation' of the Scriptures. An example of this would be the association of Martha with the active life, and Mary with the contemplative life. Brendan Freeman, OCSO, *Come and See: The Monastic Way of Today* (Collegeville, MN: Liturgical Press, 2010), 188-189, also refers to a distinct 'very monastic way of interpreting the Scriptures', identifying both a literal ('putting the reading into practice') and a spiritual interpretation.

[53] Mk 10: 17 (NRSV).

[54] Mk 10: 21 (NRSV).

[55] Mk 10: 28 (NRSV).

[56] Mk 10: 29-30 (NRSV).

behind, in order to follow Jesus, will be compensated in abundance with other kinds of relationships and possessions, already in this life.

The difference is that the new life, additionally, presages persecutions that could take the form of interior or external sufferings. Recurring references in monastic sources indicate experiences of individual interior sacrifices. The first steps of the monastic journey, especially, were often considered the hardest ones. Amma Syncletica, one of the early Desert Christians, acknowledged the reality of a slow and painful process towards transformation for those who converted to an ascetic life:

> All must endure great travail and conflict when they are first converted to the Lord but later they have unspeakable joy. They are like people trying to light a fire, the smoke gets in their eyes, their eyes begin to water, but they succeed in what they want. It is written, "Our God is a consuming fire" (Heb 12:29), and so we must kindle divine fire with tears and trouble.[57]

The way of renunciations and daily dying to self have remained a constant challenge in monastic life, as may be evidenced by the answer of a contemporary Catholic sister in a recent survey (2009). She wrote to an open-ended question, '*What do you find most challenging about religious life?*':

> To daily die to self so as not to take back the gift I offered to God – not to take back or desire the things I gave up for the love of God.[58]

The above response expresses the sacrifice of giving up, or foregoing, some things in life for the love of God. A similar dynamic is found in the text of the contemporary Benedictine monks of the Monastery of Demeure Notre Père in France. They explain the triple renunciations of family, possessions, and one's will to give themselves entirely to God, to be alone with him. These triple renunciations reflect the evangelical counsels of chastity, poverty, and obedience:

---

[57] *Sayings*, 15. Similarly, John Climacus in *The Ladder of Divine Ascent* 75 laments: 'Violence (cf. Matt 11:12) and unending pain are the lot of those who aim to ascend to heaven with the body, and this especially at the early stages of the enterprise, when our pleasure-loving disposition and our unfeeling hearts must travel through overwhelming grief toward the love of God and holiness. It is hard, truly hard'.

[58] Johnson, Wittberg, and Gautier, *New Generations of Catholic Sisters*, 106.

For the Kingdom, we relinquish founding a home. We forego the receipt of human love. We enter with Jesus in this *very first threshold of monasticism*, alone with God.

What we possess on this earth, we deliver to Jesus in the person of his poor, to stay poor with him all our lives...

Then we enter with Jesus in the mystery of his obedience to the Father, with all the consequences that this commitment can entail for the rest of our lives. He, who gives his will, gives himself entirely. He leaves the care of his existence to the Lord.[59]

The liminal, almost existential, vulnerability expressed by these Benedictines bears a resemblance with the words of the Apostle Peter in the previous passage of the 'monastic reading' of Mark's Gospel: 'Look, we have left everything and followed you'.[60]

It is worth highlighting that the three key categories—liminality, relationship, and eschatology—are captured concisely in the above text from the French Benedictines. The monks give up a home, foregoing human love and family in the *eschatological hope for the Kingdom*, and enter, with Jesus, in the margins of the society, in the *liminal 'threshold of monasticism'*, alone but in *relationship with God*. They know they will stay poor all their lives. They commit their will and their lives to God, leaving their entire existence in his care.

Some early sources suggest a progression, a sequence, in relation to monastic renunciations. John Cassian identifies three sorts of renunciations in a Conference with Abbot Paphnutius[61]:

1. Renunciation of all the wealth and goods of this world;
2. Rejection of vices and former affections of soul and flesh;
3. Detachment of the soul from all present and visible things to contemplate only things to come, setting the heart on what is invisible.

As proposed by Pierre Miquel, OSB, it is possible to view these as threefold 'successive renunciations'[62]: initially from renouncing what is

---

[59] Monastère Demeure Notre Père, *Livre de vie monastique: Chemin d'Évangile* (Paris: Editions Saint-Paul, 1984), 191. Translation and italics mine.

[60] Mk 10: 28 (NRSV).

[61] Cassian, *Conférences*, Conf. 3, Ch. VI.

[62] Pierre Miquel, *Lexique du désert* (Bégrolles-en-Mauges: Abbaye de Bellefontaine, 1986), 137.

transitory—through internal purification— towards contemplating eternal goods instead of present and visible things. These three successive renunciations could, therefore, be associated with the progression of the monastic journey:

1. Withdrawal at the start of the journey
2. Internal purification during the middle of the journey
3. Setting heart on eternal goods and things to come at the end of the journey

In conclusion, at this stage, the above is consistent with the dynamism of the monastic journey and the categories: (1) liminality of withdrawal at the start of the journey; (2) deepening relationship with God during the journey; (3) eschatological hope at the end. This suggests a dynamic sequencing of temporalities: secular time → monastic time → divine time, eternity. In this context, liminality can be viewed as a separation from the purely secular concept of time, leading to dedicated monastic time to grow in relationship with God, and thus pointing towards eternity and eschatological hope through the convergence of human and divine temporalities.

3.5   MOTIVATIONS FOR WITHDRAWAL

Following on the general review on renunciation, three somewhat different but related motivations to monastic withdrawal can be identified. The first, *Break-Away*, compares the short duration of earthly life to eternity and concludes that heaven is of more value than the world. The second motivation considers *Monasticism as a Means* of reaching heaven, with adherence to a monastic rule as a method for gaining eternal life. The third approach, *Falling in Love with God*, views monastic life as a way to anticipate eternal life through an intimate relationship with God 'already in this life'.

These three approaches were initially identified through a close reading of monastic texts as motivations for entry into religious life. Further analysis indicates a possibility for an alignment of these motivations with the three categories of enclosed contemplative life and in relation to spatial, temporal, and personal aspects. The following relationships emerge:

1. **Break-away** highlights the abrupt break from the past, the *liminality* of leaving one's past life behind and entering a new enclosed monastic way of life, in the margins of the society. This involves certain spatial distancing from the secular society.
2. **Monasticism as a means** is associated with a temporal orientation towards eternity with the *eschatological* hope to find a secure proven way to salvation and eternal life.
3. **Falling in love with God** reflects the desire to unite with God in a loving personal *relationship* during monastic life, experienced already here on earth but to reach fullness in the new life in heaven.

It would be premature, and possibly incorrect, to suggest that the three proposed motivations for withdrawal have been subject to historical development. Rather, and more likely, they have coexisted through centuries. It should be acknowledged that even an individual's withdrawal decisions may have multiple motivations. Motivations can also evolve and take different emphases in the course of one's temporal history (Fig. 3.3).[63]

The field of social psychology of religion has also engaged in research to investigate ways of being religious or spiritual. The findings of various studies point towards three dimensions, or ways, of being religious: means, end, and quest.[64] However, these definitions and especially the attempt to specify a developmental sequence between them remain speculative. In the absence of longitudinal studies in which the same individual's scores on all three religious orientation dimensions would be measured at a number of points of time, no evidence of a typical pattern has been produced and more empirical evidence would be needed.[65] The three suggested approaches to monastic motivations for withdrawal could be identified with the three dimensions of being religious:

[63] This kind of evolution and personal maturing is found, for example, in Rousseau's study on the fourth-century monastic founder Pachomius. Rousseau suggests that from what may have been a naïve generosity and a crude fear of hell, Pachomius progressed to a careful balance between many acknowledged social obligations and a self-effacing but ardent desire for union with God. See Philip Rousseau, *Pachomius: The Making of a Community in Fourth-Century Egypt* (Berkeley, CA: University of California Press, 1999), 133.

[64] See C. Daniel Batson, Patricia Schoenrade and W. Larry Ventis, *Religion and the Individual: A Social-Psychological Perspective* (New York, NY: Oxford University Press, 1993), 155-190.

[65] Batson, Schoenrade and Ventis, *Religion and Individual*, 182-183, 188.

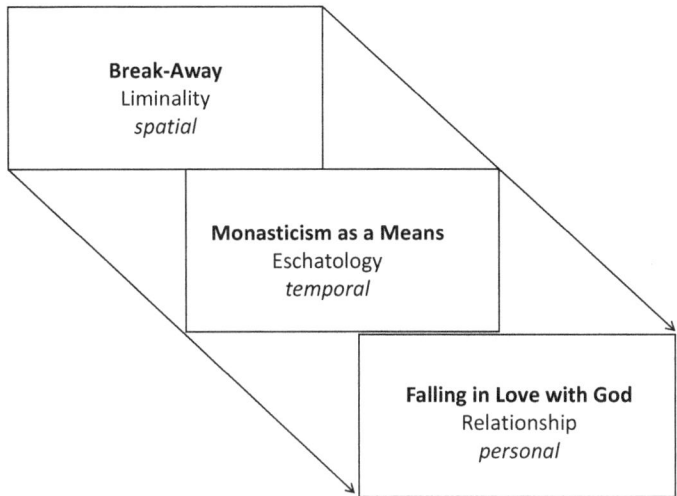

Fig. 3.3 Motivations for enclosed contemplative life

1. 'end' (intrinsic) aligned with 'break-away' to pursue the aim and the destination
2. 'means' (extrinsic) associated with 'monasticism as a means' of reaching the end
3. 'quest'[66] representing the search for a relationship with God

However, further research would be required to consider if the suggested three religious dimensions could be theoretically applied into monastic journeys, whether these dimensions are independent, and whether a sequential development can be identified. The following subsections will explore the three motivations in more detail.

3.5.1 Break-Away

Scholars of the Early Church have analysed the historical context of the birth of the monastic movement in the third century. The radical

---

[66] See Batson, Schoenrade and Ventis, *Religion and Individual*, 181: The basic components of the quest orientation were summarised as (1) readiness to face existential questions without reducing their complexity, (2) self-criticism and perception of religious doubts as positive, and (3) openness to change.

'renunciation unto death'—solitude, asceticism, and suffering endured as consequences of withdrawal—could be understood as bloodless or white martyrdom[67] at the time when the persecutions of early Christians were still ongoing, or in fresh memory.[68] Referring to the writings of Clement of Alexandria and Origen, Church historian Henry Chadwick concludes that ascetical theology was 'dominated by the ideal of the martyr who hoped nothing in this world but sought for union with the Lord in his passion'.[69] After the persecutions ended, the ascetics continued in the spirit of martyrdom, striving to achieve the same 'self-sacrificing detachment from the world'.[70]

Greg Peters, an American theologian, has identified two main historical motivations behind the early monastic lifestyles. First, the persecutions of the Christians, which did not stop until the fifth century, led some to flee from the world to deserts either from fear or self-protection or to seek persecution in their own terms in Christ-like self-denial to fight one's desires, anxieties, and sinful self-will. Second, some early Christians assumed that Christ's return was imminent, and therefore they chose countercultural lifestyles, giving up societal expectations and norms to live in immediate eschatological anticipation.[71] The eschatological expectation appears to have, at least to some extent, provided a motivation for the early monastic movement.

During the first centuries, when Christian monasticism was emerging, those who wanted to withdraw from the secular society had little previous experience on which to rely. No ready blueprint was available for a

---

[67] King, *Western Monasticism*, 76; Labrousse, *Saint Honorat*, 44.

[68] See W.H.C. Frend, *The Rise of Christianity* (London: Darton, Longman & Todd, 1986), 318-328, for Decian and Valerian persecutions (in years 250-260); and 440-463, for Diocletian persecution (in years 270-305).

[69] Chadwick, *The Early Church*, (London: Penguin Books, 1993), 177.

[70] Chadwick, *The Early Church*, 177. See also, for example, the Profession Note of Thérèse of Lisieux in *The Prayers of Saint Thérèse of Lisieux: The Act of Oblation* (Washington, D.C.: ICS Publications, 1997; trans. A. Kane) writing at the eve of her profession: "Jesus, may I die a martyr for you. Give me martyrdom of heart or of body, or rather give me both....", 38.

[71] Greg Peters, *The Story of Monasticism: Retrieving an Ancient Tradition for Contemporary Spirituality* (Grand Rapids, MI: Baker Academic, 2015), 33-34. Peters relies partly on Henri Chadwick's seminal work, *The Early Church*, which was first published in 1967 and is directly referenced above. Peters here adds value to the arguments from his specific research focus, the early history of monasticism.

Christian version of 'philosophical life',[72] although different ascetical groups already existed among Greek and Roman philosophical schools, in Judaism[73] and other religions.[74] Among the earliest experimenters of dedicated Christian ascetic piety were the 'apostolic wanderers' of third-century Syria, who embraced celibacy, poverty, and homeless wanderings in the mountains.[75] Therefore, also young Anthony, whose classic break-away withdrawal story[76] is accounted below, had rather limited options around year 270. As Athanasius explains: 'there were not yet so many monasteries in Egypt, and no monk at all knew of distant desert; but all who wished to give heed to themselves, practiced the discipline near their own village'.[77]

Anthony (ca. 251–356) was born into a wealthy Christian family. At the age of eighteen or twenty, he inherited the family assets after the death of his parents. The decisive moment came when young Anthony one day entered the church and heard the Gospel being read. It was the passage where Jesus says to the rich man: 'If you wish to be perfect, go, sell your possessions, and give the money to the poor, and you will have treasure in heaven; then come, follow me'.[78] Moved by these words, as if read directly for him, Anthony immediately gave his land possessions to the villagers,

---

[72] See Samuel Rubenson, 'Monasticism and the Philosophical Heritage' in Scott Johnson, ed. *The Oxford Handbook of Late Antiquity*, (Oxford: Oxford University Press, 2012), 487-512; 505, on monasticism as 'philosophical life'. See also Augustine Holmes, *A Life Pleasing to God: The Spirituality of the Rules of St Basil* (Kalamazoo, MI: Cistercian Publications, 2000), 9-11.

[73] Kallistos Ware, 'The Way of the Ascetics; Negative or Affirmative?', in Vincent L. Wimbush and Richard Valantasis, eds. *Asceticism* (New York-Oxford: Oxford University Press, 1998), 3-15: 4.

[74] Diarmaid MacCulloch, *Silence: A Christian History* (London: Penguin Books, 2014), 71.

[75] Daniel Caner, *Wandering, Begging Monks: Spiritual Authority and the Promotion of Monasticism in Late Antiquity* (Berkeley, CA: University of California Press, 2002), 50-77. This form of asceticism continued to be practised alongside the emerging monasticism. Adalbert de Vogüé, *Le monachisme en occident avant saint Benoît* (Bégrolles-en-Mauges: Abbaye de Bellefontaine, 1999), 22, mentions that the piety of wandering Syrian monk Isaac was documented in Western sources as late as the sixth century. This form of wandering asceticism predates Christianity; see, for example, Peters in *The Story of Monasticism*, 29, on holy men called 'wanderers' who practised extreme asceticism as early as the sixth or seventh century BC.

[76] Athanasius's classic account on Anthony's life is considered influential also because it attributed to the conversion experience of Augustine. See Augustine, *Confessions*, VIII. 12.

[77] Athanasius, *Life of Anthony*, 4.

[78] Mt. 19:21 (NRSV). This is also an example of 'monastic reading' of Scriptures.

and later sold the remaining movable property and gave the money to the poor.[79] Anthony then withdrew to the Egyptian deserts for an ascetic life for the rest of his years.

It may be worth noting, in this context, that the Gospel passage which Anthony heard began with the rich man's question: 'Teacher, what good deed must I do to have eternal life?'[80] From Athanasius's account, it is not entirely clear to what extent young Anthony's decision was initially motivated by the desire for eternal life. But as the story unfolds, during his years in the desert Anthony developed a distinct temporal conviction about life's brevity compared to eternity:

> For the whole life of man is very short, measured by the ages to come, wherefore all our time is nothing compared to eternal life... And though we fought on earth, we shall not receive our inheritance on earth, but we have promises in heaven; and having put off the body which is corrupt, we shall receive it incorrupt.[81]

Equally, in the spatial sense, for Anthony, the whole world is very small compared to heaven:

> Let us not be faint nor deem that the time is long, or that we are doing something great... Nor let us think, as we look at the world, that we have renounced anything of much consequence, for the whole earth is very small compared with all the heaven.[82]

Anthony's radical withdrawal to Egyptian deserts influenced others. Palladius in *The Lausiac History* refers to several similar radical withdrawal stories along these lines: 'A man named Apollonius, a merchant, who had renounced the world and come to live on Mount Nitria',[83] and 'Pior, a young Egyptian, having renounced the world, left his father's house and in an excess of zeal gave his word to God that he would never see any of his relations again'.[84] Nicholas Molinier notes that, for Palladius, such

---

[79] Athanasius, *Life of Anthony*, 1-3.
[80] Mt. 19:16 (NRSV). This initial question is not included in the account of Athanasius in *Life of Anthony*
[81] Athanasius, *Life of Anthony* 16.
[82] Athanasius, *Life of Anthony*, 17.
[83] Palladius, *The Lausiac History*, XIII.
[84] Palladius, *The Lausiac History*, XXXIX.

brief descriptions are sufficient to characterise 'a radical change of life'.[85] The concept of 'fleeing from the world' was already known in Greek philosophy, not necessarily as a physical departure, but rather as 'increased attention to spiritual values'.[86] However, *The Lausiac History* gives examples of less extreme forms of withdrawal, where ascetics sold most of their possessions and distributed some of the revenues to the poor while keeping some properties outside cities where they retired to lead a 'godly life' and to provide hospitality.[87] What characterises the *Break-Away* approach is primarily the motivation to withdraw from the secular society and its values to devote time for the Divine. This manifests itself in a form of 'self-imposed marginalisation'.

It can be noted that the radical renunciation and break-away approaches of the early ascetic traditions appear less frequently as motivation for withdrawal in later monastic sources. The two other motivations become more prevalent in later centuries with the development of regulated monastic cenobitic traditions. Interestingly, the same pattern is observed by the Turners in the context of pilgrimage. They write about holy shrines:

> The first pilgrims tend to arrive haphazardly, individually, and intermittently, though in great numbers, "voting with their feet"; their devotion is fresh and spontaneous.[88]

This 'haphazard' and individual movement is evident among the first ascetics like Anthony and the other Desert Dwellers. Equally, as the ascetic movement grew more institutionalised through monastic rules and orders, the historical development of pilgrimage, identified by the Turners, could apply to monastic journeys as well:

> Later, there is progressive routinization and institutionalization of the sacred journey. Pilgrims now tend to come in organized groups, in sodalities, confraternities.[89]

---

[85] Nicholas Molinier, *Ascèse, contemplation et ministère* (Bégrolles-en-Mauges: Abbaye de Bellefontaine, 1995), 57.

[86] Molinier, *Ascèse, contemplation et ministère*, 57.

[87] Palladius, *The Lausiac History*, LXI, LXII, LXVI.

[88] Turner and Turner: *Image and Pilgrimage in Christian Culture*, 25.

[89] Turner and Turner: *Image and Pilgrimage in Christian Culture*, 25.

The following section introduces a slightly different motivation for withdrawal as monasticism develops further.

3.5.2   Monasticism as a Means

It did not take long until the cenobitic way of life became the dominant form of monasticism in the East.[90] In the *Conferences*, Cassian relates how, at the time of his stay in Egypt (c. 385–400), cenobites already represented the majority of monks dwelling throughout the whole of Egypt.[91] In the late sixth century, various reports of religious life indicate that approximately one out of every four monks lived as a solitary in Italy, while in France the relationship was one in three.[92] It could be argued provisionally, that the development of cenobitic monasticism shifted the emphasis from an abrupt 'break-away' from secular societies to lead ascetic solitary lives in deserts towards an idea of 'religious life as a means of salvation'—with rules and a membership in a monastic order—which started to take form in the fifth century.

This second approach is exemplified by the deliberations of Honoratus (ca. 370–430) upon his decision to withdraw into religious life. With reference to 1 Jn 2: 16-17,[93] Honoratus considered that everything in this world is vanity and will pass away, while he who does the will of God lives forever, just as God himself lives forever. He was convinced that in exchange for the worldly pleasures, he would be granted loftier joys: 'All that exists in this world is vanity and concupiscence for the eyes and the world will pass with concupiscence, but he who has fulfilled the will of God abides forever, as God himself abides forever'.[94] Worth noting here is the temporal link between God's eternity and one's goal for eternal life. Honoratus considered the entry to religious life as an 'exchange' between transitory temporal joys and the following of a monastic rule:

---

[90] Cenobitic refers to the communal monastic approach, distinguished from an eremitic (hermit) way of life.

[91] Cassian, *Conferences*, Conf. 18, IV.

[92] de Vogüé, *Le monachisme en occident avant saint Benoît*, 141.

[93] NRSV: 'for all that is in the world—the desire of the flesh, the desire of the eyes, the pride in riches—comes not from the Father but from the world. And the world and its desire are passing away, but those who do the will of God live forever'.

[94] Hilaire d'Arles, 'Sermon sur la Vie de Saint Honorat', in Labrousse, *Saint Honorat*, 108. Translation mine.

May my joy be in my salvation, wisdom my wife, my pleasure in the practice of virtues, may Christ be my treasure! He will give me, in exchange for ephemeral joys, better joys. He will grant me in this life the pleasure and the honor of following his Rule with ardor and *thus* becoming worthy of the kingdom of heaven.[95]

The text could be read as an indication that Honoratus saw the monastic life as a way of salvation. He believed that Christ would give him, in this life, the pleasure and honour of following the monastic rule ardently and thus (*'ainsi'*, in the French text), by this means, becoming worthy of the kingdom of heaven.

Another early reference to monasticism as a 'proven method' for the journey from transitory to eternal is provided by Horsiensius (c. 300–388), the successor of Pachomius. Horsiensius compared monks to liberated slaves who follow the monastic path to heaven: 'We are free; we have cast from our necks the yoke of enslavement to the world... And let us think of the traditions of our father as a ladder which leads to the kingdom of heaven'.[96] The Rules of Pachomius themselves appear to imply that adherence to his monastic tradition would aid for a successful passage through heaven's gate on Judgement Day.[97] There is a similar reference in the Rule of Saint Benedict: 'faithfully observing his teaching in the monastery until death, we shall through patience share in the sufferings of Christ that we may deserve also to share in his kingdom'.[98]

This approach of *'Monasticism as a Means'* could be further observed during the emergence of the mendicant orders in the thirteenth century. In this epoch, as stated by Francisco Rafael de Pascual, OCSO, numerous legends appeared on the supernatural origins of the habit of the main religious orders. The religious habit, already converted into a sacred sign of belonging to the order, was considered a guarantee of salvation not only for the monk or the friar, but also for those faithful Christians who had the

---

[95] Hilaire d'Arles, 'Sermon sur la Vie de Saint Honorat', *108*. Translation and italics mine.

[96] *Pachomian Koinonia III*, (Kalamazoo, MI: Cistercian Publications, 1982; trans. A. Veilleux), 171. Quoted in Harmless, *Desert Christians*, 158.

[97] Pachomius, in *The Rules of Pachomius* (Great Britain: Aeterna Press, 2014; trans. G.H. Schodde), 24, concludes his last set of rules with a reference to the Final Judgement: 'If ye observe this [ordinance] and do it, ye will find my voice on that day at the narrow portal during the terrible judgement. And he, the Lord, will aid you to do this commandment, to whom be glory to all eternity, Amen'.

[98] *The Rule of St. Benedict in English* (Collegeville, MN: The Liturgical Press, 1982; trans. T. Fry), Prologue 50.

privilege of wearing it on their deathbed.[99] This symbolic attribution of monastic habits as a means, or as hope, for salvation has continued from the thirteenth century to modern times.[100] In recent sources, a Carthusian Father speaks, on the occasion of a cloister monk taking the Carthusian habit, about 'clinging to what is eternal' as he addresses the monk in his homily: 'Your taking of the habit today symbolises a deep commitment to orientate all your forces and desire towards the kingdom of heaven'.[101] The connection between the habit (as a symbol of monastic life) and the monk's commitment and desire towards the heavenly kingdom is clearly identifiable in this text.

Adalbert de Vogüé (1924–2011), OSB, a monastic scholar, contributes the moment of his religious calling—at the age of ten—to his reading of a book that raised questions about the vanity of earthly life.[102] Among the monastic sources, de Vogüé's personal account represents a distinctly philosophical-intellectual temporal (time vs eternity) argumentation as a motivation to enter monastic life. He records his realisation of the 'incomparability of time and eternity', and its consequences as an instantaneous resolution:

> Between time and eternity, there was no common measure. What would come to an end, must be sacrificed or subordinated to what would last forever. Life must be made into a preparation; everything must be staked on what was definitive and absolute. Christ's appeal to leave all to follow him was the very expression of this demand and this truth. There was nothing else to do here below and I would do it.[103]

[99] Rafael de Pascual, '"El hábito no hace al monje": formas y simbolismos de los hábitos', 25-30. See also, for example, a Carmelite *confrater* wearing the scapular on their deathbed and to be buried in it, in Frances Andrews, *The Other Friars: Carmelite, Augustinian, Sack and Pied Friars in the Middle Ages* (Suffolk: The Boydell Press, 2015), 30. In association, regarding to secular Christians' wishes to be buried in monastic precincts and on the practice of lay burials in Medieval Cistercian monasteries, see Emilia Jamroziak, *The Cistercian Order in Medieval Europe 1090-1500* (Oxon: Routledge, 2013), 101-107.

[100] For example, Isabel Allende's *Retrato in Sepia* (Barcelona: Plaza & Janés Editores, 2003), 16, tells a story about a businesswoman, who at the end of her colourful life wished to wear the sombre Carmelite habit on her deathbed and to be buried in it. The historical setting of this novel is in early twentieth-century Chile: 'ella deseaba irse a la tumba con el hábito triste de las carmelitas y que se ofrecieran misas cantadas durante varios años por el reposo de su alma'.

[101] A Carthusian, *The Spirit of Place*, 15-16. The homily is dated in 1991.

[102] de Vogüé, *To Desire Eternal Life*, 7-16.

[103] de Vogüé, *To Desire Eternal Life*, 9.

From that moment, the evidence that one should consecrate one's life to God and to eternity remained an indubitable 'primary truth' for him.[104] Adalbert de Vogüé makes both temporal and spatial distinctions: between time/eternity and between 'here below'/heaven. He writes that monastic life, aroused by the desire for heaven, is an anticipation of heaven here on earth. He suggests further that there is only an external relation between the reward and what merits the reward, in the same way as there is a relation between an object for sale and the price by which one buys it, and concludes: 'It is by leading a heavenly life already, that one goes to heaven'.[105] It appears that he is not far from inferring that it is by leading a monastic life that one goes to heaven. Equally, one could interpret that in the above passage 'reward' means heaven, and 'what merits the reward' refers to monastic life. These statements can be understood to reflect the idea of 'Monasticism as a Means'. This inference can be detected again in the context in which de Vogüé discusses the early monastic approach as described in the *Life of Saint Anthony*. He begins the chapter on 'Monastic Tradition' by stating: 'From the earliest document onwards, the monastic life appears as a life polarized by the desire for eternity'. At the end of the same chapter, he reminds about the transactional approach of an 'exchange' by quoting Anthony: 'In this world every object is sold at its just price, and everything is exchanged with another of the same value, but the promise of eternal life is bought at a ridiculously low price'.[106] This transactional reference bears a similarity with the 'exchange' between worldly pleasures and loftier heavenly joys that was deliberated also by Honoratus.[107]

---

[104] de Vogüé, *To Desire Eternal Life*, 9. Note that this comparison, or rather incomparability, between the transitory temporality and eternity bears similarity with monk Anthony's considerations.

[105] de Vogüé, *To Desire Eternal Life*, 41. It appears that here 'reward' means heaven and 'what merits the reward' refers to monastic life.

[106] de Vogüé, *To Desire Eternal Life*, 40-42.

[107] In other sources, Nieremberg in *A Treatise on the Difference between Temporal and Eternal*, published originally in 1640, writes about the happiness of those who renounce temporal goods for the securing of the eternal: 'those who are poor in spirit, and have forsaken their possessions for Christ, are in this world filled with joy, peace and comfort, and in the next enjoy the kingdom of heaven. O how happy are they who understand this, and know how to exchange earth for heaven!', 383-384. This indicates monastic poverty as a means for heavenly riches. However, Nieremberg also identifies love for God as a motivation to accommodate one's self poverty, in dedication to undivided love for God, 397.

To summarise, 'the life which leads to heaven is itself a heavenly life'.[108] This statement is a notable transition towards the approach of 'Falling in Love with God' and experiencing a foretaste of heavenly life already here and now, which is the topic of the following subsection.

3.5.3   Falling in Love with God

Instead of the thought of death, life in the fullness of love can be an attraction and a motivation to monastic life. In a recent survey (2009), the researchers found that especially younger generations of American Catholic sisters used 'spousal' and 'bride of Christ' images in open-ended questions relating to their attraction to their way of religious life. They wrote, for example, 'I fell in love with the Lord and realized he was calling me to be His spouse', and in relation to their order: 'Their realization that they are brides of Christ, first and foremost'.[109] This idea of spousal relationship is distinctly expressed by Mother Imelda, a contemporary Carmelite nun:

> God is my husband. That is how I think about Him... I talk to Him about my family, and I feel He really does care. He's so real to me, so alive. I know I've given some things up, yet I'm enclosed within a greater love.[110]

Three phrases are worth noting. First, Mother Imelda refers to renunciation, saying she has 'given some things up'. Second, the word '*enclosed*' is meaningful because as an enclosed contemplative, she makes a simultaneously *spatial and relational* statement of being 'enclosed within greater love'. Third, the phrase 'my family' possibly refers to her role as the 'mother' of her community.

An expression of a transformational 'personal love relationship' is how Carmelite Sister Kinga of the Transfiguration, OCD, described the path which led her to monastic vocation while she was completing her university studies in the 1990s:

---

[108] de Vogüé, *To Desire Eternal Life*, 44.

[109] Johnson, Wittberg and Gautier, *New Generations of Catholic Sisters*, 86. See also, for example, Thérèse of Lisieux in *The Prayers of Saint Thérèse of Lisieux*, opening her Profession Note with the words: 'O Jesus, my divine spouse!', 38 and referring to Carmelite sisters as 'little brides' of Jesus, 41.

[110] Marcelle Bernstein, *Nuns* (London: Collins, 1976), 39.

I realized that someone was paying attention to me, surrounded me with love, and was directing me step by step to where I needed to be. It was so simple that I have trouble expressing it, but for the first time in my life, I realised that God cared for me with a loving, active… personal love. I knew it already, but now I was experiencing that God is not an abstract concept, nor the inaccessible centre of goodness that watches over billions of little human beings, like me. I realized that God is a Person who is able to love, that we can come into contact with Him not only in an abstract way, but in reality, that He holds my destiny in his hand, that He loves me personally, that his love is tender and strong, capable of making me happy, of totally fulfilling my life as the greatest love-passion.[111]

The desire to be with God as a motivation for monastic life is also evident in the interviews of Trappist nuns in the recent television documentary *Hidden: A Life All for God*[112]:

I wanted to know God, to really know God…
Being here, I didn't choose it. It was God who asked this of me.
God offered this to me, and I just said 'Yes'.
(Sr. Francesca Molina, OCSO)
When I ask myself:
Why did you come? It's Him.
Whom do you seek? It's Him.
Why do you stay? I can't live without Him…
(Sr. Karla Goncalves, OCSO)

In terms of dynamic progression of this relationship, it is possible to propose an allegorical sequence where the relationship matures during the monastic journey:

1. Falling in love with God in the beginning
2. Engagement during the monastic life
3. Wedding in the end, through death as a transition to eternal life

This progression can be understood in the context of the deepening commitment in the monastic profession as the individual moves through

---

[111] Kinga de la Transfiguration, *Je ne me suis pas dérobée…*, 16-17. Translation mine.
[112] *Hidden: A Life All for God*. The CatholicTV Network, 2018.

the initial stages (falling in love) towards permanent vows (engagement). Thus, time in the monastery becomes preparation for the wedding feast.

This experience of an intimate and dynamic relationship with God relates to the call for a radical renunciation associated with the enclosed contemplative life.[113] A contemporary Carthusian novice master considers the idea of monastic life as a life-changing transfiguration, a transformation. He acknowledges the 'radical demand' of hating even life itself to be Christ's disciple[114] with the understanding that hating one's life means that one must, in a word, die.[115] He argues:

> Death gives rise to transfiguration, a passage to higher life... This is a Christian truth that can be applied to all without exception. The monk seeks the realisation of this death within himself, in the present, in this world, *in order to have eternal life in God in this life.*[116]

This statement represents the Carthusian's perception of time, of death 'in the present, in this world' and simultaneously enjoying 'eternal life in God in this life'. It seems to go beyond the simple concept of exchanging the pleasures of the current life to a better reward in eternity by implying enjoyment of eternal life in God 'already here and now', in this life.

Jane Foulcher's study of monastic traditions equally points towards an orientation of the monastic project which is different from and richer than a mere expectation of a heavenly reward after one's physical death. She suggests that this eschatological orientation concerns an 'open heaven', the way in which divine life opens to human existence, the way in which eternity is (partly) realised in the present.[117] Similarly, Irénée Hausherr, SJ, summarises the simultaneity of 'timeless' salvation as perceived by Desert

---

[113] Nieremberg in *A Treatise on the Difference between Temporal and Eternal*, 398, argues: 'If we love our God truly, who so much loved us, we must resolve to lose honours, wealth and pleasure, in serving and requiting him'. He posits that if we consider him to be God, who is infinitely beautiful, good, wise, powerful, eternal, immense, immutable... how can we then, since our heart is limited—and the object of our love, God, is infinite—spare any part of our heart for the things of this life?

[114] Lk 14: 26-28, 33.

[115] A Carthusian, *The Call of Silent Love*, 47-48.

[116] A Carthusian, *The Call of Silent Love*, 46. Italics mine.

[117] Foulcher, *Reclaiming Humility*, 311.

Fathers: 'Salvation is *both eternal* happiness *and, in this life*, the paradise of peace through the health of the soul'.[118]

In summary, the idea of building an intimate relationship with the Divine as an attempt to partly share, or participate, in eternal life with God 'already here' could be identified in different sources as a motivation for entering the monastery. First, the 'love-passion' for God was quoted as the preliminary attraction for the vocation by, for example, Sister Kinga of the Transfiguration. Second, the intimate relationship with God, 'first on earth and then in heaven', was identified by monastics and scholars as an experience of monastic traditions.

The exploration of monastic journeys started with withdrawal from the world. Having gone through various aspects of enclosed monastic liminality, it is time to consider some of the ways in which monastics contribute back to the world through their roles as liminal intermediaries.

3.6 CONTRIBUTION TO THE WORLD

The beginning of the monastic journey was associated with rather negative images of death, renunciation, and withdrawal. These forms of symbolic or real deliberate acts led to liminal statuses (as professed religious) in liminal spaces between earth and paradise (cloisters) and liminal times (temporality and eternity). These rather painful processes, however, can give rise to counterbalancing positive metaphors of new life, birth, and contribution.

Carmel Bendon Davis refers to liminality as a central phase of the rite of passage where the liminal stage has frequently been likened to death, to being in the womb. She suggests that, in the assumption of solitude, the contemplative enters a state that is 'dead' to the world but alive to spiritual possibilities. And, in undertaking such a life, the mystics may be viewed as individuals standing for all Christians whose ultimate aim is to attain

---

[118] Irénée Hausherr, *Penthos: The Doctrine of Compunction in the Christian East* (Kalamazoo, MI: Cistercian Publications, 1982; trans. A. Hufstader), 121. Italics mine. See also McDannell and Lang in *Heaven: A History*, 30, where they describe the monastic experience as one in which the more the individual was drawn to God, the more the world shrunk in comparison: 'Life as we normally experience it, would not compete with the intensity of life with God'. And, 'to rest in God, first on earth and then in heaven, meant not to focus on worldly cares but to concentrate on preserving the intimate relationship with the divine and the religious community'. Note here the reference to the 'intimate relationship' with both the Divine and the religious community.

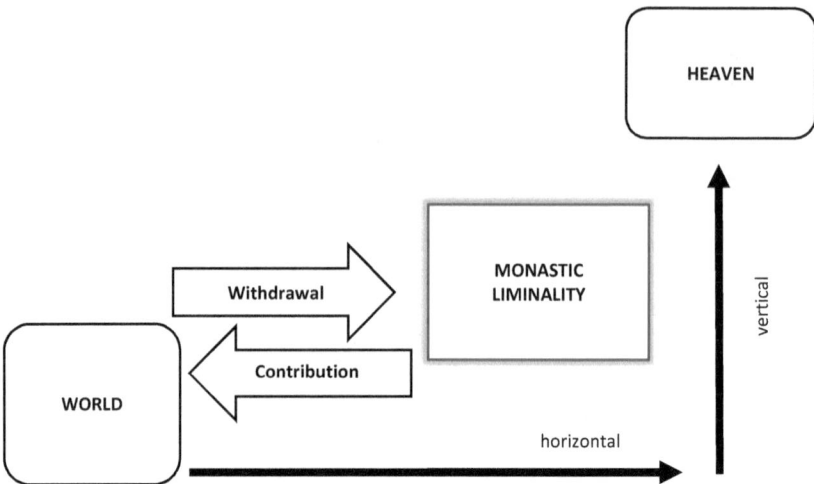

Fig. 3.4 Monastic liminality at the intersection between the world and heaven

everlasting union with God.[119] It is worth noting that she refers to two levels of intermediary liminal states: withdrawal to the contemplative life and the role as an intermediary between fellow Christians and God.

This can be described as a trajectory where liminality becomes a conduit for a transformation:

Withdrawal from World -> Liminality -> Contribution to World

The symbolic death to the world (withdrawal) allows the contemplative individual to become alive for spiritual possibilities. For the individual, contemplative life represents a liminal rite of passage. The resulting liminal status allows the contemplative to become an intermediary who stands for all Christians whose ultimate aim is to attain everlasting union with God. This is shown in Fig. 3.4.

The references to womb and birth as a rite of passage relate to Nicodemus's question (in Jn 3:3-8) on 'how does one enter the kingdom of God', to which Jesus replied that 'no one can see the kingdom of God

---

[119] Davis, *Mysticism and Space*, 87.

without being born from above'.[120] The interplay between 'death to old life' and 'birth to new life in Christ' is associated with the Christian sacrament of Baptism. It could be added that the metaphorical reference of the womb—through 'monastic reading' of the text—could also be understood as a 'birth to a new way of life'. This monastic interpretation is indeed identifiable in the Carthusian Statutes which make the connection between Baptism, withdrawal from the world, and union with Christ. It speaks of monks as acting as witnesses to the world of a new life won by Christ's redemption:

> *The monk, already by baptism dead to sin* and consecrated to God, is *by Profession still more totally dedicated to the Father* and *set free from the world,* in order to be able to strive more directly towards perfect love; linked with the Lord in firm and stable pact, he shares in the mystery of the Church's indissoluble union with Christ, and *bears witness to the world of that new life won for us by Christ's redemption.*[121]

A homily held on the occasion of the first profession of a Carthusian cloister monk, similarly, refers to birth and self-transcendence. The Father Prior addresses the young monk: 'So you must accept your part of the birth-pangs in Christ and follow him in his mysterious yet willing poverty and renunciation to the glory of the totally undreamed of newness of eternal life'.[122] In this case, birth is associated with the participation of Christ's journey by entering into the painful process of birth through poverty and renunciation. Yet, this mysterious path eventually leads to the glory and newness of eternal life. Taken together, there is a progressive path, a passage from experiences of death leading to births into a new life, in temporality and eternity: baptised Christian professed religious eternal life.

---

[120] See Jn 3:3-8 (NRSV) for the conversation between Nicodemus and Jesus on how one enters the kingdom of God: 'Very truly, I tell you, no one can see the kingdom of God without being born from above'. Nicodemus said to him, 'How can anyone be born after having grown old? Can one enter a second time into the mother's womb and be born?' Jesus answered, 'Very truly, I tell you, no one can enter the kingdom of God without being born of water and Spirit. What is born of the flesh is flesh, and what is born of the Spirit is spirit. Do not be astonished that I said to you, "You must be born from above. The wind blows where it chooses, and you hear the sound of it, but you do not know where it comes from or where it goes. So it is with everyone who is born of the Spirit"'.

[121] Carthusian Statutes, Book 1, Ch. 10.1. Italics mine.

[122] A Carthusian, *The Spirit of Place*, 110.

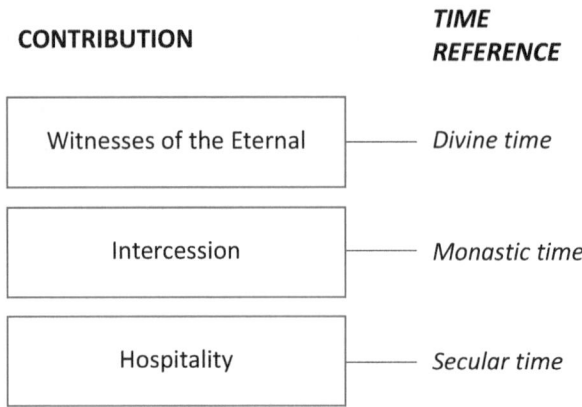

Fig. 3.5 Elements of contribution and concept of time

Moving on to the topic of 'contribution to the world', we identify three broad areas in which the religious contribute back to the world as liminal intermediaries between God and fellow humans. These, in turn, relate with divine/monastic/secular temporalities, as summarised in Fig. 3.5.

The brief analysis of each area of contribution relates to the hierarchy of temporalities, starting from what is most closely linked to the concept of divine time.

3.6.1 Eschatological Meaning: Silent Witnesses of the Eternal

German theologian Peter H. Görg, in his study of the Desert Fathers, suggests a relationship between the idea of monastic withdrawal and hope for heaven and eternal life. According to him, the monk and the ascetic plainly deny the self-sufficiency of earthly life and of this world and deliberately prefer a renunciation that can be explained only by the hope of heaven and eternal life. By doing so, he claims, they also are like an uncomfortable thorn in the flesh of Christians who are in danger of settling down in this world.[123] Donato Ogliari, likewise, points towards the eschatological end

---

[123] Görg, *The Desert Fathers*, 116. See also *Verbi Sponsa*, 7, which suggests that the religious are considered to have a special eschatological role within the Church. Living in and by the Lord's presence, nuns are a particular foreshadowing of the eschatological Church immutable in its possession and contemplation of God; they 'visibly represent the goal towards which the entire community of the Church travels... The Church advanced down the paths of time with her eyes fixed on the future restoration of all things in Christ'.

of monastic life. He argues that the end (*telos*) of monastic life does not pertain to the world (*saeculum*), but to the end of time. Therefore, monks voluntarily become eloquent signs of the 'penultimate' character of worldly reality, of the transitoriness of worldly existence. Making themselves 'strangers to the world's ways', they effect, as Ogliari claims, in advance a change in what concerns the meaning and destiny of human life, anticipating, though imperfectly, the final goal. This final goal is eternal life, with reference to the Rule of Saint Benedict:

> And if we wish... to reach eternal life, while there is still time and we are still in this body, and there remains time to accomplish all this in the light of this life, we must run and accomplish now what will profit us for eternity.[124]

There is a paradoxical calling of the silent, hidden solitary to witness 'visibly', through contemplative life, to the absolute priority of God to any created thing. The priority of God over created things relates to the proposition that a purely secular worldview with its exclusion of God leads into a self-referential 'this-worldly' loop. Seen through the lens of this study, monastic traditions are acutely aware of the transitory nature of both mortal humans and of the world, recognising their role as countercultural witnesses of the Divine and of the eternal. It invites the world to consider the possibility of self-transcendence and eschatological hope. In the words of a contemporary Carthusian monk:

> Making him who is the exclusive centre of our lives through our Profession, we testify to a world, excessively absorbed in earthly things, that there is no God but him. Our life clearly shows that something of the joys of heaven is present already here below; it prefigures our risen state and anticipates in a manner the final renewal of the world.[125]

The positive contribution of the enclosed contemplative monastics to this world 'excessively absorbed in earthly things' would highlight the apostolic value of monastic enclosure. According to Jean-Charles Nault, OSB, contemplatives reveal the primacy of the 'vertical' relationship. The Divine Office and silent adoration are the monk's main apostolate through which he reminds the world of the gratuitous character of time 'wasted' on God,

---

[124] Ogliari, 'Tempus Monasticum', 37-38, with references to the Rule of Saint St. Benedict Prologue 43-44, and Prologue 35-37, RB 50 and 73.8.
[125] A Carthusian *The Wound of Love*, 239.

from which flows a wealth of graces for the entire Church.[126] Similarly, Anders Arborelius, OCD, links contemplative life with the apostolic endeavours of the Church.[127] However, he rejects the attitude of 'being useful at any cost' and claims that 'Prayer is a waste of time, and it should be a waste of time, because God is worth it'.[128] This then leads his argument to the eschatological goal of contemplative life: to start here below the adoration and glorification of God, which will be our full-time occupation in God's eternal kingdom.[129]

Garcia M. Colombas, OSB, a monk and monastic scholar, suggests that the consecrated religious give a witness to the whole world of the existence of a future life, not by words but by raising and sanctifying it, in a certain way, through the transformation of their own spirit and heart which is reflected in their bodies. The faithful monk reminds all people that they are not made for this earth, that this life is not the real life; he is a 'living sign of eschatology'. According to Colombas, the monk lives in a union with the Divine as he is occupied in the continuous singing of the Psalms, prayer, meditation of the Holy Scriptures, contemplating in nature the reflections of God's perfections, discovering in the succession of seasons, months, days, and hours the projection of a celestial rhythm. He concludes that in this way, the religious are, *already now*, inhabitants of Paradise. Their singing of Psalms, prayers, and continuous contact with the word of God prepare them for the eternal dialogue which awaits them in heaven; 'they get used to the language of the angels', as Colombas puts it. For such people, the future life appears very close, or rather, for them, the future life will only be a glorious revelation of *what they already possess*.[130]

The above passage from Colombas summarises some central themes of monasticism. Firstly, the religious here are described as 'living signs of eschatology'. And, while on the journey, they not only are learning the

---

[126] Jean-Charles Nault, *The Noonday Devil: Acedia, the Unnamed Evil of Our Times* (San Francisco, CA: Ignatius Press, 2015), 163.

[127] Anders Arborelius, *Carmelite Spirituality: The Way of Carmelite Prayer and Contemplation* (Irondale, AL: EWTN Publishing, 2020), 93-101.

[128] Arborelius, *Carmelite Spirituality*, 116.

[129] Arborelius, *Carmelite Spirituality*, 119.

[130] Garcia M. Colombas, *Paradis et Vie Angélique: Le Sens Eschatologique de la Vocation Chrétienne* (Paris: Les Éditions du CERF, 1961, trans. S. Caron), 285-286. Translation and italics mine.

'language of the angels' which prepares them for the 'eternal heavenly dialogue', but, in a way, 'already now' possess the blessed future life.

John Paul II, addressing Carthusians in 1984, touched upon the interconnectedness of the apostolic mission of the Church in the world and the role of enclosed contemplatives:

> Mankind needs to seek the absolute, and to see it confirmed, as it were, by a living witness. It is your task to show them this. For their part, those sons and daughters of the Church who devote themselves to the apostolate in the world, in the midst of changing and transient things, need to rest in the stability of God and His love. This stability they see manifested in you who, during this earthly pilgrimage possess it in an especial way.[131]

It is interesting to note that John Paul II, in the final sentence of the above quote, refers to both stability (permanent liminality) and pilgrimage (dynamic liminality). He identifies the 'living witness' role of the enclosed contemplatives for the Church's apostolic work in the changing and transient world. Further, he refers to the stability [of God and His love] that other members of the Church see manifested in them during this earthly pilgrimage.

Paradoxically, this silent witness of the primacy of the Eternal has been carried out (in time) through centuries and (in space) throughout the world even though the contemplatives themselves have chosen a life in silence, enclosure, and hiddenness. What appears to be contemplative 'inactivity' translates into action that is 'beyond activity' through this hidden contribution. Davis suggests that while mysticism begins as a private and personal approach to God, it results in a return of benefits to society as a whole. In this way, mystics are more easily and obviously exemplars of the sacred for their community, situated to be visible to the members of their society, 'living icons' who provide a service for their community by their example.[132] If we accept the image of the icon as a representation of the monastics, the Eastern Orthodox view of the icon as 'a visual

---

[131] John Paul II quoted in Robin Bruce Lockhart, *Halfway to Heaven: The Hidden Life of the Sublime Carthusians* (London: Thames Methuen, 1985), 138.
[132] Davis, *Mysticism and Space*, 89.

anticipation of the eschatological kingdom of Christ'[133] further emphasises the role of monastics as silent but visible witnesses of the eternal. It can be inferred that a living icon (a monk or a nun) represents a visual symbol of the eschatological hope and the kingdom to come.

Not only are the religious themselves perceived as signs or icons, but also external symbols, such as the monastic habit, can be considered as a means of non-verbal communication with secular society. As noted by Augustine Holmes, a scholar of early monasticism, 'The clothes of the ascetic signify separation from the world, but they are also a sign to the same world'.[134] A similar claim could be made about enclosed monastic buildings which impose boundaries that signal a visible separation from their external surroundings but simultaneously remind the secular society about the religious values represented by the monastery.[135] These dual symbolic references to (1) stability of enclosed monastic life (permanent liminality) and (2) pilgrimage to heaven (dynamic liminality) may serve as a witness to laypersons in the surrounding world. As suggested by Diarmaid MacCulloch, a British historian of Christianity, specifically in the turbulent times of the ninth and eleventh centuries in Europe, the Benedictine regulated communal life; their liturgy and architecture represented order and reassurance for lay people who viewed monasteries modelled like the City of God, an image of heaven.[136]

[133] Leonid Ouspensky, 'Icon and Art' in Bernard McGinn, John Meyendorff, and Jean Leclercq, eds., *Christian Spirituality: Origins to the Twelfth Century* (London: SCM Press, 1996), 382-394: 391. According to Ouspensky, an icon manifests the participation of human nature in divine life, representing the realisation of the Patristic formula: 'God became man so that man might become God', 390. See also Mother Thekla, *Eternity Now: An Introduction to Orthodox Spirituality* (Norwich: Canterbury Press, 1999), 4-6, who considers icons as a visual explication of Christ's Incarnation. The baby Jesus's face is often painted as wrinkled with age and his body as long and un-childlike. 'This is because for him there can be no time, he is ever man, and he is ever God', 6.

[134] Holmes, *A Life Pleasing to God*, 207.

[135] Harmless, in *Desert Christians*, 125, notes that high walls were the most distinctive feature of a Pachomian monastery and 'these served as the very visible boundary separating monastery from the outside world'.

[136] Diarmaid MacCulloch, *A History of Christianity: The First Three Thousand Years* (London: Penguin Books, 2010), 359.

3.6.2 Guarding the Walls: Intercession and Prayer

The *Lausiac History* includes a story in which Palladius was disturbed by his lack of progress and was tempted to leave the monastery. He went to Macarius of Alexandria who advised him to say to his thoughts: 'For Christ's sake I am guarding the walls'.[137] According to W. K. Lowther Clarke, this refers to the monastery as a protecting wall interposed between the enemy and the people of Egypt who live their life in the world, exposed to many temptations. The monks' prayers were helping to guard that wall. And from this, Clarke continues: 'If we believe in prayer as the noblest and most fruitful activity of man's nature, we shall probably be led to believe that God separates some to a life of prayer, and that the mass of mankind dwell in greater security, thanks to the protecting wall of the prayers of the separated ones'.[138]

This early Desert Dwellers' understanding of 'monastery as a fortress with protective walls against the enemy' has carried on through the centuries. Similarly, a website of Carmelite sisters explains their cloistered way of life today:

> The monastery walls not only guard against the world so peace, prayer and holiness can blossom, but they also stand as the towers of a fortress where spiritual war is waged against sin and evil. Carmelites taste of struggle as much as they taste of the sweetness of contemplation and spiritual joy. They live an austere life of penance and renunciation to make reparation for the sins of us all and to implore God's pardon. They ask Heaven's blessing upon our lives, and they continually beg for the salvation of our souls. With this, it is evident how greatly needed in these times are their life and beautiful vocation.[139]

Katja Ritari suggests that while the eschatological orientation of monasticism influenced the monastics' relationship with this world, it did not necessarily mean rejection of the world as such.[140] Monasteries served the needs of the wider community as powerhouses of prayer, representing conduits between God and the earthly society; by offering a glimpse of the

---

[137] Palladius, *The Lausiac History*, Ch. XVIII.
[138] Introduction by W.K. Lowther Clarke in Palladius, *The Lausiac History*, 13.
[139] https://sistersofcarmel.org/carmelite-order-history. Accessed 27/06/2020.
[140] Ritari, *Pilgrimage to Heaven*, 178.

heavenly reality, they gave hope and encouragement to all Christians threading the earthly path to salvation.[141]

If a monastery can be viewed as an intermediate place between earth and heaven, then, by extension, monastic contemplatives may, through their prayers, become intermediaries between God and their fellow humans. Samuel Rubenson argues that, because the monk was independent of ordinary society, even almost independent of bodily needs, he could be trusted as a mediator not only of God but also of other human beings.[142] Patristic theologian and Eastern Orthodox bishop Kallistos Ware (1934–2022) went further, suggesting that ascetics essentially help their fellow humans by just being what they are: 'According to the early Christian worldview, the solitaries were assisting others simply by offering prayer – not just through prayer of intercession, but through any kind of prayer... The ascetic in the desert, that is to say, helps his fellow humans not so much by anything that he does, but rather by what he is'.[143]

Contemplatives themselves appear to hold a firm conviction that they have a special function in the Church and the world; yet, despite their hiddenness, they remain closely connected to fellow humans. A Carthusian monk writes: 'If therefore we are truly living in union with God, our minds and hearts, far from shut in on themselves, open up to embrace the whole universe and the mystery of Christ that saves it'.[144] He admits that only those who have experienced the love for solitude and silence of the hermitage can describe the benefit and divine delight it brings to them. He continues:

> Yet, in choosing this, the best part, it is not our advantage alone that we have in view; in embracing the hidden life we do not abandon the great family of our fellow men; on the contrary, by devoting ourselves exclusively to God we exercise a special function in the Church, where things seen are ordered to things unseen, exterior activity to contemplation.[145]

[141] Ritari, *Pilgrimage to Heaven*, 178.

[142] Samuel Rubenson, 'Christian Asceticism and the Emergence of the Monastic Tradition', in Vincent Wimbush and Richard Valantasis, eds., *Asceticism* (New York-Oxford: Oxford University Press, 1998), 49-57: 55.

[143] Kallistos Ware, 'The Way of the Ascetics: Negative or Affirmative?', 7-8.

[144] A Carthusian, *The Wound of Love*, 239.

[145] A Carthusian, *The Wound of Love*, 239.

Likewise, the Benedictine monks of the Monastery of Demeure Notre Père view their role as 'people who have been called by God to consecrate their whole life for prayer in a certain exclusive way'. According to them, monasteries, within the Church and the world, are places of prayer, praise, and adoration. But the monks remain in the presence of God, not only in their own name but in the name of all God's people. They see themselves being consecrated by the Church as a living presence of the people in front of God; the monks are their prayer, their adoration, their liturgy, and their expectation of eternal goods.[146]

By praying for the world, contemplative monastics can be considered as participants on earth of the heavenly mission of Christ 'who is at the right hand of God, who indeed intercedes for us'.[147] This calling was also mentioned by a Catholic sister in a survey conducted in 2009 as the reason which most attracted her to join a religious institute: 'I was attracted by… our primary charism of perpetual adoration. In adoring Our Lord exposed in the Blessed Sacrament, we aid the Church in a special way by always interceding for those in need'.[148]

3.6.3   Monastic Hospitality and Words of Wisdom

During the second half of the fourth century, the Desert Fathers in Egypt were constantly visited by individuals who were looking for words of wisdom; it was considered axiomatic that the sayings of those who lived so close to God would be inspired.[149] Those who could not make the journey to the deserts were able to read the pilgrimage stories such as *Historia Monachorum in Aegypto* and *The Lausiac History* to 'get a glimpse of the face of the holy'.[150]

The liminal role of acting as intermediaries between God and fellow humans, from the royalty[151] to the anonymous poor, involving interactions with the secular world and contemplative monastic enclosure, appears to require a careful balance. Emilia Jamroziak, a British scholar of

---

[146] Monastère Demeure Notre Père, *Livre de vie monastique*, 21-22. Translation mine.
[147] Rom 8:34 (NRSV).
[148] Johnson, Wittberg, and Gautier, *New Generations of Catholic Sisters*, 103.
[149] Henry Chadwick, *The Early Church*, 178.
[150] Harmless, *Desert Christians*, 298.
[151] See, for example, MacCulloch, *Silence*, 122: Carthusian and Bridgettine orders became much favoured by nobility and monarchs during the late medieval period across Northern Europe and England.

medieval religious history, observes that a pragmatic approach chosen by the Cistercians—an ability to adapt to local conditions and to respond flexibly while yet maintaining Cistercian observance and values—served the order well in medieval Europe. This took the form of hospitality for the living and burials for the dead; equally, the obligations to feed the poor and pray for the benefactors were central to Cistercian monasticism.[152]

The symbolism of the monastic enclosure is mentioned by John W. Kieser in a passage where he describes the architecture of the cloister as one of interiorised space; it presents to the world a protective exterior that shelters inner privacy. And at the same time, he further observes, monasteries place great importance on the virtue of hospitality.[153] This paradox of enclosed interiority, the hermitic nature of monastic life, and the hospitality extended to visitors by the hermits is encountered already in the early texts of Cassian.[154] It could be proposed that the 'exterior hospitality' which monasteries offer to visitors could be viewed as an extension of the 'interior hospitality' offered for the world through the prayers of the religious.

---

[152] Jamroziak, *The Cistercian Order in Medieval Europe 1090-1500*, 115-116. See also: Martin Heale, *Monasticism in Late Medieval England, c. 1300-1535*. (Manchester: Manchester University Press, 2009), evidencing that religious houses in late medieval England served not only the spiritual needs but also social needs such as hospitality, education, and charity, 188-200; provided employment and generally enhanced the economies of their localities, 201-212; Janet Burton and Julie Kerr, *The Cistercians in the Middle Ages* (Woodbridge: The Boydell Press, 2011), *191-194*, on the Cistercians' influence on (and being influenced by) the world which, in the Middle Ages, involved social, economic, political, and spiritual developments such as welcoming guests, burials, writing letters of advice, prayers, charity and alms-giving, caring for the sick, poor, and needy.

[153] John W. Kieser, 'An Algerian Microcosm: Monks, Muslims, and the Zeal of Bitterness' in *Cistercian Studies Quarterly* 38, no. 3, 2003: 337-354: 342-343, quoted in Foulcher, *Reclaiming Humility*, 285.

[154] Cassian, *Conferences*, Conf. 19, Ch. V. Note that this is still true today as the website of a Benedictine Abbey explains: 'St Benedict did not envisage his monasteries as existing primarily for the purpose of receiving passing guests. In fact, he saw them as sanctuaries for those who wished permanently to put aside the distractions of the world and seek Christ alone. Yet St Benedict recognised the attraction monasteries held for those in the world, and resigned himself with goodwill to making provision for guests, that they be **welcomed as Christ** (RB 53:1)'. In https://douaiabbey.org.uk/guesthouse.php, accessed 27/04/2021.

The radical monastic message of the primacy of God seems to find its way back to the world, often through literary sources.[155] Julie Kerr, a British historian, notes in her study on medieval cloisters that the Carthusians spent much of their time copying and binding books in the solitude of their cells, both for their own use and for dissemination to others. She suggests that '[in] this way they "preached with pen" and communicated the Word while remaining secluded from the world and immersed in silence'.[156] This literary dissemination of the—paradoxically hidden and silent—monastic message was undertaken early on by writers such as Athanasius. Athanasius's *Life of Anthony* ends with the suggestion to 'read these words' to others so that they may learn about the life of monks.[157] He reminds the reader that the Lord leads those who serve him unto the end, *not only to the kingdom of heaven, but here also*—'even though they hide themselves and are desirous of withdrawing from the world'— making monks illustrious and well-known everywhere on the account of their virtue and the help they render to others.[158] Athanasius's words proved indeed insightful as his biography of the monk Anthony later played an instrumental role in the conversion of Augustine.[159]

3.7 CONCLUSIONS

Monastic sources indicate three motivations for the withdrawal from the world: break-away, monasticism as a means, and falling in love with God. This leads to 'self-imposed marginalisation' from the society to devote more time for a relationship with God and to seek salvation, a way to eternal life. However, it can be argued that it is precisely through their dynamic and permanent states of liminality that the enclosed contemplatives contribute in various ways back to the society from which they withdrew. This is summarised in Fig. 3.6.

---

[155] See, for example, King, *Western Monasticism*, 245-248, on the role of Carthusians copying and promulgating devote books like *Cloud of Unknowing* and their influence on the *Devotio Moderna* with *Imitation of Christ* its masterpiece; and Lawrence, *Medieval Monasticism*, 147, on books distributed by medieval Charterhouses serving a missionary purpose.

[156] Julie Kerr: *Life in the Medieval Cloister* (London: Continuum, 2009), 183.

[157] Athanasius, *Life of Anthony*, 94.

[158] Athanasius, *Life of Anthony*, 94.

[159] See Augustine, *Confessions*, VIII.12; Henry Chadwick, *Augustine of Hippo: A Life* (Oxford: Oxford University Press, 2010), 25-31.

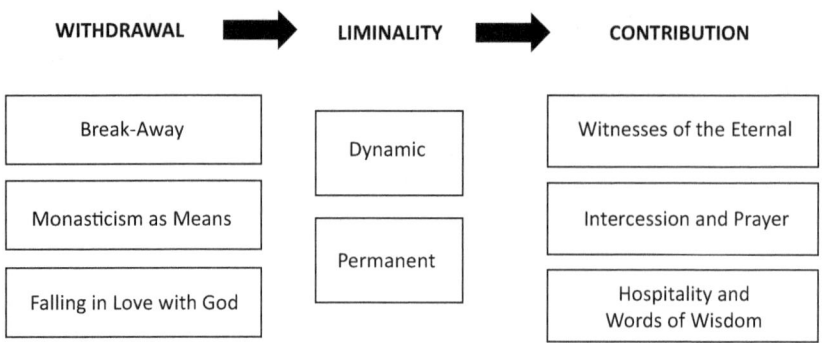

Fig. 3.6 Liminality as a conduit between withdrawal and contribution

Monastic withdrawal represents, in a way, preparation for death by learning to abandon earthly possessions, relationships, and own will during one's lifetime. This means ultimately abandoning one's life and soul into God's hands. It allows for the monastic freedom to travel light without distractions and excess baggage. A Catholic priest who served as a chaplain to Carmelite sisters describes how he understood the sisters' cloistered life inside the walls. Looking at the stars at the patch of the heavens above, he writes, 'It occurred to me that the walls kept me from seeing a lot of beautiful things but at the same time helped me to focus intently on one part of the sky – and that this was what [the sisters'] life was about: to limit the peripheral vision of distractions in order to contemplate God'.[160]

CHAPTER 4

Middle of the Journey: Time in Monastery

Prayer of a Nun.
Thou, the today in every act of my life,
Thou, the today who lights up all monotony,
Thou, the today in the unfolding adventure,
Thou, the today in the life that blossoms.[1]

It is through the gates of the monastery that one enters first to the status and the place of liminality. However, liminality remains an enduring feature throughout the monastic journey. It becomes a 'perpetual', permanent state. Moving on to consider the middle of the monastic journey, a different turn of the 'kaleidoscope' emerges. We take a look at monastic relationality with the view shifting towards the divine perspective.

---

[1] Prayer of an anonymous nun, lines 1–4, from a booklet included in the documentary DVD film on Carthusian nuns in *Une vie en Chartreuse* (2018), 21. This expresses the middle of the journey of an enclosed nun with recurring references to 'today' (present) as the predominant temporality in the life that is experienced as monotonous (stable) and as an unfolding adventure (dynamic).

R. Hujanen, *Monastic Perspectives on Temporality*,
https://doi.org/10.1007/978-3-031-34808-2_4

4.1   Relationship

There is no better way to introduce the idea of a divine call to monastic life and to a union of 'intimate love' with the Trinity than to quote the Carthusian Statutes[2]:

> To the praise of the glory of God, Christ, the Father's Word, has through the Holy Spirit, from the beginning chosen certain men, whom he willed to lead into solitude and unite to himself in intimate love. In obedience to such a call, Master Bruno and six companions entered the desert of Chartreuse in the year of our Lord 1084 and settled there.

This call from God began with a physical journey to the desert of Chartreuse.[3] Here already, the key elements of monastic enclosure, solitude, and union with God, emerge. It is a special relationship that is initiated by God, based on a personal calling, and marked by intimate love. The entry to the monastic life, therefore, establishes a new kind of 'defining' relationship with the Divine. Three specific aspects of this relationship emerge:

1. **Dynamic Relationship** which is built through participation in Christ's journey. This is where the Incarnation, humility, temporality, and God's immanence are most 'visible'.
2. **Permanent Relationship** which is based on God's temporal and spatial omnipresence in the life of the religious. This is associated with an experience of enjoying a relationship with God 'Already Here and Now'.
3. **Contemplative Relationship** which relates to Ascent, a transcendent journey that reaches upward or 'beyond' but also towards a greater degree of interiority. From the temporal perspective, it can be described as 'an instant suspended into eternity'.

While these three forms of relationships will be examined separately for clarity, in practice they would coexist simultaneously. These somewhat differentiated relationships can be explored in the context of God's immanence and transcendence, which relate to the dual ways of understanding

---

[2] Carthusian Statutes, Book 1, Ch. 1.1 (Prologue).

[3] The 'desert of Chartreuse' likely refers to the early monastic tradition to enter desert to dedicate time to be 'alone with God' in a community of like-minded companions.

or describing God. For example, the divine nature can be perceived both as dynamic and as permanent/stable. One must therefore become comfortable with the notion that some statements which appear 'paradoxical' or 'contradictory' are indeed not mutually exclusive but, instead, can be true simultaneously. Franciscan theologian and philosopher Bonaventure (1221–1274), notably, approaches God from this perspective, as he describes 'the most pure and absolute Being' who is the origin and consummating end of all things:

> Because it is eternal and most present, it therefore encompasses and enters all duration as if it were at one and the same time its center and circumference. Because it is utterly simple and the greatest, it is, therefore totally within all things and totally outside them and thus "is an intelligible sphere whose center is everywhere and whose circumference is nowhere". Because it is most actual and unchangeable, therefore "while remaining stable, it gives motion to all things."[4]

Therefore, in a balanced way, enclosed contemplatives can enter into a relationship with God who is simultaneously dynamic and stable, because he is also:

Three in One.
   Immutable Mover.
   Temporal and Timeless.
   Mysterious and Intimate.
   Immanent and Transcendent.

Thus, the enclosed contemplative 'paradoxical' monastic way of life can simultaneously accommodate *ora et labora*, suffering and joy, enclosure and love for humankind, death and life, time and eternity. From the theological perspective, and specifically with our interest in temporalities, God's immanence and transcendence are key concepts in understanding the category of relationship. This is illustrated in Fig. 4.1.

---

[4] Bonaventure, *The Soul's Journey into God*, Ch. 5.7.

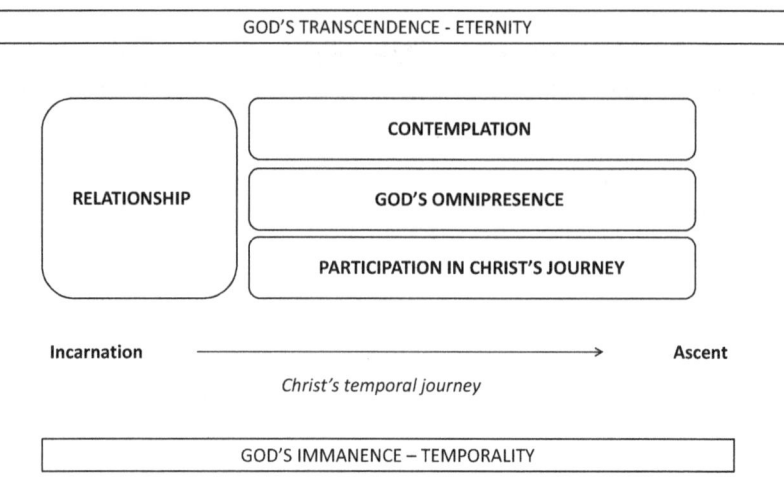

Fig. 4.1   Relationship with God in enclosed contemplative life

4.1.1   The Ontological Difference

Returning to the 'main problem of religion': how to bridge the gap between the human and the Divine?[5] This relates specifically to the challenge presented by the ontological difference. Clyde Lee Miller, an American scholar of ancient and medieval philosophy, in his article on contemplative vision writes about the 'chasm between finite and infinite'. He argues, 'The chasm between finite and infinite cannot be bridged from the human side. What remains is to believe what God will accomplish in and through Christ—our way into and through the cloud and the darkness to some taste of the divine'.[6] How can this 'chasm' be bridged? Thus, the return to the initial temporal research question: how can the mortal and the Eternal meet?

While interpersonal relationships between human beings can be complicated enough, this 'chasm' between finite and infinite represents a very different challenge altogether. David Foster, OSB, writes about the 'strangeness' and the fundamental ontological difference between

---

[5] As proposed by McDannell and Lang in *Heaven: A History*, 54.

[6] Clyde Lee Miller, 'Seeing and Being Seen in Nicholas of Cusa's The Vision of God' (1453), in *The Downside Review*, Vol. 131, No. 464, July 2013, 147–155: 154.

creature and Creator.[7] He reflects on the meeting and the relationship between the two ontologically different parties in prayer through the concepts of 'liminality' and 'threshold':

> In the liminal experience of prayer… there is a limit I cannot cross which is more fundamental than the threshold that separates me from another human subject. This threshold puts me in question more fundamentally than any human relationship. But even there is a relationship, and the possibility of an exchange.[8]

This is where the category of liminality is encountered again, in the relationship between human and the Divine. The two categories identified in the current study overlap here. Foster suggests that a possibility of an exchange is realised in the act of prayer which serves as a liminal threshold that enables creatures to negotiate the ontological limit recognised as God's profound 'otherness' while simultaneously responding to an invitation for a loving relationship with their Creator:

> This is fundamentally what I think happens in prayer, where we cannot cross the ontological limit between creature and creator, but where my recognition of God's otherness as an openness and invitation to love constitutes a threshold I negotiate in prayer.[9]

This possibility of an exchange—in prayer—offers a way to bridge the 'chasm' or 'gap' between human and Divine, the finite and the Infinite, a profound connection where 'deep calls to deep'.[10] It is a liminal encounter; as Foster puts it: 'The other does not displace me entirely, however much his otherness forces me to recognize my finitude. The threshold is a place of *relationship*'.[11] Foster sees this experience of a relationship, the personal dimension in prayer as a structure that helps us to understand how it is possible to cross a threshold of liminality between the finite and Infinite: 'even though I have no other way of seeing myself in relation to

---

[7] Foster, *Contemplative Prayer*, 108–109.
[8] Foster, *Contemplative Prayer*, 112.
[9] Foster, *Contemplative Prayer*, 112.
[10] Ps 42:7 (NRSV).
[11] Foster, *Contemplative Prayer*, 112.

this person; the unknowability, the sheer elusiveness is about all I can point to in order to name the person "behind" it as God'.[12]

Liminality appears to be part of the contemplative experience itself. Contemplation becomes the liminal point of intersection where the eternal God and the finite human interact. David Foster writes about the metaphorical world of Pseudo-Dionysius where apophasis is described in terms of the ascent of a mountain, of an approach to God who, however, remains beyond view in material or conceptual terms, leading to the fundamental point where the boundary between created and uncreated is being reached.[13] This 'ascent' theme (which is associated with the Contemplative Relationship) will be discussed in more detail towards the end of this chapter.

Foster concludes that the connection between faith and prayer is fundamental because it is what makes the shift possible in the liminality of our experience of finitude to a sense of a threshold that opens up to what is beyond, as the recognition of God. The threshold state is ambiguous, one which we cannot cross but where we are engaged by what is beyond, in terms of the dynamics of intersubjectivity in our relationship with God in prayer.[14]

This liminal threshold experience of a contemplative, intimate, and transformational relationship with God—who is simultaneously 'radically other and radically close'—through Christ is also reflected by a contemporary Carthusian novice master. The Carthusian, referring to Hebrews 9:24, suggests that, to enter the true sanctuary, 'we must die to "our" prayer' and have to receive the prayer of Christ by being transformed through his death into his risen state—a condition realised in our whole life and whole being. 'In this way, we shall have access, in the spirit, to the face of the Father, to his intimacy, his Glory, radically other, yet radically close'.[15]

This idea of the Father as 'radically other, yet radically close' calls to mind Evelyn Underhill's classical finding. She reminds that researchers of contemplative experience must be prepared to accept and use many different descriptions in our enquiry into the nature of contemplative's perceptions of the Absolute. Typically, the evoked emotions fall into two groups:

---

[12] Foster, *Contemplative Prayer*, 113.
[13] Foster, *Contemplative Prayer*, 135.
[14] Foster, *Contemplative Prayer*, 199.
[15] A Carthusian, *The Wound of Love*, 235.

(1) the strange, dark, unfathomable Abyss of Pure Being; (2) the divine and loved Companion of the soul.[16] But rather than seeing these emotions as two separate expressions, it appears that they can coexist for a contemplative mind. God is experienced simultaneously as intimate and mysterious. Underhill indeed reminds us that all the apparently contradictory first-hand descriptions of pure contemplation such as Remoteness and Intimacy, Darkness and Light represent not the Transcendent but the overwhelming impression felt by the contemplative during his communion with a Reality which is One.[17]

This twofold human experience of God is repeatedly found in contemporary research on the psychology of religion. As a summary, many scholars have contrasted:

1. Numinous or prophetic experience of the divine as an awareness of a 'holy other' beyond nature, with which one is felt to be in communion. The term 'numinous' is based on Latin *numen* denoting a power implicit in the sacred object (God, transcendent) which elicits a response from the subject (human, creature). The numinous consciousness of humans is both compelled to seek out and explore the transcendent object (*mysterium fascinans*), and to be repelled in the face of the majesty and awfulness of this object, in whose presence one's own 'creatureness' is accentuated (*mysterium tremendum*).[18]

2. Mystical experience which can be described by a religious experience of unity. This can take the form of 'extrovertive mysticism' when unity is found within the world in which all objects are unified into a perception of totality of oneness. Unity can further be felt in the form of 'introvertive mysticism' where the mystical experience is devoid of perceptual objects. Perceptual objects disappear and the unity in introvertive mysticism is with a pure consciousness devoid of objects of perception, literally an experience of 'no-thing-ness'.[19] It has been also found that mystical experiences are common in

[16] Evelyn Underhill, *Mysticism: A Study in Nature and Development of Spiritual Consciousness* (Breinigsville, PA, 12th Revised Edition, 1930), 252.

[17] Underhill, *Mysticism*, 251.

[18] Ralph W. Hood, Jr., Bernard Spilka, Bruce Hunsberger and Richard Gorsuch, *The Psychology of Religion: An Empirical Approach* (New York, NY: The Guildford Press, 1996), 225–226.

[19] Hood, Spilka, Hunsberger and Gorsuch, *The Psychology of Religion*, 225.

nature and in meditative prayer—two conditions that are often solitary. Hence, it is possible that factors that meaningfully enhance solitude facilitate the report of mystical experience.[20]

Researchers of the psychology of religion Ralph W. Hood, Jr., Bernard Spilka, Bruce Hunsberger, and Richard Gorsuch note that empirical studies use measurements that tend to emphasise experiences of either a sense of presence (favouring numinous experiences) or a sense of unity (favouring mystical experiences). However, they point out that although it is possible to separate the numinous and the mystical as two poles of religious experience, they appear to be ultimately united.[21]

How are these 'two poles of religious experience' of God's presence and sense of unity reflected in monastic literature? Irénée Hausherr, a monk and scholar of early monasticism, in his study of *penthos* (mourning) describes the paradoxical combination of the effect of purificatory mourning. The monk who has travelled through this road finds that 'he has the sense not only of having sinned but of *being* a sinner, and the confidence—almost the observable certainty—of having entered in God's grace'.[22] Further, this dual experience is described as: (1) suffering unworthiness and estrangement from God; (2) being enfolded in divine nearness and tenderness:

> It is from having suffered estrangement from God, to the point of tears, that he will tremble the more with joy at nearness to him. He knows that he is still unworthy of this divine tenderness which enfolds him; he even grasps more clearly the contrast between what he deserves and what he is receiving.[23]

As Underhill suggested above, these different expressions likely reflect the dual human experiences *of God* rather than any actual duality *in God*. Likewise, Simon D. Podmore, a systematic and philosophical theologian, points to a profound ontological distinction which, in the research of spirituality, presents challenges to interpreting the God-relationship and to the

---

[20] Hood, Spilka, Hunsberger and Gorsuch, *The Psychology of Religion*, 265. Empirical research suggests that mystical experience and solitude are linked but the causality is not evidenced. One could therefore ask: Is it that mystics are drawn to solitude, or is it that solitude engenders mystics?

[21] Hood, Spilka, Hunsberger and Gorsuch, *The Psychology of Religion*, 226.

[22] Hausherr, Penthos, 138.

[23] Hausherr, Penthos, 138.

limits of knowing both God and the 'self'. He suggests that the experiences of the unknown, the dark night, the *contemplation* of the darker side of God and oneself, and the Negative Numinous associated with the concept of *mysterium horrendum* are within the liminal space between God and the creature rather than *in God* (the numen) or *in me* (the creature).[24] Podmore, therefore, appears to locate the experience of the terrifying ontological distance between the Creator and the creature in a separate liminal space rather than in the object (God) or in the subject (human) themselves.

This 'liminal space' is the threshold that opens up an opportunity for a relationship between the Creator and creature to be formed in contemplative prayer. Nevertheless, despite the relationship (and even the possibility of a union) between the human soul and God, the radical ontological difference will remain.

4.1.2   Ladders and Other Methods of Ascent

How, then, to deal with this ontological challenge? How to cross the chasm between the Creator and the creature? As Claude Lee Miller argued in the previous subsection, this cannot be done from the human side. Nevertheless, Foster also above suggested prayer as the way to negotiate this ontological difference between the Divine and human. What are, therefore, the monastic solutions for this dilemma? The following brief historical review summarises some suggested methods from the human side.

The earliest Christian monastic traditions were preoccupied with the study and development of methods for spiritual progress, both in practice and in theory. Typically the early efforts were a combination of physical (ascetic), moral, and spiritual practices. Ascetic self-control and discipline were the means for fighting against vices and progressing towards virtues. Practised virtues and the resulting passionlessness would enable progress to contemplation and knowledge of the Trinity. An example of such an approach, developed by Evagrius Ponticus (c. 345–399), constructed a trajectory of a spiritual progress from Ascetic Practice to Mystical Knowledge. The beginning of *Ascetic Practice* was faith and fear of God

---

[24] Simon D. Podmore, '*Mysterium Horrendum*: Mystical Theology and Negative Numinous' in Louise Nelstrop and Simon D. Podmore (eds.), *Exploring Lost Dimensions in Christian Mysticism: Opening to the Mystical* (Farnham: Ashgate Publishing, 2013), 93–116: 115–116.

with passionlessness as the goal. This goal was to be attained through the purgative cleansing of harmful passions (gluttony, impurity, avarice, sadness, anger, *acedia*, vainglory, pride) and the acquisition of virtues (temperance, charity, continence, patience, courage, wisdom, understanding, prudence). The beginning of *Mystical Knowledge* was contemplation of nature (*physike*) with the purpose of ridding oneself of ignorance in order to reach the higher goal: knowledge of the Trinity (*theologia*).[25]

Around the same time, Cassian introduced the image of a lofty spiritual tower which, built on the rock of the gospel and founded on deep humility, shall reach the sky.[26] He reflected on the priorities for monastic life in the *Conferences* with a reference to the fundamental 'end purpose'. According to Cassian, the *end* of monks' profession is the kingdom of God, or kingdom of heaven, but the *immediate aim* is purity of heart without which no one can gain that end. Therefore, secondary means such as fastings, vigils, meditation on the Scriptures, self-denial, and abnegation of all possessions are not perfection, but aids to perfection. Through the illustration of Martha and Mary, Cassian concludes that the Lord makes the 'chief good' consist of divine contemplation: all other virtues should be put into second place.[27]

Some scholars have criticised the early ascetic agenda as predominantly preoccupied with this-worldly egocentric self-transformation efforts. For example, Adalbert de Vogüé compares how the early monastics defined the summit of ascent. He argues that according to Cassian, humility leads to charity, the perfection of Christian life here below, while the sixth-century anonymous monastic author 'Master'—without neglecting this summit—looks further and is much more interested in the heavenly 'reward'.[28] He moreover distinguishes Cassian's approach as 'a theory of spiritual perfection here on earth' in contrast with 'a ladder to be climbed to heaven' referring to the eschatological perspective introduced later in the Rules of the Master and Benedict.[29]

---

[25] Evagrius, *The Praktikos & Chapters On Prayer*, 15–39. See also Harmless in *Desert Christians*, 346 for a useful illustration of Evagrius's approach.

[26] Cassian, *Conferences*, Conf. 9, Ch. II-III.

[27] Cassian, *Conferences*, Conf. 1, Chapters IV-VIII; Harmless notes in *Desert Christians*, 391, that what Cassian calls 'purity of heart', Evagrius had called 'passionlessness' (*apatheia*).

[28] Adalbert de Vogüé, *A Critical Study of the Rule of Benedict, Vol. 2* (Hyde Park, NY: New City Press, 2014; trans. C. M. McGrane), 223–224.

[29] de Vogüé, *A Critical Study of the Rule of Benedict, Vol. 2*, 236.

John Bamberger, OCSO, notes that one of the chief accusations made against Desert spirituality is that it is egocentric.[30] One cannot escape the notion of a certain self-preoccupation in the solitary struggles endured by the early ascetics in *Sayings*, *The Lausiac History*, and *The Historia Monachorum in Aegypto*. David Brakke, for example, concludes in his study on early Christianity: 'At its core, the monk's combat with the demons was an individual effort, an unrelenting struggle to maintain the integrity of one's self in the face of continual assault as one sat alone in the cell'.[31] This vulnerability in a solitary struggle only intensified as progress was made. The monk, who managed to conquer his own will, was rewarded with even more severe attacks, exemplified by Moses, who journeyed alone up the mountain to see God.[32]

What is common with these observations is the period they refer to: (1) the era of early asceticism; (2) the solitary combats of the hermits in the desert. The other side of the argument is that religious heroism, taken to an extreme, can lead to unrealistic expectations. David Foster, OSB, offers some cautionary remarks:

> Christian ideas about contemplation can turn into fantasies about tops of grandiose mountains. We do not bear in mind the actual conditions in which, in the biblical sources of this image, God actually revealed himself to people like Moses, Elijah or Jesus. We look for the high ground rather than the little Way, of a Thérèse of Lisieux... We think, with suitable equipment and technology, that we can tough out the fierceness of the mountain and deserts of the spiritual journey. We forget the disposition and dereliction of the journey to Calvary.[33]

Here, the ascent to God is complemented with a reminder about the painful journey to Calvary. Ascent and resurrection come only after the descent to humility, suffering and death. With progress and ascent, there is a prize to gain but also a price to pay.

---

[30] Bamberg in Evagrius, *Chapters on Prayer*, 123, footnote 55.

[31] David Brakke, *Demons and the Making of the Monk: Spiritual Combat in Early Christianity* (Cambridge, MA: Harvard University Press, 2006), 147.

[32] Brakke, *Demons and the Making of the Monk*, 147.

[33] Foster, *Contemplative Prayer*, 93. On ascent and suffering see also Colombas, *Paradis et Vie Angélique*, 106. Colombas, OSB, referring here to the ladder of Jacob (as a symbol of asceticism and purification notes that as the religious cry and suffer while climbing upwards, the world and all that it contains, for them, becomes small—'ridiculously miniscule'—while at the same time heaven becomes closer.

Paradoxically, progress on the vertical level may initially lead downward. There is a parallel in the life of Christ who, before ascending to heaven, descended into hell.[34] Another downward/upward trajectory is presented by Dante's allegory in *Divina Commedia*; the journey begins with the descent into hell, followed by a climb up the mount of purgatory, before the final ascent through the heavens until the vision of God is reached.[35]

Following from the earliest traditions, the Rule of Saint Benedict introduced the ladder of humility as the monastic way of progression.[36] Augustine, previously, had developed a number of different ladder schemes as his theological thinking evolved.[37] In the seventh century, *The Ladder of Divine Ascent* by John Climacus further expanded the idea of monastic life as a ladder stretching from earth to heaven which, by God's grace, the monks mount step by step. His ladder has thirty rungs or steps. The ascent starts with initial conversion—the break with the world—and continues with the practice of the virtues in 'active life' (*praxis, praktiki*) and finally transitions to the 'contemplative life' (*theoria*) in union with God.[38]

In the Carthusian tradition, Guigo II, the ninth Prior of the Grande Chartreuse in 1173–1178, outlines reading, meditation, prayer, and contemplation as the four rungs of a ladder by which monks are lifted up from

---

[34] *Catechism of the Catholic Church*, Part One, Section Two, Chapter Two, Article 5, 631: He who descended is he who also ascended far above all the heavens.

[35] Cunningham and Egan, *Christian Spirituality*, 54. The descent/ascent dynamics is also displayed in the *Sayings*, 38, where a monk who has fallen to sin is compared to a person who has fallen from a higher state to a lower and must work hard until he rises again. He is comparable to a ruined house which nevertheless can be rebuilt with the right materials. Likewise, a newcomer will find himself 'low down on the ladder of religion'. In this respect, a fallen monk is considered equal to a beginner who is starting from the bottom of the ladder.

[36] *The Rule of St. Benedict in English*, Ch. 7.

[37] Kenney, *Contemplation and Classical Christianity*, 94.

[38] Kallistos Ware, Introduction in Climacus, *The Ladder of Divine Ascent*, 10–13. Ware suggests that Climacus accepts, in general terms, the distinction drawn by Evagrius between the active and contemplative life. However, in contrast to Evagrius, Climacus holds that the supreme end of the spiritual way is not contemplation or *gnosis* but love, which is the final step of the ladder. On these distinctions, see also Rik van Nieuwenhove, 'Aquinas on Active and Contemplative lives' in *The Thomist*, Vol. 81, No.1. (January 2017), 1–30: 13. In his article on Aquinas's position on this, van Nieuwenhove argues that 'while the active life prepares us for the contemplative life, the latter is pursued for its own sake and has, furthermore, an eschatological dimension: eternal life is nothing but the consummation of the contemplative life, which constitutes a foretaste of the beatific vision of God'.

earth to heaven.[39] The lower end of the ladder (reading) rests upon the earth but the top (contemplation) 'pierces the clouds and touches heavenly secrets'.[40] This line of tradition, throughout the following centuries, generated several additional classics of monastic spirituality that could be labelled as 'ascent' or 'ladder' literature,[41] such as *The Soul's Journey Into God* by Bonaventure (d. 1274), *The Scale of Perfection* by Walter Hilton (d. 1396), *The Cloud of Unknowing* (latter half of the fourteenth century), *Interior Castle* by Teresa of Ávila (d. 1582) as well as *Dark Night of the Soul* and *Ascent of Mount Carmel* by John of the Cross (d. 1591). The two sixteenth-century Carmelites, it could be argued, brought the 'ascent' genre into perfection. It took another Carmelite, Thérèse of Lisieux, to take up the subject of ascent again, but from a somewhat different perspective. Instead of climbing the 'rough stairway of perfection', she introduced a new way of ascent. Writing in 1897 she wanted to 'seek out means of going to heaven by a little way, a way that is very straight, very short, and totally new':

> We are living now in an age of inventions, and we no longer have to take the trouble of climbing stairs, for, in the homes of the rich, an elevator has replaced these very successfully. I wanted to find an elevator which would raise me to Jesus, for I am too small to climb the rough stairway of perfection.[42]

And she discovered: 'The elevator which must raise me to heaven is Your arms, O Jesus! And for this I had no need to grow up, but rather I had to remain *little* and become this more and more'.[43] Within the tradition of 'ascent' spirituality, therefore, Thérèse of Lisieux modernised and simplified the journey, making it shorter and straighter. Yet, all the elements of Cassian's original tower construction remain:

---

[39] Guigo II, in Robin Bruce Lockhart (ed.), *Listening to Silence: An Anthology of Carthusian Writings* (London: Darton, Longman and Todd, 1997), 20. According to Peeters in *When Silence Speaks*, 189, later authors reduced the ladder to the first three steps because 'the gift of contemplation is quite rare'.

[40] Guigo II, in *Listening to Silence*, 20.

[41] The terms 'ascent literature' and 'ladder literature' in this sense are used by Cunningham and Egan, *Christian Spirituality*, 53.

[42] Thérèse of Lisieux, *Story of a Soul*, 328.

[43] Thérèse of Lisieux, *Story of a Soul*, 329.

1. Gospel (Jesus) as the rock
2. Humility (littleness) as the foundation
3. What is sought: the kingdom of heaven

The shared method in the monastic 'ascent literature' to attain the kingdom of heaven (the goal) therefore appears to be humility and relationship with the Divine, regardless of the analogy used. More recently, Thomas Merton (1915–1968), OCSO, follows a similar path of acknowledging the ontological difference between God and human by finding a unitive relationship through contemplative monastic life:

> That is the meaning of the contemplative life, and the sense of all the apparently meaningless little rules… they all serve to remind us of what we are and Who God is – that we may get sick of the sight of ourselves and turn to Him: and in the end, we may find Him in ourselves, in our purified natures which will become the mirror of His tremendous Goodness and of His endless love.[44]

In summary, according to this tradition, the way of progress goes through purification and humility with an ascent towards God aimed at knowledge of the Holy Trinity and transformation, that is, to become God-like. Interestingly, the timelessness of this monastic path, originating from the fourth-century Desert Dwellers, still echoes today in the words of a twenty-first-century cloistered contemplative:

> Humility is the foundation of the spiritual life and our holy ancestors have tried to teach us this lesson right from the beginning. The humbler we are the greater edifice God can build in our souls![45]

4.2   The Chain of Mysteries

The previous subsections introduced: (1) the challenge of the ontological difference; (2) a brief review of means and methods within monastic traditions in response to how to cross the chasm; how to *ascend* towards God. This subsection introduces the Chain of Mysteries as God's response; in other words, his salvific plan on how to *reach down* (*kenosis*) to humans.

---

[44] Merton, *The Seven Storey Mountain*, 372.
[45] Email from 'Mel', a cloistered contemplative, 06/05/2017.

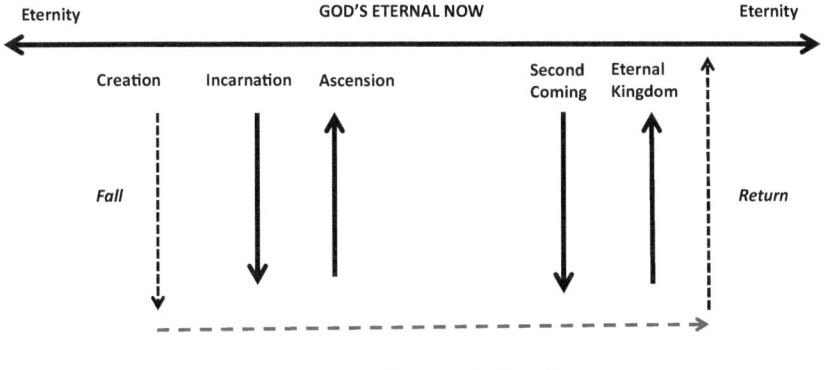

Fig. 4.2 Chain of Mysteries

The Chain of Mysteries originates from the eternity (before all ages); enters into temporality with creation and is followed by the Incarnation as the First Coming of Christ in humility (descent) to his Ascension back to heaven (ascent). What remains is the eschatological anticipation of the Second Coming of Christ in his glory (descent) and his final return to heaven (ascent) with the foundation of the eternal Kingdom. The Chain of Mysteries incorporates the temporal eternal/historical dimensions with the spatial vertical/horizontal dimensions (Fig. 4.2):

This Chain of Mysteries indicates the temporal link between the Incarnation and Eschatology, between the history of humankind and God's Eternal Now. Donato Ogliari notes that while monastic life appears constant, cyclic and repetitive, in an eschatological perspective it acquires a linearity 'which is the increasing mark of the history of salvation and that runs like a red thread through every hour of the day and night, today like yesterday and tomorrow like today'.[46] This linearity in monastic life is, according to Ogliari, 'marked by different time, by the attraction that the Eternal exercises on it in an ever new and unpredictable manner'.[47] He makes the connection between eternity and the history of salvation through the Incarnation:

---

[46] Ogliari, 'Tempus Monasticum', 41.
[47] Ogliari, 'Tempus Monasticum', 41.

This is due to the real immanence of the divine, which has impregnated the time of the universe and of human history in the Incarnation.[48]

Ogliari underlines the convergence of human temporal and horizontal time (diachronic) with divine eternal vertical time (synchronic) which has the salvific power:

> During the "diachronic" dimension of monastic time, lived as an epiphany of the history of salvation, there is a meeting with the "synchronic" dimension of this presence which saves. It impresses its seal on the "here and now" of the multiform search for God inscribed in the monastic experience.[49]

Ogliari here links the linear history of salvation with the dynamic plans of the Eternal in time. He suggests that the monk tries to live in a 'concentrated time', a time in which he tries to discover and receive the newness of the presence of God in 'today'.[50] The monk's day is therefore repetitive only in appearance. Within it there is a history, personal and communal, which is interlaced with the *history of salvation* and illumined and invigorated by it.[51]

This thought process presents us with an elaborate configuration of God's time and human time over the personal history of the religious, as well as humankind. By living the present time in the constant search of God, the 'here and now' experience of monastic life intersects with God's eternity. The historical Chain of Mysteries and the annual liturgical calendar transform into a personal journey of salvation. For example, to a contemporary cloistered contemplative:

> [Advent] not only commemorates the actual historical event, but His coming to us by grace and His final coming at the end when He will save us and bring His faithful ones to Heaven. As we renew this longing love for Him, we trust that He will grant... an ever greater desire for the only one thing necessary: eternity.[52]

---

[48] Ogliari, 'Tempus Monasticum', 41.
[49] Ogliari, 'Tempus Monasticum', 43.
[50] Ogliari, 'Tempus Monasticum', 41.
[51] Ogliari, 'Tempus Monasticum', 42.
[52] Email from 'Mel', a cloistered contemplative, 11/12/2018.

Similarly, Lucie Rivière, a Carmelite author views the cloister as a place where *chronos* time and *kairos* time intersect, in the manner of a chain or a weaving of the monastic life. With the contemplation of the Paschal Mystery of the Crucified-Resurrected the Carmelite learns to cross over her own sin, suffering, evil, death. It is the same union of two poles of times (*chronos* and *kairos*) that represents the same movement of the soul towards God that has integrated times in the Mysteries of the Incarnation and the Redemption.[53]

4.3   The Incarnation

The Incarnation is the paradox of the Eternal Divinity being born as a child in the temporal history of this world. The unique ontological nature of the Son of God could thus establish the possibility of a liminal relationship between the mortal human and the eternal God.[54] The Incarnation created the bridge between the Divine and human, between temporality and eternity, between immanence and transcendence. Accordingly, John Cottingham, an English philosopher, sees the Incarnation as the key concept for understanding the intersection between the vertical and the horizontal: the 'inaccessible light' of the divinity becomes visible in the person of one human being who is the 'icon of the invisible God'.[55] He argues:

> If we are to respect the otherness, the transcendence of God yet at the same time avoid becoming lost in a silence that risks being elided into agnosticism, we need a transition, a way of understanding God in human terms. And the life of Christ provides… such a transition, *an intersection point between the vertical and the horizontal*, which, as has often been observed, is

---

[53] Rivière, *Un temps supérieur à l'espace*, 34–35.

[54] The Nicene Creed confesses that the Lord Jesus Christ was 'born of the Father before all ages… begotten, not made, consubstantial with the Father', therefore eternal like God the Father, and present in creation; 'through him all things were made'. The Chalcedonian Creed, in 451 AD, established the orthodox view that Christ has two natures (human and divine) that are unified in one person. See also *Catechism of the Catholic Church*, Part One, Section Two, Chapter Two, Article 3, Paragraph 1. III. 464: 'The unique and altogether singular event of the Incarnation of the Son of God does not mean that Jesus Christ is part God and part man, nor does it imply that he is the result of a confused mixture of the divine and the human. He became truly man while remaining truly God. Jesus Christ is true God and true man'.

[55] John Cottingham, *The Spiritual Dimension: Religion, Philosophy and Human Value* (Cambridge: Cambridge University Press, 2005), 162–163.

symbolised in a unique way by the central image of the Cross. Contained here in this sign… is the secret 'hid for long ages' of our human redemption, of our access to God, of the mystery that is 'Emmanuel' – God with us.[56]

Similarly, Ogliari suggests that in the Incarnation of Christ, God has 'temporalized' eternity by entering into the evolving life of the universe and of human history.[57] The mystery of the Incarnation establishes an entry point for the intersection of divine and human temporalities. This intersection is essential for the God-human relationship. Accordingly, Jean-Philippe Houdret, OCD, proposes the idea of participation: individuals are not *enclosed* in their temporality but called to *share* with the divine life in the eternity.[58]Houdret argues that any attempt to try to compare human existence in relationship to God through geometric images—such as progressing from two-dimensionality to three-dimensionality—will fall short in explaining something that is rather beyond such comparisons. He claims that actually 'it is the question of moving from a destiny which is restricted by the limits of temporality to a destiny which opens to the infinity of God'.[59] For the Christian, eternity—present in this time—is inseparable from participation in God's eternal life.[60] Like several other monastic writers, Houdret connects this participation with the Incarnation:

> In the Incarnation, the divine life irrupts into time and confers on us the absolute gift of the eternal. It is in this temporal time that the eternal is already communicated to us. The important thing, therefore, is to receive the eternal in time, and not to seek to escape time to join it. It is in time that our eternal destiny is played out: with God or without God, according to whether we accept his love or not.[61]

Note that temporality—time and eternity—here is relational: it derives its meaning from one's response to God's love, from the relationship with the Divine.

---

[56] Cottingham, *The Spiritual Dimension*, 162. Italics mine.
[57] Ogliari, 'Tempus Monasticum', 51.
[58] Houdret, 'Le temps et l'éternité', 9. Translation mine. Italics mine.
[59] Houdret, 'Le temps et l'éternité', 9.
[60] Houdret, 'Le temps et l'éternité', 13.
[61] Houdret, 'Le temps et l'éternité', 13.

Andrew Louth, a Greek Orthodox patristic theologian, points towards the Incarnation as God's descent into the world, offering to humans the possibility of a relationship with God. Such a communion was not possible for them by nature, despite 'man being made in the image of God':

> Within the Platonic framework the soul's search for God is naturally conceived as a return, an *ascent* to God... Christianity, on the other hand, speaks of the Incarnation of God, of his *descent* into this world that he might give to man the possibility of a communion with God that is not open to him by nature. And yet man *is* made in the image of God, and so these movements of ascent and descent cross one another and remain – as a fact of experience – in unresolved tension.[62]

This experienced 'unresolved tension' could also be expressed as the ontological difference between God and humans as well as the tensions between 'here and there' (spatial) and 'now and then' (temporal). From the perspective of eternity, these experienced tensions could to some extent be overcome through the Christian virtue of hope. While still on the journey, not having reached the destination yet, the experience of God's temporal and spatial omnipresence can give the daily hope needed to keep on moving onwards (horizontal) and upwards (vertical). In other words, the human journey from transitory to eternal is reciprocated, or rather enabled, by Christ's journey from eternal to temporal and transitory. These 'vertical' salvific movements occurred within the 'horizontal' history of humankind, at a specific time and space, in temporality.

The association between time and motion, which contributes to our metaphor of the journey, leads us back to Augustine. Augustine's thinking, as summarised by Simo Knuuttila, a historian of philosophy, is based on a distinction of time and timelessness. Time depends on movement, but because God is unmoving, there is no time before creation. The

---

[62] Andrew Louth, *The Origins of the Christian Mystical Tradition: From Plato to Denys* (Oxford: Oxford University Press, 1981), xiv.

creation is an actualisation of God's eternal and immutable decision: to will a change does not imply a change of will.[63]

This is consistent with Scott MacDonald's interpretation of Augustine's theology regarding God's divine eternity: Augustine supposes that a being that experiences time necessarily changes, for its cognition will be (successively) affected by the temporal modalities of future, present, and past. By contrast, the divine being, that which truly *is*, cannot change this way, and so must comprehend all things in the eternal present. Augustine further argues that time itself is among God's creatures and comes into existence with the creation of the universe.[64] Continuing from Augustine's reasoning, this would imply that 'Because God exists, also time exists as a result of creation'; which would not exclude the statement that 'because God is unmoving, his existence is also timeless'.

While contemplative life and mysticism are not synonyms, it is worth considering Carmel Bendon Davis's central conclusion that '*the simultaneous recognition of God's transcendence and immanence* is possibly what the definition of mysticism, as an unmediated apprehension of the Divine, is really encapsulating'.[65] As suggested by Catholic theologian, Maurice Emelu, this revelation is reflected in the God-Moses encounter where God reveals his identity to Moses as 'I AM', 'a name that at the same time is no name… The *immanent* God at the burning bush is, at the same time, the God of *transcendence*, the *eternal* "I AM"'.[66] The omnipresence of 'I

---

[63] Simo Knuuttila, 'Time and Creation in Augustine' in Eleonore Stump and Norman Kretzmann (eds.), *The Cambridge Companion to Augustine* (Cambridge: Cambridge University Press, 2006), 103–115: 106. Further, Augustine assumed that time as a duration is not dependent on any specific motion, but if nothing passed or arrived or existed, there would be no past, future of present times. For example, time would still pass even if the sun stood still, 111.

[64] Scott MacDonald, 'The Divine Nature' in Eleonore Stump and Norman Kretzmann (Eds.), *The Cambridge Companion to Augustine* (Cambridge: Cambridge University Press, 2006), 71–90: 85.

[65] Davis, *Mysticism and Space*, 249. Italics mine.

[66] Maurice Emelu, *Our Journey to God* (Irondale, AL: EWTN Publishing, 2017), 27. Italics mine. See also Rowe and Neyrey, 'Christ and Time – Part Three', 83–90, where the authors argue that the sense of heavenly time is best expressed in the appropriation by Jesus of the divine name 'I am who I am' spoken to Moses. They claim therefore that the Fourth Gospel leads its readers to think that Jesus enjoys eternal duration because he had no beginning in the past and will have no ending in the future. Accordingly, Jesus has the role and status as a 'timeless' figure, whose 'time' is that of God: uncreated, non-contingent, eternally existing 'I AM'.

AM'—the perfection of Being—is revealed by his name. The Incarnation, therefore, represents the temporal inflection point when the eternal Word became flesh as the transcendent and the immanent converged.

Among contemporary monastic sources Garcia Colombas, OSB, however, cautions against what he sees as a modern tendency of Christianity to focus on the immanent. He admits that Christianity, undoubtedly, is the religion of the Incarnation, but the only Son of the Father did not descend to our world to remain here and found an earthly kingdom; rather, he came to gather humankind and to bring it with him to his heavenly kingdom, his real homeland. Colombas maintains that 'Christianity is *at the same time* the religion of the Incarnation and of the Ascension'.[67] His arguments in this account indicate a balanced view between God's immanence and transcendence. This is reflected in the themes of the Incarnation and Ascension, temporal and eternal, earthly and heavenly.

4.4   Dynamic Relationship: Participation in Christ's Journey

The 'monastic reading' of the Gospels would suggest that certain aspects of religious life imitate the way the Lord led his earthly life. He was celibate, poor, and obedient to his Father, lived in community with a chosen group of 'brothers' (the disciples), having left his home and family relations to follow a different path in a dedicated religious life. In a deeper way, he was aware of his 'liminal' role as an intermediator between humankind and the Father, and of the salvific journey that was mapped for him. This obedient and humble route would take him through the suffering of Via *Crucis* and death to the joy of Resurrection and Ascension. Jesus was also aware of the eschatological destiny of the world, even if he did not know precisely 'the day and hour'.[68]

For the religious, sharing in Christ's journey means taking up one's cross, enduring the suffering and joys of daily life (imitation of Christ), participating in the works of God (*opus Dei*) and continuous prayer. This kind of association or even assimilation of roles is expressed by a contemporary cloistered contemplative:

---

[67] Colombas, *Paradis et Vie Angélique*, 281. Translation and italics mine.
[68] Mt. 24:36 (NRSV).

Look at the Son of God on the cross. When one meditates truly upon this mystery, one discovers the complete love that God has for the sinner. Who would take on such madness, so to speak, as to suffer and die such a cruel death for an ungrateful sinner? And yet, Christ did. His was not madness, it was LOVE. There was no other way to express His love for humanity than by suffering to the extreme. Suffering and love are one and the same. In Religious Life, it is the same. We are here to live the life of Christ: to love, to suffer, to give, to be at peace, to have joy.[69]

The sentence 'Suffering and love are one and the same' is worth highlighting. Here, suffering is seen as a divine form of love. The God who loves is also the God who suffers.

Ogliari suggests that the monk tries to live in a 'concentrated time', a time in which he tries to discover and receive the newness of the presence of God in 'today'. This means that the monk assumes existentially the exterior and interior rhythms of the monastic day. The exterior alterations refer to elements such as light and darkness; while interiorly the monk experiences alterations of joys and sufferings, of mystical insight and aridity.[70] In addition to the changes of light and darkness, many daily events are liturgical, related to the succession of solemnities, feasts and memorials which embellish the ordinary course of the Divine Office. Some are occasional events that mark the course of the monastic days such as the passage of pilgrims and travellers in the monastery, the arrival of new postulants, professions, sickness, and death.[71]

The dynamic relationship as 'participation in Christ's journey' is also found in the Vatican *Verbi Sponsa* document which defines monastic enclosure as 'a special way' of living the Paschal Mystery: 'withdrawal from the world in order to dedicate oneself in solitude to a more intense life of prayer is nothing other than a special way of living and expressing the Paschal Mystery of Christ'.[72] *Verbi Sponsa* further identifies cloistered life as a 'true encounter with the Risen Lord, a journey in ceaseless ascent to the Father's house'.[73] We can identify in the last sentence several recurrent monastic themes: Relationship (encounter), journey, 'ceaseless' ascent,

[69] Email from 'Mel' a cloistered contemplative, 17/08/2016.
[70] Ogliari, 'Tempus Monasticum', 41.
[71] Ogliari, 'Tempus Monasticum', 42.
[72] *Verbi Sponsa*, 3.
[73] *Verbi Sponsa*, 3.

and heaven (Father's house). The Carthusian Statutes, likewise, indicate a dynamic relationship through participation:

> By penance, moreover, we have our part in the saving work of Christ, who redeemed the human race from the oppressive bondage of sin, above all by pouring forth prayer to the Father, and by offering himself to him in sacrifice. Thus, it suggests that we, too, even though we abstain from exterior activity, exercise nevertheless an apostolate of a very high order, since we strive to follow Christ in this, the inmost heart of his saving task.[74]

There is a profound relationship, and there is a shared redemptive mission. Participation in Christ's journey becomes a transitional dynamic relationship where the Son leads the soul to know and love the Father: 'Those who love me will keep my word, and my Father will love them, and we will come to them and make our home with them'.[75] The Ascension of the Resurrected Lord sets the hope of a shared destiny: 'I am ascending to *my* Father and *your* Father, to *my* God and *your* God'.[76] This dynamic participation in Christ's journey, furthermore, has the potential to open up the soul towards others—seeing every human being as a brother or sister in Christ. The direction of travel is away from self towards knowing God, as well as sharing life and the Faith with others. A Carthusian prior, in his sermon on the perpetual donation of a brother, advises him: 'The fatigue and occasional sufferings of each day and of a tired body and mind can be associated with the sufferings of Christ and become the source of redemptive grace of fellow human beings that you may never know'.[77]

The relationship between God and a religious is dynamic because it evolves over time, as relations between persons do. This is not due to changeability in God; it indicates the inherent dynamism of relationships. The deepening of this bond with the Eternal is expected to continue after death for all eternity. As Dom Dysmas, O.Cart., explains the liaison with God: 'Like any relationship, it has a history, it develops.... With God, this movement has no end, since he is infinite'.[78]

---

[74] Carthusian Statutes Book 4, Ch. 34.4. Italics mine.

[75] Jn 14:23 (NRSV).

[76] Jn 20:17 (NRSV). Italics mine.

[77] A Carthusian, *The Spirit of Place*, 119.

[78] Robert Sarah, *The Power of Silence: Against the Dictatorship of Noise* (San Francisco, CA: Ignatius Press, 2017; trans. M. Miller), 211.

4.5   PERMANENT RELATIONSHIP: GOD'S TEMPORAL AND SPATIAL OMNIPRESENCE

How might God's temporal and spatial omnipresence be reflected in the experience of enclosed contemplatives? A poem written by a Carthusian monk provides a glimpse of a day lived in an intimate relationship with God. His poem *Gazing* covers the cycle of a day lived in the constant presence of God.

Gazing

> God is always gazing at me: I feel
> His gentle gaze throughout the day in face
> And voice, in sunlight splintering clouds, in rain
> And rumbling skies, in multitudinous greens,
> In labour and in pain, the work of love.
> When nature turns to sleep and silence lays
> Its hand on the overactive mind to calm
> Its undue agitations I feel his gaze
> As intimacy. I feel the rags I am
> So vividly yet that is fair in love.
> He loves me because he loves me; I ask not why
> God gives himself so recklessly. I gaze
> At him in the night and ache to see his face.
> The darkness covers me and all I see
> Is God's creative gaze. O God of Love!
> "Abba!" cries the child awakened by
> Your presence. My soul's an eternal child in you
> Content to rest upon your bosom, the vast
> World of peace and overflowing joy.
> Your eyes are flames of everdawning love....[79]

The intimacy of this relationship and God's presence finds various forms in this poem. It is expressed by: (1) the sovereign divine love 'He loves me because he loves me'; (2) Father-son relation, 'My soul is an eternal child in you'; (3) nature—'sunshine, rain'—as well as daily work and pain. The general theme is that of being seen and loved. Importantly, there is mutuality in the relationship. God gazes at the monk, the monk gazes at God, longing and aching to see his face. The presence of God is

---

[79] A Carthusian, *In Praise of Silence*, 23.

felt and sought during the whole course of the day, even in the darkness of the night. One can imagine the daily Divine Office further intensifying this experience of being in the constant presence of God.

Another experience of God's presence in time comes from Thomas Merton, OCSO, who writes about 'the reality of the present' in solitude that is 'divorced from past and future':

> I shall remember this time and place of this liberty and this neutrality which cannot be written down. These clouds low on the horizon... the big cedars tumbled and tousled by the wind. Standing on a rock. Present. The reality of the present and of solitude divorced from past and future. To be collected and gathered up in clarity and silence and to belong to God and to be nobody else's business.[80]

Merton's experience relates to the sense of belonging to God alone, in the enclosure of his Trappist monastery. The elements of 'present' and 'presence' are tangible in the moment. Time stands still, the monk stands on a rock. The only motion is in the wind that moves the branches of cedar trees.

Merton's 'reality of the present' is related to Ogliari's focus on the 'instant' as an element of monastic time. In the eyes of the religious, Ogliari claims, every instant is precious because at every instant they are offered the possibility of receiving and experiencing the efficacious and providential presence of God, which guides the history of the individual and of the community:

> Thanks to this presence, everything, from the greatest events to the smallest and apparently least significant, takes a sacred aspect and is transformed into a concrete *possibility of harmonization with the eternity of God*.[81]

Ogliari furthermore defines monastic time as a sort of 'theology of the instant' as he sees 'instant' closest to the experience that monks have of time.[82] He associates monastic time with the relational dimensions of 'the search of God' and of 'the living perception of the presence of God':

---

[80] Merton, *The Sign of Jonas*, 246.

[81] Ogliari, 'Tempus Monasticum', 43. Italics mine, to stress the impact of God's omnipresence as a possibility to harmonise the present time with the eternity of God.

[82] Ogliari, 'Tempus Monasticum', 42–43.

> The search of God, which is the leitmotiv of the monastic vocation, and the living perception of the presence of God in the day of the monk, are... the ultimate reasons not only why the monastic time is not repetitive, but also why time itself is precious and unrepeatable.[83]

This draws attention to the significance of the personal relationship with God as the leading motivation for religious life. It could be argued that monastic time is relational because it is lived in relationship with God. But it is also relative because time itself has no intrinsic value: the value of monastic time is derived from God, directed towards God, and lived in relation with the Divine.

Ogliari argues that the organisation of time in Benedictine monastic life can be understood as a regimentation that is based on the consciousness that the values of God's eternity are already impressed on the present time.[84] 'This present is the *here and now* that is daily offered to us so we might exercise our humble and faithful responsibility. In its attempt to make us perceive the time of God in human time, and vice-versa, the RB reminds us that monks do not escape time and history'.[85]Ogliari sees monks, in contrast, embracing time and letting themselves be embraced by it so as to transfigure time from within.[86] Monastic time therefore becomes an intermediary between divine time and human time, and hence the values of God's eternity are transported into human life.

Adalbert de Vogüé provides another 'Already Here and Now' experience related to temporal convergence through the relationship with the Son and the Father:

> To believe in the Son is therefore to *have* eternal life, and this is nothing else but to know him and his Father. The eternity hoped for passes from the future into the present. This actualization, which transfigures earthly life, can only sharpen man's attention to the mystery of the ultimate state into which he has already entered.[87]

Worth highlighting here is the phrase 'mystery of the ultimate state into which he has *already* entered'. While still on the journey and while getting

---

[83] Ogliari, 'Tempus Monasticum', 42.

[84] Ogliari, 'Tempus Monasticum', 50.

[85] Ogliari, 'Tempus Monasticum', 50–51. (RB is abbreviation for The Rule of St. Benedict.)

[86] Ogliari, 'Tempus Monasticum', 50–51.

[87] de Vogüé, *To Desire Eternal Life*, 22.

to know God better, one already possesses eternal life. In this *anticipation* and *transfiguration* of time, divine eternity 'hoped for' passes from the future and 'already' enters into the human present. This apparent complexity of converging temporal and atemporal references relates to the paradoxical dynamism and stability of monastic time. Monastic 'time' from this perspective presents itself as a peaceful 'space'—not necessarily a place of rest—but rather an environment for gradual transfiguration and transformation, of 'being' while 'becoming'.

Similarly, a Carthusian novice master instructed his novices in 1928 about allowing them to be transformed by the Divine Will through being crucified and glorified in Christ. This Carthusian indicates that the transformation towards eternal life begins while one is still on earth, led by God. It goes through ultimate humility, the descent to 'nothingness', where one accepts 'to be content to be divine'. The Carthusian novice master explains:

> Rare are the souls which really dare to be nothing, and which, in that very act, are humble enough to be content to be divine and to be sons of the Most High, but it is precisely this miracle of miracles that the Divine Will wishes to lead those of us who allow ourselves to be transformed, to be in short crucified and glorified in Him... beyond every temporal striving; in God alone: that is where life eternal begins for us even while we are still here on earth.[88]

This thought is quite paradoxical: that one's ascent to divinity is found in descent and ultimate humility. It involves participation in Christ's crucifixion and glorification; abandoning oneself to the Divine Will which performs this transformation in the religious. As a result, eternal life in God begins already here and now. Specifically, eternal life is associated with God alone, 'beyond' temporality.

Among the enclosed contemplative traditions, God's omnipresence is regarded as a 'very Carmelite thing'. Contemporary Carmelite sister Angela Thérèse describes her experience of God's presence in all aspects of her life:

---

[88] *A Carthusian Speaks*, notes taken in 1928 by a novice during the Novice Conferences given by the Novice Master of the Charterhouse of La Valsainte. The notes were translated into English and published by Peter Van der Meer de Walcheren in his book *The White Paradise* (New York, 1952). http://transfiguration.chartreux.org/ Accessed on 20 July 2019.

I see God more as a presence, both within us and without, because He is everywhere all the time, and within us as well. That's a very Carmelite thing – the practice of the presence of God. We call it the Divine Indwelling, the idea that He's with us everywhere all the time. He's with us amongst the pots and pans as much as He is when we're in the choir on our knees.[89]

Elizabeth Obbard, OCD, argues that God's continual presence, as part of the Carmelite spiritual tradition, allows the religious to 'ask the right questions and realize ultimately that God is *all*. In God we have everything, including, and indeed most especially, our deepest humanity, for he is Emmanuel: God-with-us'.[90] Here, God's spatial omnipresence refers to the recognition of his immanence and transcendence while God's temporal omnipresence refers to his temporality and timelessness. The divine omnipresence reaches down to the human temporal and transitory condition. The elements of 'here and there' (spatial) and 'now and then' (temporal) converge.

How can we understand this experience of 'being with God already on earth' as expressed by the contemplatives above? An answer is found through the Ascension: Christ is 'seated at the right hand of the Father' but has also promised to be with his disciples 'always to the end of the age'.[91] A contemporary Carthusian Father speaks about the Lord who has ascended into heaven, yet is also present on earth in the Church through the gift of the Spirit, the Word and the sacraments.[92] Following from this, he argues that monks too are called to respond to this 'paradox of Ascension': 'In Christ, we too share his risen life and we too live on earth,

---

[89] Loudon, *Unveiled*, 29. Sister Angela Thérèse's description resembles that of Brother Lawrence of the Resurrection (1611–1691), in *The Practice of the Presence of God and the Spiritual Maxims* (Mineola, NY: Dover Publications, 2005): 'The time of business... does not with me differ from the time of prayer; and in the noise and clatter of my kitchen... I possess GOD in as great tranquillity as if I were upon my knees at the blessed sacrament', 16. This thought originates from Teresa of Ávila, in *Book of the Foundations* (London: T. Jones, 1853; trans. J. Dalton): 'when obedience calls you to exterior employments (as, for example, into kitchen, amidst the pots and dishes), remember that our Lord goes along with you, to help you both in your interior and exterior duties', 27.

[90] Elizabeth Obbard, *To Live is to Pray: An Introduction to Carmelite Spirituality* (Norwich: Canterbury Press, 1997), 104.

[91] Mt. 28:20 (NRSV).

[92] A Carthusian, *The Spirit of Place*, 103–104. The sacraments were first linked to Ascension in Leo the Great's *Sermon 74: On the Ascension of the Lord*, II.

or rather, Christ lives in and through us in space and time'.[93] The monks become participants in the paradox of Ascension. They represent Christ on earth while, through their contemplative life, they anticipate Christ's risen life in heaven.

4.6   CONTEMPLATIVE RELATIONSHIP: ASCENT TO GOD

Contemplation is a complex term which eludes precise definition. It is sometimes identified as the unitive stage of the traditional threefold model of 'purgation–illumination–union'[94] where union as a relational term can be associated with the God-human Relationship. Contemplation, in addition to relationality, is traditionally associated with verticality. The classical sentence from Evagrius, 'Prayer is an ascent of the spirit to God',[95] indicates a vertical movement, an ascent which lifts the human spirit to God. According to the twelfth-century Carthusian Guigo II, 'Contemplation is when the mind is in some sort lifted up to God and held above itself, so that it tastes the joys of everlasting sweetness'.[96] These definitions of contemplation are associated with ascent,[97] where the soul is directed upwards and above itself towards God, in line with the idea of *vertical* enclosed contemplative journeys.

Contemplation also differs from meditation. Carthusian Dom Dysmas distinguishes these forms of mental prayer by describing meditation as an intellectual activity to 'grasp' while contemplation refers to 'marvelling' and 'abandoning' to God's love that is 'beyond' human understanding:

---

[93] A Carthusian, *The Spirit of Place*, 103–104.

[94] See, for example, Benedict J. Groeschel, *Spiritual Passages: The Psychology of Spiritual Development* (New York, NY: Crossroad, 1983), 160–188.

[95] Evagrius, *Chapters on Prayer*, Ch. 35.

[96] Guigo II, In *Listening to Silence*, 20.

[97] Ascents can take various forms. See Cunningham and Egan, *Christian Spirituality*, 53: In spiritual theology, the images of ladder and mountain, for example, have been used to map out the steps or stages which had to be taken to move up from this world to the world of God. In the Bible, God's presence is associated with nature-related ascent metaphors, such as cloud surrounding a mountain (Lk 9:43) and mountain (Ex 19:21). See also Mircea Eliade, *The Sacred and the Profane: The Nature of Religion* (New York, NY: Harcourt, 1987; trans. W. Trask), 36–44, on how mountains in various civilisations express a sacred symbolic connection between heaven and earth; spatial links also designate a point of intersection—and hence communication with the transcendental world—while implying also the difference in ontological status between cosmic planes.

> Contemplation is nourished more by what we do not understand. In medi-
> tation, a man seeks to grasp something of a mystery. In contemplation, he
> marvels and abandons himself to God's love, which surpasses us.[98]

Contemplation is moreover considered a grace, similar to faith and salvation.[99] These are gifts from God which may be sought but not achieved
solely by human volition or effort. They can only be 'received', not 'taken'.
The question arises, then: why do certain monastic orders call their
approach specifically 'contemplative'?[100] One answer may lie in that contemplation is considered a desirable state—the closest experience to being
in union with God—and achievable even if it may be experienced only
momentarily and transiently. Such a type of prayer is patiently sought
through the intimate relationship with the Divine. This means that, from
the perspective of the individual, if contemplation is considered a grace
(rather than a result of employing a designed meditative technique or
method), the only way to receive it is to humbly wait on God. Perhaps, by
faithfully persisting in God's Work (*opus Dei*), one trusts that God does his
work in one's life and in the lives of others, in due course, over time.

Another answer could be found in using broader definitions of 'contemplation' and 'contemplative'. In the Carthusian usage, these terms
appear to cover their entire way of life: an approach that penetrates both

---

[98] Sarah, *The Power of Silence*, 219. Cf. John of the Cross in *A Spiritual Canticle of the Soul
and the Bridegroom Christ*, Stanza XXVII, 3 appears to connect contemplation with love,
knowledge and will, as he writes: 'This science is mystical theology... which spiritual men call
contemplation. It is most full of sweetness because it is knowledge by love, love is the master
of it, and it is love that renders it all so sweet. Inasmuch as this science and knowledge are
communicated to the soul in that love with which God communicates Himself, it is sweet to
the understanding because knowledge belongs to it, and sweet to the will, because it comes
by love which belongs to the will'. Contemplation, according to John of the Cross, here is
defined as 'knowledge by love' but it is communicated to the soul by God, in love. In stanza
XXXIX, 17, John of the Cross further distinguishes between 'dim contemplation' (here
below) and 'clear contemplation' (serene vision of God above).

[99] Teresa of Ávila in *The Way to Perfection*, Ch. 17 stresses that contemplation is something
given by God. It is not necessary for salvation and God does not ask it of the religious before
He gives them their reward. The religious should make themselves ready for God to lead
them by the contemplative road if He so wills but the whole point of *true* humility is to
consider oneself happy either way, 124; there is always greater safety in humility, mortification, detachment and other virtues, 126; God's judgements are His own and we must not
meddle in them, 127.

[100] Louth in *The Origins of the Christian Mystical Tradition*, 100, makes the intriguing
observation that we find no word about contemplation in the Rule of Saint Benedict.

'the mundane nitty-gritty of life, the immense spaces of living solitude, the monastery itself' and the 'mystical aspiration, the living sense of the transcendent, the ineffable mystery of God'.[101]Carthusians, therefore, speak about 'perennial' and 'mystical' contemplation in the heart of the spiritual life *in its totality, the hidden dimension of all its activity* instead of an extraordinary sphere. This means that mystical contemplation is not a special degree of prayer but a more or less enduring transaction, involving the gift of wisdom. God is able to infuse it in the context of other forms of prayer (such as the Divine Office) or even during manual work. 'Intimacy with God' is the essential vocation of a Carthusian.[102]

As it is beyond the scope of this study to arrive at the exact meaning of the terms 'contemplation' and 'contemplative', it is reasonable to conclude that within monastic traditions there appears to be: (1) a broader definition that refers to the contemplative way of life, a perennial attitude; (2) a narrow definition with reference to a specific state of contemplation which is momentary and episodic. The implication of this will be reviewed next.

4.6.1 Humility

It has been said that Augustine was obsessed with time but he was also a searcher of contemplation. According to Kenney, Augustine realised that contemplation of God was a momentary, episodic experience. Abbreviated and arrested ascents were due to the fallen nature of the human soul. The fallen soul has only a limited capacity for unmediated contemplation in this life.[103] Thus the soul needs to maintain its focus on divine wisdom through the power of grace. This can be done by daily meditation upon scripture and the practice of Christian discipline.[104] Kenney reframes Augustine's conclusion: while progress in the beatitudes grows into a renewed likeness of God and contemplation of the divine truth, a continuous loop leads back to humility and constant following of the path of the beatitudes.[105] This interpretation of Augustine's findings would suggest that the monastic journey is not done in a straight line but is rather a com-

[101] A Carthusian, *The Way of Silent Love*, 68–69.

[102] A Carthusian, *The Way of Silent Love*, 68–68.

[103] Kenney, *Contemplation and Classical Christianity*, 157.

[104] Kenney, *Contemplation and Classical Christianity*, 154. Augustine, *Confessions*, X.2 and XI.30–31.

[105] Kenney, *Contemplation and Classical Christianity*, 155.

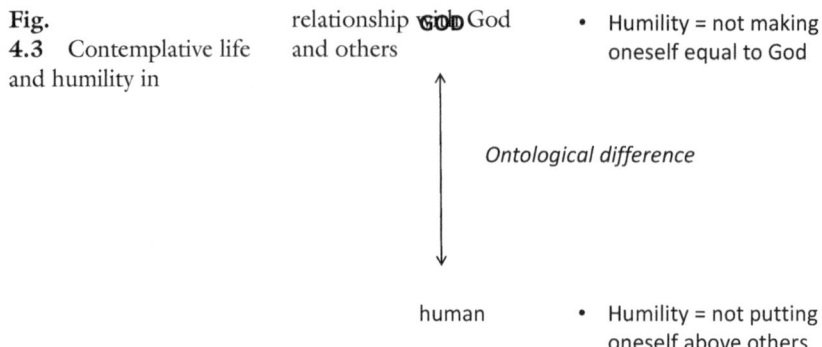

Fig. 4.3 Contemplative life and humility in

bination of staying steadily on a progressive path and simultaneously experiencing 'a continuous loop' between humility and contemplation.

One might ask, why bring up the topic of humility only here, in connection with contemplation. Is not humility supposed to characterise the beginning of the journey, as the foundation of monastic life? Perhaps humility is foundational in the sense that it covers the whole journey. Indeed, Desert Fathers reminded that one should expect to be tempted all the way to the very end.[106] Yet, it seems that humility is particularly closely connected with contemplation. One reason for this could be found in the ontological difference. As one approaches the divine transcendence in contemplation, one becomes ever more acutely aware of one's unworthiness. In the words of Mathois, a Desert Father: 'The nearer a man comes to God, the more he sees himself to be a sinner'.[107] Furthermore, humility grows from increasing self-knowledge. A humble attitude has twofold consequences. First, the acknowledgement that one is a sinner reflects one's correct attitude in relation towards God, and second, it should lead to non-judgement of fellow humans. This dual meaning of humility is shown in Fig. 4.3.

This search for self-knowledge and non-judgemental attitude with its temporal and eternal consequences is expressed in the dialogue between two Desert Fathers:

---

[106] *Sayings*, 148: 'Our great work is to lay the blame for our sins upon ourselves before God, and to expect to be tempted to our last breath'.

[107] *Sayings*, 157. Further on the connection between humility and ascent/descent in the ladder of contemplation see John of the Cross, *Dark Night of the Soul*, Book II, Ch. XVIII.2.

Joseph: Tell me how to become a monk?

Poemen: If you want to *find rest in this life and the next*, say at every moment, 'Who am I?' and judge no one.[108]

Jane Foulcher notes that, on one hand, the monastic tradition speaks of a way of imitating the humble Christ. On the other hand, the monastic tradition protects the graced nature of this quality, which can never be found by human effort but is the by-product of a life oriented towards God.[109] Foulcher suggests that the monastic traditions she has examined all understand human life as oriented towards an end (*telos*), variously expressed as the vision of God, the kingdom of heaven, eternal life, purity of heart, and love.[110] According to this perspective, the desire for God is met by a *sense of the distance* between the Divine and the human, an *eschatological humility*.[111] Human beings are limited, broken creatures with divine vocation but paradoxically, in facing and acknowledging these limits we are able to transcend them.[112]

This relates to the ontological difference, as the 'sense of distance', as the gap between the Divine and the human. The terms 'eschatological humility' (used by Foulcher) and 'eschatological hope' (used in this study) therefore refer to the need of self-transcendence: how to bridge the gap and close the distance. This distance is experienced at multiple levels: temporal (time/eternity), spatial (earth/heaven) and relational (human/God). Contemplative monastic life is therefore characterised by 'eschatological longing'. Yet, monasticism is not an end in itself, but rather a means, as well as a sign that points towards what is 'beyond'.

As a conclusion of the discussion between contemplation and humility, the monastic experience seems to encompass a multiform setting:

---

[108] Sayings, 85. Italics mine.

[109] Foulcher, *Reclaiming Humility*, 309. Foulcher suggests here that humility, which was never a virtue in the Greco-Roman world, came in the early Christian era to signal a radically different way of conceiving the human journey. Subsequently its trajectory found a place in the theology and practice of Western monastic expressions.

[110] Foulcher, *Reclaiming Humility*, 310. Foulcher studied Desert Monasticism, The Rule of Saint Benedict, Bernard de Clairvaux, Christian de Chergé and the Monks of Tibhirine.

[111] Foulcher, *Reclaiming Humility*, 310. Italics mine.

[112] Foulcher, *Reclaiming Humility*, 310.

contemplation juxtaposed with humility in reliance on God's grace.[113] Here, God's grace manifests itself through the initial calling at the beginning of the journey, through his providence during monastic life and finally in the hope of God's mercy at the Day of Judgement.[114] The individual's correct response is to receive these gifts—God's invitation to a relationship in time and eternity—with humility and gratitude.

4.6.2   Upward Journeys

Following from the 'descent to humility', we return to the topic of 'ascent through contemplation'. Selected classic descriptions of the Contemplative Relationship as a vertical upward journey are presented first.

Gregory of Nyssa (c. 335–395) wrote about the ascent of Moses to Mount Sinai where he presents the paradox of 'standing still' and 'being on the move'. He writes, 'For he who ascends certainly does not stay still, and he who stands still does not move upwards'.[115] Yet, according to Gregory of Nyssa, it is precisely through standing still that the ascent occurs. This stillness, in monastic terms, can be associated with enclosure, which enables contemplation by vertical ascents. The initial ascent becomes a continuous desire for the soul to push upwards:

> If nothing comes from above to hinder its upward thrust (for the nature of Good attracts to itself those who look to it), the soul rises ever higher and will always make its flight yet higher – by its desire for heavenly things.... Made to desire and not to abandon the transcendent height by the things already attained, it makes its way upward without ceasing.[116]

This leads to what Gregory of Nyssa calls *epektasis*, or the constant pursuit of God that is also paradoxically the enjoyment of his presence.[117] 'This

---

[113] This fine balance is expressed by Innocent Le Masson (Prior of the Grand Chartreuse in 1675–1703) in Lockhart, *Listening to Silence*, 65 through the image of 'two wings'—confidence and humility—which must serve the contemplatives to keep them 'balanced between heaven and earth'.

[114] See *Catechism of the Catholic Church*, Part Three, Section One, Chapter Three, Article 2, 2021: 'Grace is the help God gives us to respond to our vocation of becoming his adopted sons. It introduces us into the intimacy of the Trinitarian life'.

[115] Gregory of Nyssa, *The Life of Moses* (New York, NY: HarperCollins, 2006; trans. A. Malherbe and E. Ferguson), 107.

[116] Gregory of Nyssa, *The Life of Moses*, 103.

[117] McGinn, *The Essential Writings of Christian Mysticism*, 14.

truly is the vision of God: never to be satisfied in the desire to see him', Gregory of Nyssa concludes and continues: 'Thus, no limit would inter- rupt growth in the ascent to God, since no limit to the Good can be found, nor is the increasing of desire for the Good brought to end because it is satisfied'.[118] The elements of enjoyment of God's presence 'already here' and the eschatological 'looking forward' are identifiable in this early ascent text.

Pseudo-Dionysius the Areopagite, a Christian theologian and Neoplatonic philosopher of the late fifth and early sixth centuries, in *The Mystical Theology*, similarly recounts the narrative of Moses' holy ascent to Mount Sinai. This journey, which leads to an encounter with God, begins with purification followed by a departure from those who have not under- gone this experience. Moses then pushes ahead to the summit of the divine ascents but does not meet God himself. He contemplates not him who is invisible, but rather where he dwells. Finally, Moses breaks free of the things perceived with the eye of the body or the mind, away from what sees and is seen and plunges into the truly mysterious darkness of unknow- ing. Here, renouncing all that the mind may conceive, wrapped entirely in the intangible and invisible, he belongs completely to him who is 'beyond' everything.[119]

According to Pseudo-Dionysius, the more we take flight upward, the more our words are confined to the ideas we are capable of forming. As we plunge into that darkness which is 'beyond' intellect, we find ourselves not simply running short of words but actually speechless and unknowing. When the direction of travel rises from what is 'below', 'up' to the tran- scendent—and the more it climbs—the more language falters 'and when it has passed up and beyond the ascent, it will turn silent completely, since it will finally be at one with him who is indescribable'.[120] As suggested by Kevin M. Clarke, an American scholar of Early Christianity, for Pseudo- Dionysius, the one who ascends into the luminous darkness is one who rises into a state of union with God. And God is the one who acts upon the soul, deifying it and suffusing it with his light. Therefore, when Moses

---

[118] Gregory of Nyssa, *The Life of Moses*, 106.

[119] Pseudo-Dionysius, 'The Mystical Theology' in *The Complete Works*, (Mahwah, NJ: Paulist Press, 1987, trans. C. Luibheid), 133–141: 136–137.

[120] Pseudo-Dionysius, *The Complete Works*, 139.

has unknown everything that is not 'beyond', he belongs completely to God.[121]

Augustine, in *Confessions*, further relates ascent to an upward journey initiated by the Holy Spirit, leading to eternal peace and stability in the heavenly Jerusalem:

> By your gift, the Holy Ghost, we are set aflame and borne aloft, and the fire within us carries us upward. Our hearts are set on an upward journey, as we sing the song of ascents. It is your fire, your good fire, that sets us aflame and carries us upward. For our journey leads us upward to the peace of the heavenly Jerusalem... There, if our will is good, you will find room for us, so that we shall wish for nothing else but to remain in your house for ever.[122]

The direction is upwards because that is where the heavenly Jerusalem is situated. This represents a vertical trajectory towards God. However, there is also a horizontal dimension to the journey, which takes place at the level of interiority. The internal horizontal journey takes two different directions: (1) an inward movement, to deeper interiority; (2) a trajectory of going-out, away from self.

How does contemplation as an upward movement relate to inward movements? In the previous section, the passages from Gregory of Nyssa and Pseudo-Dionysius represent the apophatic tradition that sees God as mysterious, 'beyond' all creaturely language, distinctions, or definitions. This differs from, or is paired with, the cataphatic tradition which, in simple terms, takes the opposing view that affirmative statements can indeed be made about God using human language and concepts.[123]

The idea of 'internal' and 'contemplation' is of interest here. It refers to the simultaneous movements of 'upward' and 'inward' in contemplative

---

[121] Kevin M. Clarke, 'Moses's Dark Cloud, Teresa's Dark Night and the Soul's Entrance to the Divine Presence' in *Logos*, Vol 22:1 (Winter 2019), 131–146: 135.

[122] Augustine, *Confessions*, XIII.9.

[123] Cf. Merton in *The Ascent to Truth* (London: Hollis & Carter, 1951), 217–218 claims that there is no essential difference between the mysticism of 'light' and the mysticism of 'darkness'. The difference, according to Merton, lies in the language in which they try to express the essentially same experience of God in contemplation. The mystics of 'light' (such as Bernard of Clairvaux) emphasise the delight rather than the anguish of the ascent to God. The mystics of 'darkness' (such as John of the Cross) insist on the transcendent character of the mystical experience and emphasise its attainment in a 'cloud of unknowing'. In either case, the experience of God in contemplation is one in which love outstrips the intelligence and attains to Him immediately, beyond all our ideas.

prayer, marking a return to Augustine. In his synthesis of Augustine's epis-temology, Denys Turner, philosopher and theologian, identifies self-reflection as the interception point of the individual's horizontal axis in time and the vertical axis, where the eternal Trinity dwells. For Augustine, a person's true selfhood is in her interiority and the place where the self and interiority intersect opens out to God, eternal Light of Truth, who is above. 'Therefore, that which is most interior to me is also that which is above and beyond me. The God who is within me is also the God I am in'.[124] Denys Turner concludes:

> if through successive phases of self-reflection, the memory tracks horizon-tally along the paths of my identity in time, that memory, so to speak, stum-bles across the eternal light of Truth which shines upon it from above. At that point, then, where greatest inwardness has been achieved, the memory is also projected 'above' itself on a contrary, vertical axis. Here, where time intersects with eternity, the mind's most intimate interiority is also its 'high-est' point... the place 'in' it which overlaps with the eternal Light it is in. It is this point at which the mind can most truly contemplate the Trinity and in which the Trinity dwells by participating image'.[125]

Edward Howells, a British theologian, reflects on Augustine's idea that humans can participate in a relationship with God and distinguish his pres-ence within us through love. According to Howells, Augustine suggests that God can be known in the same manner as love. This suggests a pos-sibility that we can distinguish God's presence in us through participation, by an awareness of being in intimate relation to him. In short, this is the kind of awareness we have of love, when we love.[126] In *On the Trinity*, Howells further notes:

[124] Denys Turner, *The Darkness of God: Negativity in Christian Mysticism* (Cambridge: Cambridge University Press, 1999), 99–100.

[125] Turner, *The Darkness of God*, 99–100. Turner also notes that the reference to mind's 'highest point' relates to Augustine's concept of hierarchical ascent: the 'higher' a thing is the more it approximates to the eternity, necessity and immutability of Truth itself; the 'lower', the more it lapses into temporality, contingency and into changeableness, 100.

[126] Edward Howells, 'Understanding Augustine's *On the Trinity* as a Mystical Work', in Louise Nelstrop and Simon D. Podmore (eds.), *Christian Mysticism and Incarnational Theology: Between Transcendence and Immanence* (Burlington, VT: Ashgate Publishing, 2013), 155–164: 161.

Augustine seeks to develop tools (such as self-knowledge) that serve to raise our awareness of this kind of knowing within us, so that we can move more easily to knowing God face to face, as the goal of the journey of faith. By personal engagement with the Trinity, we are learning the shape of 'face-to-face' vision now, in a transformation that moves away from understanding God as an object outside us and towards finding God as the inward presence of truth and love.[127]

This is a journey of increasing knowledge (of self and of God). It is progressive discovery within a relationship, in personal engagement with the Trinity. Esther de Waal, a scholar in the Benedictine and Celtic traditions, describes the dual task found in the Cistercian tradition: the need to know our own selves as we set out to make our way back to God. We have to understand how our human nature works, and what is natural to a human being made in the image and likeness of the triune God. Accordingly, de Waal posits, the re-establishment of the integrity of human nature is the central problem which Cistercian mysticism addresses. We are given the responsibility of making the journey of restoration of what has been lost. This task of recovery, monastic conversion, is one of return of the prodigal son to the loving father. In this way, humility, knowledge, and love are interconnected. Love, which is given to us by God, makes it possible to know him. Love is the necessary condition of any knowledge of God. If we had nothing in ourselves of what God is we would be incapable of knowing him. Through this, de Waal appears to link self-knowledge and knowledge of God; and therefore, through loving and knowing, one participates in what that person (God) is, and becomes like that person.[128]

In temporal terms, contemplation can be defined as an intersection of time and eternity. What about in spatial terms? From the perspective of interiority, the 'place' of intersection is the human immortal soul that carries the image of eternal God. Here, we find Bonaventure combining various directions of the soul's contemplative journey. This indicates trajectories pointing to 'outside, within and beyond', as summarised by William Harmless[129]:

[127] Howells, 'Understanding Augustine's *On the Trinity* as a Mystical Work', 160.

[128] Esther de Waal, *The Way of Simplicity: The Cistercian Tradition* (London: Darton, Longman and Todd, 1998), 104–114.

[129] William Harmless, *Mystics*, (New York, NY: Oxford University Press, 2008), 250.

finding God *outside* us through and in creation;
    finding God *within* us through and in God's image in the soul;
    finding God *beyond* us through and in his name as oneness and Trinity.
    The arrival of the journey is in ecstatic union with the Crucified Christ.[130]

The Carmelite tradition, in parallel to Augustine's and Bonaventure's reasoning, identifies interiority and the human soul as a meeting place with the Divine. The thematic framework of Teresa of Ávila's *Interior Castle*, it could be argued, is indeed a movement and progression through the spaces of increased interiority towards the centre where God is found.[131] John Welch, O.Carm., referring to John of the Cross's finding that 'The soul's center is God', notes that a constant admonition from the Carmelite saints is to *keep the center open*. He therefore concludes: 'It is there, at the center, that the human spirit and the spirit of God meet and burn into one flame'.[132]

Moving on to the other horizontal internal dimension—away from self—this is related to the idea of a transformational monastic path from an egoistic self-centred existence towards a union with God. Elizabeth Obbard, OCD, a Carmelite novice master, writes about a journey from the 'self' towards God. This demands simplicity and self-forgetfulness, a real death involved in leaving self-preoccupation.[133] The contemplative practice of adoration, according to Obbard, means the *continual forgetting of self* so as to attend to the Divine at each moment,[134] a union which

---

[130] Note the references to death as a way to this union in Bonaventure, *The Soul's Journey Into God*, Ch. VII. 2: 'with Christ he rests in the tomb, as if dead to the outer world, but experiencing, as far as possible in this wayfarer's state, what was said on the cross to the thief who adhered to Christ: *Today you shall be with me in paradise*' and Ch. VII.6: 'Whoever loves this death can see God because it is true beyond doubt that "*man will not see me and live*". Let us, then, die and enter into the darkness; let us impose silence upon our cares, our desires and our imaginings. With Christ crucified let us pass *out of this world to the Father*'.

[131] Teresa of Ávila in *Interior Castle*, Sixth Mansions, Chapter IV, for example, writes: 'The soul becomes one with God. It is brought into this mansion of the empyrean Heaven which we must have in the depth of our souls; for it is clear that, since God dwells in them, He must have one of these mansions', 106.

[132] John Welch, *The Carmelite Way: An Ancient Path for Today's Pilgrim* (Mahwah, NJ: Paulist Press, 1996), 145.

[133] Obbard, *To Live is to Pray*, 93.

[134] Obbard, *To Live is to Pray*, 93. Italics mine.

begins here on earth.[135] Obbard quotes another Carmelite, Elizabeth of the Trinity,[136] regarding this union:

> Indeed I have found heaven on earth because heaven is God and God is in my soul. The day I understood this everything became clear to me.[137]

This profound insight of Elizabeth of the Trinity encapsulates several of the monastic themes:

1. **Eternity of the Eternal.** Elizabeth's central finding is 'heaven is God'. We could say that she conflates heaven (transcendent eternal place and time) and God (the Eternal Person).
2. **Already Here and Now.** For Elizabeth, God is heaven and heaven is God. And when God is in her soul, she is essentially already now in heaven here on earth.
3. **God's Omnipresence.** Elizabeth expresses the conviction that God can live in her soul and simultaneously he also represents 'heaven' which she distinguished from 'earth'.
4. **Intersection with Eternity.** Elizabeth identifies her soul as the place of intersection, the meeting point with God, where the heavenly verticality of the Eternal penetrates her soul during its horizontal journey on earth. She thus finds heaven on earth.

In one concise sentence, the quotation captures all three monastic categories: 'I have found heaven on earth' (liminality), 'God is in my soul' (relationship), and 'heaven is God' (eschatology). Elizabeth of the Trinity's discovery thus formulates a focused 'kaleidoscopic' insight that is entirely coherent.

---

[135] Obbard, *To Live is to Pray*, 94.

[136] Elizabeth of the Trinity, OCD, born Élisabeth Catez (1880–1906), was a French Discalced Carmelite professed Religious. She was canonised as a Catholic saint on 16 October 2016. In his doctoral dissertation, Christian-Marie Michel, OCD in *Le Ciel sur la Terre: Élisabeth de la Trinité et la spiritualité sacerdotale* (Toulouse: Éditions du Carmel, 2017), 182–185, argues that Sister Elizabeth's theology is '*eschatologically* Trinitarian', with different eschatological elements presented as the 'red thread' and the 'epicentre' of her thinking. Among these, Michel identifies: Sister Elizabeth's idea of the soul living in an 'anticipated heaven'; her apophatic adoration; her vision of religious life as Advent (of God who comes) that prepares the Incarnation in souls.

[137] Obbard, *To Live is to Pray*, 94.

Similarly, as with Augustine's continuous loop between humility and contemplation, a perpetual loop within the horizontal dimension exists: (1) towards greater interiority so as to find God in the centre of one's soul; (2) away from self, from self-preoccupation and egoism towards God. This is what seems to happen at the personal horizontal level.[138] On the vertical level, the ascent, the contemplative encounter with God continues to rise upwards until—in the eschatological fulfilment—it reaches complete assimilation. As described by the sixteenth-century Carmelite John of the Cross:

> But until that day, however high the point the soul may reach, there remains something hidden from it – namely, all that it lacks from assimilation in the Divine Essence. After this manner… the soul continues to rise above all things and above itself, and to mount upward to God. For love is like fire, which ever rises upward with the desire to be absorbed in the centre of its sphere.[139]

This is how John of the Cross ends his discourse in the *Dark Night of the Soul* on the 'secret ladder' which leans on God. But before reaching the ultimate goal, the soul has been required to gain practice of knowledge of God and of oneself. This involves the perfect love of God and contempt of self, exaltation, and humiliation, ascending and descending. These movements will not cease until one has reached the summit of the ladder where the soul attains to God and becomes united with him.[140]

In summary, it can be concluded that enclosed contemplative journeys are dynamic, creative, and progressive because they are lived as a relationship with Personal God. These journeys can follow various different trajectories but there is a common ultimate goal: union with God.

---

[138] Pierre Miquel, *La voie monastique* (Bégrolles-en-Mauges: Abbaye de Bellefontaine, 1986), 7, compares the monastic life to a labyrinth that presents obstacles and options; one has to enter the labyrinth, then move to the centre, and finally leave at the other end. Similarly, he argues, a monk's monastic journey involves first going into one's centre and then leaving oneself.

[139] John of the Cross, *Dark Night of the Soul*, Book II, Chapter XX. 6.

[140] John of the Cross, *Dark Night of the Soul*, Book II, Chapter XIX. 4.

4.6.3   Instant Suspended for Eternity

Contemplative Relationship was previously discussed in terms of 'spatial' vertical and horizontal movements towards ascent to heaven and God's transcendence. In this subsection, we encounter contemplation as a convergence of temporalities.

Ogliari writes about the 'profound sense of being a monk (*monos*)', a person unified by the search for and contemplation of God. He quotes D. de Vincentiis Fazzino who identifies contemplation with a temporal—or rather, atemporal—experience where an instant becomes suspended for eternity:

> And perhaps (the monk) will also be the only one able to have the experience of contemplation in the temporal sense, as attraction to the totality of time... (a closed space designed to receive within itself the density of time), in an atemporal and metaphysical instant suspended for eternity, a point of time when all the different levels of temporality converge.[141]

This quotation is remarkably condensed; it compares the experience of contemplation to an 'atemporal and metaphysical instant suspended for eternity' and paradoxically, this moment becomes 'a point of time when all the different levels of temporality converge'. Contemplation is seen as an *instant* with simultaneous (1) suspension towards eternity and atemporality; (2) convergence of all temporalities into one. Perhaps contemplation can be best understood as an atemporal experience, an instant where time intersects with eternity. Interestingly, there is also reference to 'closed space' as a place in which contemplation receives within itself the density of time. In some sense, there seems to be an awareness of the spatial element for experiencing the atemporal metaphysical experience.

Thomas Merton, OCSO, in a similar way, appears to collapse temporalities into one 'atemporal instant' where eternity *is present* in the present. He also brings eternity spatially into very close *proximity* as he claims: 'Eternity is in the present. Eternity is in the palm of the hand'.[142] In another passage, Merton describes how he sits in a sunny room sur-

---

[141] Ogliari, 'Tempus Monasticum', 47, footnote 54.

[142] Merton, *The Sign of Jonas*, 353. Equally, a Carthusian in *Where Silence is Praise*, 104, refers to the presence of God in the present moment as he defines contemplation as 'the plenitude of God in the present moment; receiving moment by moment the full action of God, who gives himself to us continuously'.

rounded by books and writes: 'a very happy room, in which a monk is where he belongs, in silence, with angels, his hand and eye moved by the living God in deep tranquillity. The watch ticks: but *perhaps there is after all no such thing as time*'.[143] It is as if the monk in the silence of his room gets lost in 'monastic time', somewhere in between secular time and divine time.

The convergence of different temporalities is found also in Carthusian teaching on prayer. A Carthusian novice master suggests that prayer—at this very point of time—is simultaneously linked to eternity: 'From all eternity God has wanted this prayer that I am making here and now, at this point of time, in view of a particular effect, which he has also willed from all eternity'.[144] The Carthusian gets some support from a Dominican, Emmanuel Durand, OP, who writes:

> God does not answer our prayers in the sense of conforming himself to them; in reality he involves us in the implementation of his salvific will, thereby mobilizing the efficacy of our prayers to accomplish it. We are not to imagine that the providence of God precedes our prayers in a temporal way. Eternal and simple, providence is always "contemporaneous" with our prayers.[145]

Durand notes that beyond the material or immediate object of the request, prolonged prayer affects an interior transformation in the one praying.[146] He concludes: 'The prayers of the faithful are... integrated from all eternity into the providential order of God, by reason of the primeval gratuity of his will of grace, according to which he associates human beings as free subjects with the temporal effecting of his plan'.[147] It can therefore be argued that the concept of time suggests an intersection and convergence between the human and eternal perspectives where, through prayer one's will is aligned with God's. In prayer, God's eternal plan pierces into our present time and place and, like a magnet, draws our will towards his.

---

[143] Merton, *The Sign of Jonas*, 249. Italics mine.

[144] A Carthusian, *Interior Prayer*, 45.

[145] Emmanuel Durand, 'Prayer and Providence' in *The Thomist*, Vol. 78, no. 4 (October 2014), 519–536: 535.

[146] Durand, 'Prayer and Providence', 535.

[147] Durand, 'Prayer and Providence', 536.

4.7   Conclusions

The simple conclusion is: whether it is through participation, the experience of God's temporal and spatial omnipresence, or contemplation, the monastic journeys offer a possibility for humans to become introduced to the divine concept of time. Such convergence or assimilation of temporalities is a result of the relationship with the Divine. One can assume that, as the religious 'spend time' with God, this leads to the potential for God to also transform their perception of time, along with other perspectives of life. This is in line with Bernard McGinn's central conclusion in his introduction to the anthology of Christian mystical literature that 'the pursuit of the divine mystery does not remove us from the world of space and time, but *makes us ever more conscious of the intersection of time and eternity*'.[148]

The different expressions of God-human relationship are summarised in Fig. 4.4. The forms of relationship are 'located' along Christ's temporal journey from the Incarnation to his Ascension to heaven. When these are viewed in the context of God's immanence and transcendence, the three expressions of relationships find their time and place within the Chain of Mysteries. It is worth noting that while the path from the Incarnation to

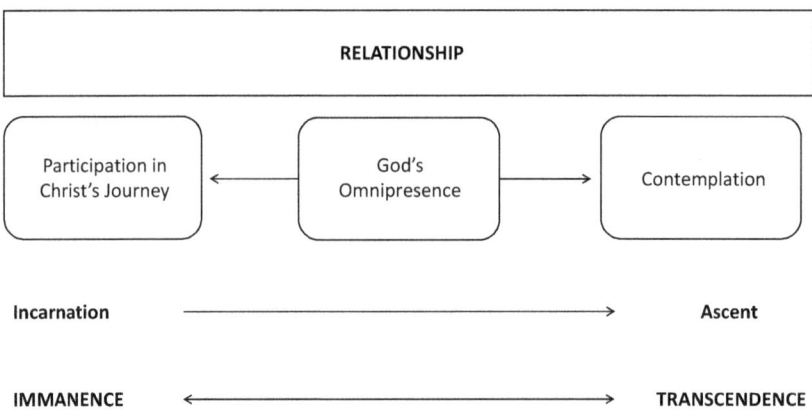

Fig. 4.4   Overlay of the expressions of relationship with theological concepts

---

[148] McGinn, ed., *The Essential Writings of Christian Mysticism*, xviii. This anthology of Christian mystical literature consists of nearly one hundred texts. Italics mine.

Ascension has a temporal historical direction God's immanence and transcendence are non-directional atemporal concepts. This atemporality is somewhat correspondingly reflected in God's temporal and spatial Omnipresence in the category of Relationship. It should be emphasised, however, that the different expressions of Relationship are not mutually exclusive or sequential. For example, the oscillation between (immanent) self-reflection and (transcendent) self-forgetfulness is notable in the works of monastic writers. Their texts frequently move between introspective analysis of their relationship with God and expressions of contemplative prayer where the writer moves 'beyond' self-directing all attention to God alone.

Figure 4.4 is essentially an amended representation of Fig. 4.1. It reiterates an overlay of the main theological concepts with the three expressions of Relationship. The figure aims to locate the forms of Relationship with the theological concepts in a dynamic way.

One might ask: why do the theological concepts of God's immanence and transcendence emerge so prominently when exploring the question of Relationship? This relates to the person-to-person relationship with the simultaneously mysterious and intimate Trinity that the religious dedicate their lifetime for. It deals with the desire to grasp some knowledge of God, of his Being. But, for individuals—being made in the image of God—there is also an opportunity for self-knowledge through this relationship. This eventually points towards one's self-transcendence, which is discussed in Chap. 5.

CHAPTER 5

End of the Monastic Journey

Prayer of an Elderly Nun

The life that springs up when my forces fail me,
The life that springs up to fill others' lives,
The life that springs up from the heart of all my cries,
The life that springs up, my life hidden in Your life.[1]

5.1 Waiting for a Bus

An allegorical story about a farewell at the roadside, told by a Carthusian monk, introduces the topic of death at the end of the monastic journey.

When he was the master of novices, Dom Dysmas once took a postulant to the six a.m. bus. During the night, the two men went down to the little main road …

In the winter, from the Grande Chartreuse onward, it was necessary to make your way through thick snow. Often, gusts of wind slowed the walk.

---

[1] Prayer of an anonymous nun, lines 13–16, from a booklet included in the documentary DVD film on Carthusian nuns in *Une vie en Chartreuse* (2018), 22. This expresses the end of the journey of an elderly nun who, despite her failing forces, sees her life springing up, hidden in God's life.

R. Hujanen, *Monastic Perspectives on Temporality*, https://doi.org/10.1007/978-3-031-34808-2_5

Below, the bus stop was not marked. An edge of the road, nothing more. Dom Dysmas and the postulant waited patiently. Headlights in the distance. The bus? No, just a car. The time had not come yet. When it finally appeared, Dom Dysmas immediately recognized its illuminated strip. They had just enough time to give each other a hug, hail the driver, load the suitcase. Farewell. One minute later, the bus disappeared in the darkness of the forest, out of sight, and Dom Dysmas remained alone on the side of the road.

For the monks, death is not so different.

"It is an old friend who drives the bus; we wave to her as she passes, indicating that, the next time, perhaps it is you whom she will take for the beautiful trip. Or someone else, who knows? But we must leave that to God."[2]

This allegory introduces several central monastic themes on temporality: struggling through the night, patient waiting in the darkness, familiarity with the expectation of death, companionship during the last moments, and trust in leaving it all in God's hands.

It has been said that at death, everyone is alone. The monastic community may accompany the individual at the moment of death but fundamentally the monk departs alone—*monos*—to meet his Maker. This chapter focuses on the end of the monastic journey, with future and eternity as the main temporalities, while the perspective is predominantly that of an individual.

What happens when the monastic journey is ending and the traveller is approaching the eternal? As this life's journey is coming to an end, the individual hopes to arrive in the heavenly homeland, an eternal dwelling place, in spatial terms. Eternal has also a temporal meaning: eternal life, existence of endless duration. Finally, in relational terms, the individual can be understood to encounter the Eternal—the personal God—face-to-face and come to a union with God's eternal Being. 'Eternal' as a concept can therefore refer to a place, time or Person (Fig. 5.1).

Chapter 2 introduced the concept 'Eternity of the Eternal' regarding divine temporalities. In other words, God is eternal Being. These dimensions—temporal, spatial, and relational—were also identified in Chap. 3 as motivations for monastic withdrawal. Here, the same dimensions are related to the meanings of 'Eternal'. Regarding the relational aspect, specifically, Chap. 4 explored the human-God relationship and the ontological difference which involves crossing the gap between human-divine temporalities. God is eternal and atemporal, but simultaneously, he

[2] Diat, *A Time to Die*, 171.

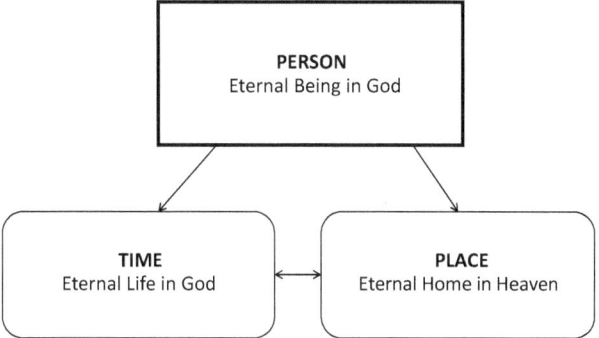

Fig. 5.1 Relational, temporal, and spatial meanings of 'Eternal'

has also assumed temporality (at least temporarily) for the sake of his love for humankind.

In this chapter, these ideas come together with some further conclusions. The figure above indicates a hierarchical structure between the three meanings of 'Eternal'. When exploring the question about the concept of 'time', we can conclude that enclosed contemplatives do think about time in general terms (although remain puzzled by it).[3] Time remains a mirage, an enigma, a mystery. However, the main finding is that time is 'relational': time is a function of the supreme category that is the Person of God. Time, as such, is a neutral concept that finds its meaning through relationship with the Divine Eternal Being. Eternal life (time) and heaven as eternal dwelling (place) ultimately receive a positive meaning only through the personal love-relationship with God. Indeed, the opposite is also true: 'being deprived of the vision of God' and 'eternal separation from God' are the very definitions for eternal damnation and hell, according to the Catholic dogma.[4] This explains the primacy of Person in the hierarchy of meanings of Eternal. 'Time' and 'place' derive their significance from the relationship with the Divine Person, which from the eschatological perspective gives the promise and hope for sharing eternal being

[3] See Dom Dysmas in Sarah, *The Power of Silence*, 219: 'The most familiar realities are full of mystery... Only someone who has not reflected on it thinks that he knows what time is'. Similar comments by Augustine, Thérèse of Lisieux and Thomas Merton on 'time as a mystery' are referenced elsewhere in this study.

[4] *Catechism of the Catholic Church*, Part One, Section Two, Chapter Two, Article 5, Paragraph 1, 633 and Part One, Section Two, Chapter Three, Article 12, IV, 1035.

in God. Consequently, when monastic sources deal with the concept of time, these considerations relate more to God than temporality itself. In other words, monastic time is 'relational'. Time is valued through the relationship with God; time spent with him is valuable. To repeat Houdret's conclusion: 'It is in time that our eternal destiny is played out: with or without God, according to whether we accept his love or not'.[5]

The perspective of this chapter is predominantly that of an individual. This applies especially to the final subsections where the matters of life and death are explored through personal monastic voices. Thus, evidence becomes more anecdotal.

5.2   ESCHATOLOGY AND CONTEMPLATIVE MONASTICISM

This section explores the eschatological meaning of monastic journeys. It proposes a parallel between 'microcosm'—an individual's life journey—and 'macrocosm' as the universe; they both are finite and, with the passage of time, are travelling towards their ends. Enclosed contemplative life has a special role as an eschatological sign and as a reminder for the Church and the whole of society of the world's final destiny. Monastic eschatology is the voice in the desert that calls to prepare a way for the Lord, for his Second Coming.

5.2.1   Hope of the Resurrection

A monastic writer, Margaret Malone, SGS, argues that there must be an eschatological dimension to ascetical endeavour, lest it degenerate into merely physical practices. The real ends of ascetical life are ultimately eschatological and transformational, in the same way as the human body (microcosm) is destined to be transformed and this will entail the experience of the transformed world (macrocosm). It can also be expressed in the meaning of the Paschal Mystery; we must die to our old life and rise to a new life.[6] The idea of microcosm and macrocosm presented by Margaret Malone can also relate to the requirement of a journey in time and space, a transformational pilgrimage which applies to the mortal body and eternal soul at the 'microcosm' level of human life. At the microcosm

[5] Houdret, 'Le temps et l'eternité', 13.
[6] Margaret Malone, *Living in the House of God: Monastic Essays* (Collegeville, MN: Liturgical Press, 2014), 41–43.

level, the transformation of the transitory body takes shape through asceticism and finally, through death, to resurrection and to the receipt of a new heavenly body. The soul's journey to eternity takes place through a transformational pilgrimage, in vertical communication with God and interior journey towards deeper self-knowledge. This microcosmic destiny is associated with the Paschal Mystery where Christ shows the way of such transformation as 'the firstborn' among the brethren.[7] He was the first to take this journey.

Along these lines, John Polkinghorne reflects on the idea that 'human destiny beyond death and cosmic destiny beyond death lie together'[8] pointing towards a possibility that in a future moment the dying cosmos will be changed into the 'matter' of the new creation, just as Jesus' dead body was transformed into his risen and glorious body. That cosmic 'Day of Resurrection' will also be the event in which the soul-patterns of all human beings, which have been held in the divine memory, will be reconstituted as embodied beings living in the new creation.[9] These microcosmic and macrocosmic transformations are therefore ultimately interconnected.

A Carthusian poet-monk reflects on the mortality of his flesh and the immortality of his soul (at a personal microcosmic level) and the hope of the resurrection in a new 'body' to be united with himself, God and all (at the macrocosmic level):

My Eternal Moments

Moments of changing things swiftly pass.
My spirit changes not nor passes. My flesh
Is constantly in flux in a world of flux.
Each change is given a different measure of time,
An hour for this, a year to that. But I
Am rooted in God's eternity. He does
Not change nor I, nor ever will. In God
I endure as he endures stripped of change
Or measurement, the least vestige of time.
In God's eternal scheme of things he released

---

[7] Col 1:18 (NRSV).

[8] John Polkinghorne, *Exploring Reality: The Intertwining of Science and Religion* (London: SPCK, 2005), 174.

[9] Polkinghorne, *Exploring Reality*, 174.

The idea of me to master the flesh and blood
Destined for me its principle, its sense
Of feeling, its unity and common-sense,

Its power to communicate, remember and will.
My soul's in God yet living a human life
Outside of God. Eventually my flesh
Will die dissolve in a billion bits of dust
While I remain unchanged robbed of heart
And brain, enriched (let's hope) by kindly deeds.
The resurrection reconnects the soul
And flesh. We will not live as angels devoid
Of body. We will be truly human and speak,
Communicate through 'body', a novel kind
Of language. Then at last I will be one
In myself, one with all in God
In Paradise, a fruitful almond rod ...[10]

The Carthusian monk's poem represents the classic Christian dogma of the resurrection and the soul's reunion with its glorified body.[11] It also represents 'monastic realism' related to physical death and simultaneously conveys the eschatological vision of a new body which 'reconnects the soul and flesh' and reunites the monk in himself and with others as one in God. Why introduce the term 'monastic realism' regarding the resurrection of the body here? This can be indirectly answered by another Carthusian, Dom Innocent, who raises his concern about modern Christianity in this respect:

> Earthly life and eternal life are intimately connected. Why fear the junction between these realities? Christians no longer really believe in the resurrection of bodies. Paradise is likened to a void of floating souls. But men are [made]

---

[10] A Carthusian, 'My Eternal Moments' in *Stillness: Poems 2020*. Unpublished collection of poems.

[11] *Catechism of the Catholic Church*, Part One, Section Two, Chapter Three, Article 11, 997: 'In death, the separation of the soul from the body, the human body decays and the soul goes to meet God, while awaiting its reunion with its glorified body. God, in his almighty power, will definitely grant incorruptible life to our bodies by reuniting them with our souls, through the power of Jesus' Resurrection'.

in the image of God. It will not be necessary to leave our humanity in order to be united with God. Eternity will be much more human than we can imagine.[12]

It appears that 'monastic spirituality' here is deeply rooted in 'monastic realism' which in turn is rooted in the Catholic dogma of the resurrection of the body.[13] Heavenly life is connected with earthly life. Eternity resembles rather a dynamic continuation of the journey already begun on earth.

The interplay between the macrocosmic and microcosmic eschatology travels through the centuries of monastic traditions. Alexander Golitzin, an American scholar of early Christianity, in his study of the seventh-century text *The Syriac Apocalypse of Daniel*—which he assumes was written by a Syriac monk—observes that the early classical monastic literature from the fourth century finds very little concern with philosophical-cum-theological questions of divine justice. Golitzin suggests that theodicy on the macrocosmic scale was a matter largely reserved for theologians and bishops such as Origen and Augustine, while monks focused on the affairs of the inner man, where the history of Israel and the salvation offered in the Church through Christ were to be

---

[12] Diat, *A Time to Die*, 166. In support of this statement, one could refer to tangible images of heaven such as Mt. 26:29 (NRSV): 'I tell you, I will never again drink of this fruit of the vine until that day when I drink it new with you in my Father's kingdom'. In the other synoptic Gospels the references to '*my Father's kingdom*' are: Mk 14:25 (NRSV): 'I will never again drink of the fruit of the vine until that day when I drink it new in *the kingdom of God*'; Lk 22:18 (NRSV): 'I will not drink of the fruit of the vine *until the kingdom of God comes*'. Note also that Matthew specifies '*with you*' which is not in the other passages. Italics mine. Related eschatological reference in Jn 6:54 (NRSV): 'Those who eat my flesh and drink my blood have eternal life, and I will raise them up on the last day'.

[13] See also Bernard of Clairvaux, 'On Loving God' in Emilie Griffin, ed., *Selected Works* (New York, NY: HarperCollins, 2005; trans. G. R. Evans), 81–85, on resurrection and restoration of bodies. Bernard asks in his treatise, referring to eternal life: 'If death is precious, what must life be, and life such as that?', and continues: 'It need not be surprising that the glorified body should seem to confer something on the soul, for it was of use to it when it was weak and mortal... Its weak body helps the soul to love God; it helps it when it is dead; it helps it when it is resurrected, first in producing fruits of patience, second in bringing peace, third in bringing completeness'. According to Bernard, the soul does not want to be perfected without what it feels has served it well in every condition. This indicates that the soul would not be complete without a body and that there is some kind of connection between the mortal and the glorified body.

discovered at the microcosmic level of the soul.[14] He softens this apparent disparity by qualifying: 'This is not to say, however, that properly monastic literature is not eschatological in its orientation. To the contrary, meditation on the last things continues to be of direct relevance to, and at the very center of, classically monastic reflection'.[15] Golitzin gives an example from the writings of East Syrian hermit Isaac of Nineveh, who died around the year 700. This text describes the process of an increasing, interior conformity, through meditation and constant reflection on things to come—the 'new world'—which is to discover its confirmation and final expression in the eschatological transformation of the risen body.[16]

The constant reflection on things to come continued in the following centuries. When reviewing the previous research on the medieval approaches to eschatology, Katja Ritari refers to the 'ever-present expectations of the end of the world' and the 'eschatological mentality' of the Middle Ages. She adds to these the anticipation of each individual's personal end and the preparation for individual judgement. According to Ritari, this individual 'smaller' eschatology colours early medieval spirituality, especially in its monastic form, and informs the monks' relationship with this world.[17] In contemporary sources, we find the Carthusian poet-monk speaking the same eschatological language of 'God's total view of time' and human salvific history flowing towards the consummation of time:

> Trust is the little door to eternity.
> Trust exalts every moment to an equal good:
> The good of entering God's total view of time,
> his wisdom. In trust we move with human history
> towards its consummation when Christ will
> have 'drawn every person to himself'.[18]

---

[14] Alexander Golitzin, 'A Monastic Setting for the Syriac Apocalypse of Alexandria' in Robin Darling Young and Monica J. Blanchard (eds.), *To Train His Soul in Books: Syrian Asceticism in Early Christianity* (Washington, D.C.: The Catholic University of America Press, 2011), 66–98: 69.

[15] Golitzin, 'A Monastic Setting for the Syriac Apocalypse of Alexandria', 70.

[16] Golitzin, 'A Monastic Setting for the Syriac Apocalypse of Alexandria', 70–71.

[17] Ritari, *Pilgrimage to Heaven*, 179. See also MacCulloch, *A History of Christianity*, 365, who suggests that eschatological millennial expectation around year 1000 contributed to the reformation of the Cistercian order and the emergence of the new mendicant orders during the eleventh century.

[18] A Carthusian, *Given-over to Providence*, lines 1–6, in *The Beautiful to Ponder*, unpublished collection of poems. Note the use of 'door' here as a liminal metaphor.

The awareness of eschatological temporality ('that this world will one day be over') and the daily orientation towards eternity constitute the real foundation for contemplative monastic life, as expressed by 'Mel', a contemporary cloistered contemplative:

> Contemplative life is a reminder to the world that God exists, that eternity exists, that this world will one day be over. We have dedicated our entire lives to this essentially this one reality: eternity.[19]

This firm dedication to eternity has daily consequences. Everything is done for God with the hope that this will provide an eternal reward for fellow humans as well as for the religious themselves. This ultimate reward is to be with eternal God forever in heaven:

> What we do every day has only that in view. All our daily works, our prayers, our sufferings, our contemplation, our joys, our misunderstandings of life, our sorrows, our labors, our writing this very email…. everything that we do in each day, is done for God, who is eternal, with the hope of winning an eternal reward for others and for ourselves, and being with God forever in Heaven.[20]

In summary, monastic sources tend to point towards the shared eschatological directions between the microcosmic and macrocosmic levels. There are parallels between the interiorly experienced developments of the human mind and body and the anticipated exterior transformation of the universe, both on a journey towards their eternal destinies. Regarding resurrection, what could be described as 'monastic realism' was identified. How can this humble, 'realistic' attitude towards the afterlife be defined?

Firstly, there is general avoidance of presumption relating to one's own eternal destiny. This is left in the hands of God. By extension, excessive speculation about heaven could be viewed as presumptuous. Instead, apprehension and humility seem to mark the monastic attitude. Secondly, true to the literal aspect of 'monastic reading' of the Scriptures, there appears to be little interest to speculate 'over and above' the biblical revelation. Some examples about visions relating to the time of death of a

---

[19] Email from 'Mel', a cloistered contemplative, 16/02/2019.
[20] Email from 'Mel', a cloistered contemplative, 16/02/2019.

monk are found in the *Sayings* and other early texts. Equally, the early sources contain warnings against relying on visions.

In conclusion: what comes to the fore at the end of life is the category of Relationship. Eternity, eternal life, and heaven are inseparably associated with the Eternal, God. Everything else is dependent on God. Heaven or eternal life without God is unthinkable. As stated by Elizabeth of the Trinity: 'heaven is God'.

5.2.2   Eschatological Meanings of Monasticism

It is necessary to distinguish first between 'Future Eschatology' and 'Realised Eschatology'. Here, 'Future Eschatology' refers to the Second Coming of Christ in his glory and the Last Events and Final Judgement. In temporal terms, this is an anticipated, yet 'unrealised' future eschatological event. In addition, scholars recognise an argument for 'Realised Eschatology', which British theologian Stephen Yates defines as follows:

> For the Christian, the end which they have been promised exists not only in the future but, in some real sense, already in the present. This is, in essence what is meant by 'realised eschatology'. The basic form of what might be called the 'Argument for Realised Eschatology' to the doctrine of resurrection in death is: because the New Testament speaks of resurrection not only as a future but as a present reality in the life of the believer, it can be expected that this resurrection life would continue unbroken through death.[21]

Yates further refers to the passage of Jn 11:24–25 where 'we see Christ correcting Martha's purely futurist view of the resurrection in 11:24 with the declaration: "I am the resurrection and the life" (11:25)'.[22] A further suggestion of a possible 'monastic reading' of this passage could be added here. Within monastic traditions, Martha represents the active life and

---

[21] Stephen Yates, 'Does the New Testament Teach Resurrection in Death?' in Andrew B. Morris (ed.) *Aspects of Doctoral Research at the Maryvale International Catholic Institute, Volume One* (Newcastle Upon Tyne: Cambridge Scholars Publishing, 2019), 16–49: 41.

[22] Yates, 'Does the New Testament Teach Resurrection in Death?', 41. See Jn 11:23–26 (NSRV): 'Jesus said to her, "Your brother will rise again." Martha said to him, "I know that he will rise again in the resurrection on the last day." Jesus said to her, "I am the resurrection and the life. Those who believe in me, even though they die, will live, and everyone who lives and believes in me will never dies'.

Mary the contemplative life. The eschatological interpretation of Yates suggests that Martha was corrected for her 'purely futurist view' in Jn 11 (in addition to having been corrected for being 'worried and distracted by many things').[23] Mary's disposition, in contrast, could be interpreted as an expression of 'Realised Eschatology' as she had chosen the better part and sat at the Lord's feet in contemplative silence. Carlos Eire, indeed, refers to monasticism as 'realised eschatology', as an entry point to one's eternal destiny. He suggests that monasticism could also be viewed on less individualistic terms, as a 'communal eschatology'. This is because, within the monastic frame of reference, heaven and eternity were not some distant horizon but rather an imminent threshold within the cloister walls.[24]

However, another approach would be the integration of 'Realised' and 'Future' Eschatology, the 'already here' (in the present, now) and 'then there' (in the future). In a mysterious way, in Jn 11:25–26, faith in Christ in this life translates into 'never dying'; and converts into 'living' even if one will die.[25] Eschatological hope then becomes a conduit that provides a meaning to the question, how can death turn into life? In a similar balanced way, Christian Salenson, a French theologian, distinguishes between: (1) a 'futurist' understanding of eschatology where the Kingdom is reached after death; (2) a 'repatriated' eschatology brought to the present [as in 'eternal life is now']; and (3) an eschatology that can be understood as '*avenir*' which puts us in a position to welcome God that comes 'today' relying on the Faith of Christ's death and Resurrection, where the victory over death opens an anticipated '*a-venir*' eschatology.[26] This anticipated hope of the resurrection thus builds a bridge between the 'eschatology now' and the 'eschatology in the future'.

Along these lines, Theo McCall, an Australian theologian, suggests that the call to self-transcendence is both an 'experience' and a 'promise'. He writes about the hope of eternity: 'Precisely because we have the hope, or the anticipation, of transcendence in the ultimate sense, it is possible to experience something of that transcendence while we are on the journey

[23] Lk 10:41 (NSRV).
[24] Cf. Eire in *A Very Brief History of Eternity*, 71–72.
[25] Jn 11: 25–26 (NSRV).
[26] Christian Salenson, *L'échelle mystique du dialogue par Christian de Chergé* (Montrouge: Bayard editions, 2016), 222–223.

toward it'.[27] In a similar way, Nicholas Molinier, an Orthodox monk, suggests that monastics are witnesses of the eschatology that has *already begun* and of the *current* divine providence.[28] In light of this, it can be argued that it is the *hope* or *anticipation* of 'Future Eschatology' that is experienced *already here* as 'Realised Eschatology' through the Relationship with God.

This anticipation of the victory of Life is celebrated by the contemporary Carthusian poet-monk who claims that: 'Death is a paradox: what follows on Life's demise is Life's triumph'.[29] Likewise, Thérèse of Lisieux expressed similar conviction during her final days: 'I am not dying; I am entering into life!'[30] A lifelong friendship with God therefore forms an everlasting bond that survives beyond the boundary of life and death. The separating veil of the transcendent becomes transparent with the passage of time. Indeed, time itself appears transitory, 'only a mirage', between the present and eternity, as Thérèse of Lisieux wrote to her sister Céline:

> Already the soul of the prophet Isaiah was immersed, just as our own soul is, in the HIDDEN BEAUTIES of Jesus …. Ah, Céline, when I read these things, I wonder what time really is? … Time is only a mirage, a dream … already God sees us in glory, HE TAKES DELIGHT in our eternal beatitude! … He feels that we understand Him, and he is treating us as His friends, as His dearest spouses.[31]

What is important for Thérèse is not 'time'—she almost seems to doubt the significance of it. What matters is the intimate relationship (as friends, as spouses) between God and souls. Furthermore, Thérèse views this from the divine perspective, imagining how God 'already' sees their souls in glory and takes delight from their eternal beatitude. She here also relates

---

[27] Theo McCall, 'Hope and Eternity: God as Transcendent Presence in the Ordinary', in David Yaden, Theo McCall, Harold Ellens, (eds.), *Being Called: Scientific, Secular and Sacred Perspectives* (Santa Barbara, CA: Praeger, 2015), 193–202: 201.

[28] Molinier, *Ascèse, contemplation et ministère*, 216. Translation and italics mine.

[29] A Carthusian, *Death Is A Paradox*, lines 16–17 in *The Outlaw: Poems 2000–2002*, unpublished collection. This verse ends: 'Life's reconstruction (based on the death of Christ, On Pillars of Wisdom) will stand as Love must stand, Head and mystic Body, in timelessness' (lines 17–20).

[30] Thérèse of Lisieux, *Story of a Soul*, 431. She wrote these words to Father Bellière in the infirmary during her final days.

[31] Thérèse of Lisieux, *General Correspondence: Volume I* (Washington, D.C.: ICS Publications; trans. J. Clarke, 1982), 630, LT 108/LC 129 in July 18, 1890.

to God's feeling that human souls understand him. For Thérèse, such deep mutual relationship, once established on earth, is timeless realised eschatology, beyond boundaries of temporality.

The eschatological meaning of monasticism is explored by Christiana Piccardo, OCSO, in a rich way, as she writes: 'Monastic life ... is a living momentum toward happiness. It is a memory that transcends time, with sights set on the eschatological fullness of the future'.[32] Piccardo defines monasticism as a vision of man and of his destiny, of being and becoming, of time and its eschatological dimension, of space projected beyond contingent limitations.[33] Significant in this text is the decisive 'leaning forward', expressed variously:

1. A living momentum toward happiness
2. Eschatological fullness of the future
3. Vision of destiny
4. Becoming
5. Eschatological dimension of time
6. Beyond contingent spatial limitations

Monastic life here takes a dynamic eschatological meaning, an orientation towards the eternity and the transcendent. The monastic concept of time is dynamic and creative. It is about 'becoming' while still on the transformative journey. There is active forward-looking movement even in 'being' as it is paired with 'becoming'. This relates to another aspect of monastic time, the future eschatology, of which Thomas Merton writes regarding his eschatological positioning:

> If it were a matter of choosing between 'contemplation' and 'eschatology', there is no question that I am, and would always be, committed entirely to the latter ... I believe that He has called me freely, out of pure mercy, to His love and salvation and that at the end ... I shall see Him after I have put off my body in death and have risen together with Him. That at the last day 'all flesh shall truly see the salvation of God'. What this means is that my faith is

[32] Piccardo, *Living Wisdom*, xxii.
[33] Piccardo, *Living Wisdom*, xxii.

an eschatological faith, not merely a means of penetrating the mystery of the divine presence and resting in Him now.[34]

Why would Merton contrast contemplation and eschatology when he claims, 'If it were a matter of choosing between "contemplation" and "eschatology", there is no question that I am, and would always be, committed entirely to the latter'? The reason could be partly stylistic or rhetoric. But Merton also seems to make a temporal argument. Eschatology is preferred over contemplation because eschatology has its end point, or *telos*, in the 'eternal' while contemplation, for him, refers to 'merely' resting in the divine presence already 'now', in temporality. However, Merton eventually finds a way to reconcile contemplation and eschatology by saying that, because his faith is eschatological, it is *also* contemplative: 'for I am even now in the Kingdom and can even now "see" something of the glory of the Kingdom and praise Him who is King'.[35] Therefore, his rhetorical 'preference' construct does not really hold. He chooses both. Merton attributes 'the union of contemplation and eschatology' to the gift of the Holy Spirit, specifically to faith and hope:

> In Him we are awakened to know the Father, because in Him we are refashioned in the likeness of the Son. It is in this likeness that the Spirit will bring us at last to the clear vision of the invisible Father in the Son's glory, which will also be our glory. Meanwhile, it is the Spirit who awakens in our heart the faith and hope in which we cry for the eschatological fulfilment and vision. In this hope there is already a beginning, a 'promise' of fulfilment ... The realization that we are on our way, that because we are on our way we are in that Truth, which is the end and by which we are already fully and eternally alive. Contemplation is the loving sense of this life and this presence and this eternity.[36]

Merton claims furthermore that contemplation and eschatology both complete each other and intensify each other.[37] This dynamic union of contemplation and eschatology places the monastic vocation at the service

[34] Thomas Merton, in Patrick Hart and Jonathan Montaldo (eds.), *The Intimate Merton: His Life from His Journals* (Oxford: Lion Publishing, 1999), 284. This is from Merton's diary in 1964.

[35] *The Intimate Merton*, 284.

[36] *The Intimate Merton*, 285.

[37] *The Intimate Merton*, 284–285.

of the Church and humankind. As Merton puts it: 'It is by contemplation and love that I can best prepare myself for the eschatological vision—and best help the Church and all men to journey towards it'.[38]

The connection between contemplation and eschatology is not unique to Merton. John Peter Kenney suggests that, within Classical Christianity, Augustine discovered an itinerary which leads from Contemplation to Incarnation and Eschatology.[39] Largely through his personal search and experiences, Augustine found that 'contemplation reveals the depth of the soul's estrangement from God, the degree of its powerlessness, the bitter distance lying between itself and its true home'.[40] This was followed by the realisation that 'the soul has no way home without divine grace achieved through the incarnation of Christ'.[41] It is therefore Christ's Incarnation that creates the bridge for the soul to return to its true home. Kenney makes a further link between contemplation and eschatology in Augustine's theology: 'Contemplation is thus indicative of the ambivalence attached to transcendence, exacerbating the soul's sense of eschatological longing'.[42]

The associations between the Incarnation and contemplation (as well as the ontological distance, the soul's estrangement from God) were discussed previously. We may now move to the final link between the two historical/temporal events (the Incarnation and Eschatology) and see the role of contemplation as the uniting element between *immanence* and *transcendence*. In temporal terms, two dimensions can be identified: the first fundamental transcendent one is 'God's Eternal Now'. The second is the temporal history of the immanent created universe and humankind. God's heavenly eternity can be understood to run limitlessly and atemporally 'above' the temporally limited history of the universe here 'below' in the world. From this perspective, relating to the transitory and eternal: Creation, the Incarnation and Eschatology are inseparable and interlinked. This leads to the proposition that *temporal time itself is transitory*, and it will converge to God's eternity, at the end of time. The final movement, therefore, is from the immanent (material temporal

---

[38] *The Intimate Merton*, 284–285.

[39] Kenney, *Contemplation and Classical Christianity*, 91–92.

[40] Kenney, *Contemplation and Classical Christianity*, 91–92.

[41] Kenney, *Contemplation and Classical Christianity*, 92.

[42] Kenney, *Contemplation and Classical Christianity*, 92. This 'ambivalence attached to transcendence' here relates to the terms 'sense of distance', 'ontological difference', and 'gap between human and God'. This in turn is expressed as 'eschatological humility/hope/longing'.

universe) to the transcendent (a completely new atemporal form of existence).

Relying on monastic sources, it is possible to argue further that monastic time is 'relative time'.[43] The meaning of 'time' is derived from the divine 'eternal now', above and beyond successive temporalities. The present time is reflected against the eschatological dimension, destiny, and existence beyond material limitations. 'Being' is reflected in the light of 'becoming'. This sets the human lifespan into immeasurably bigger, eternal perspective. Eternity gives meaning to the present. But the present also intersects with eternity, giving it a glimpse of timelessness.

Another temporal schema is presented by Michael Downey in his study of the Trappist monastic tradition. He points towards a Trinitarian movement from earth to heaven; a continuum of time which reaches from the Incarnation of Christ (past) to the daily presence of the Holy Spirit (present) towards the eschatological promise when the glory of the Father will be revealed (future):

> Through the mystery of the Incarnation, the monk is caught up in a movement with Christ toward the face of God, from earth to heaven, moving daily through the presence and power of their Spirit toward the promised future in which Christ will be all in all to the glory of God the Father.[44]

This indicates that monasticism is indeed a Trinitarian journey, a dynamic Trinitarian movement with the goal to become God-like and to see the Father who is in heaven; this can be achieved through the participation in the life of the Son, Christ, and his son-ship. Nicholas of Cusa (1401–1464) in *The Vision of God*, connects the attainment of eternal bliss to union with Jesus—God and Man. To behold God the Father and Jesus, His Son, is to be in Paradise, and it is everlasting glory. Every blissful spirit beholds the invisible God and is united—in Jesus—unto the

---

[43] For example, Houdret in 'Le temps et l'éternité', 8–10, presents three points about human orientations in relation to temporality and eternity. Firstly, as temporal beings we live in the temporality with an orientation towards eternity. Secondly, the hope of eternity puts our temporality into a relative perspective. Thirdly, the anticipation of eternity gives value to our temporality. He concludes that eternity, paradoxically, exposes the relativity of our temporality but simultaneously gives value to it.

[44] Michael Downey, *Trappist: Living in the Land of Desire* (Mahwah, NJ, Paulist Press, 1997), 73.

unapproachable and immortal God. Thus in Jesus the finite is 'united' unto the infinite, and unto that which is 'beyond union'.[45]

This Trinitarian relationship is shared through the Holy Spirit in prayer, the Sacraments, and in the reading and meditation of the Scriptures. The Carthusian poet-monk expresses this as an exchange of movements and qualities (his descent to our nothingness/our ascent to his immensity):

> *The Word descended to taste our nothingness;*
> *We ascend to enjoy his immensity,*[46]

... which essentially will lead to the eschatological enjoyment of the Trinitarian relationship:

> *To see the glory he had before the world*
> *Began at peace in the Father's bosom the Flame*
> *Of the Spirit uniting them in fecundity,*
> *In joy and wonder, in love's eternity ...*[47]

All aspects of the 'Chain of Mysteries' constitute a daily presence in the lives of the contemplative religious through the repetition of the Liturgy of the Hours, the Holy Mass, and *Lectio Divina* as they make their way through the cycle of the liturgical year. Donato Ogliari argues that, taken up and valorised by liturgical rhythm, time becomes 'univocal' and 'existential' allowing a continuous entry into communication with divine salvation.[48] In this way, the temporal horizontal time is redeemed in a *'vertical thrust that synchronizes it with the eternity of God and orients it toward an eschatological horizon'.*[49] Therefore, it can be claimed that this lived and practised theology is marked with a differentiated concept of time, an eschatological orientation experienced in daily communication with the Divine. Katja Ritari summarises well this line of reasoning: 'Monasticism can be understood as an *eschatological theology that is lived in*

[45] Nicholas de Cusa, *The Vision of God* (New York, NY: Cosimo Classics; trans. E. G. Salter, 2007), Ch. XXI, 102–105.

[46] A Carthusian, *Whatever*, lines 11–12, unpublished poem.

[47] A Carthusian, *Whatever*, lines 13–16, unpublished poem.

[48] Ogliari, 'Tempus Monasticum', 44.

[49] Ogliari, 'Tempus Monasticum', 44. Italics mine.

practice. Indeed, monastic life is a programme that allows for a translation of theological concepts into patterns of behaviour'.[50]

Examples of such 'eschatological practical theology' are not difficult to find. Ogliari, for example, notes that certain Benedictine monastic traditions can be seen as signs of eschatological anticipation such as the prescriptions regarding the lamp that ought to be kept burning in the dormitory, and the injunction to sleep clothed and with loins girt.[51] Given that the time of the Second Coming of the Lord is unknown, the monk should be vigilant and ever prepared for the coming of Christ at any time, at an unexpected hour. The passage from the Night Office to Lauds equally takes a 'paschal coloration'; the Night Office can be experienced as a 'spiritual bridge' which extends from night towards the coming dawn, from the night to the morning of resurrection.[52] Similarly, Carthusian Statutes explain the meaning of the Night Office: 'In night prayer, we keep a holy and persevering watch, awaiting the return of the Master so as to open to him as soon as he knocks'.[53] In the words of Carthusian Dom Dysmas:

> While the world sleeps, we choose to rise to unite our prayer and intercession to Christ's, so that the prayer of mankind, this vital bond between heaven and earth, may not cease. Then, when we go to bed, others, Benedictines or Cistercians, will take up the relay.[54]

Enclosed contemplatives, separated from the society, feel united in the awareness of their shared eschatological role: to stand before the living God and keep vigil on behalf of humankind.[55] This idea of 'eschatological watching' on behalf of all was also expressed by André Louf, OCSO: 'At the crack of dawn … the monk stands on that frontier between the world that is passing away and the world which is coming'. The monk does not keep watch only for himself but persists, morning after morning, in the name of the whole world. He waits for the dawn, on alert for the slightest signs which could announce the imminent return of Jesus at the end of

---

[50] Ritari, *Pilgrimage to Heaven*, 178. Italics mine.

[51] Ogliari, 'Tempus Monasticum', 46.

[52] Ogliari, 'Tempus Monasticum', 46.

[53] Carthusian Statutes, Book 3, Ch. 21.5.

[54] Sarah, *The Power of Silence*, 233.

[55] Cf. Carthusian Statutes, Book 4, Ch. 34.2: 'Apart from all, to all we are united, so that it is in the name of all that we stand before the living God'.

time. What is more, his prayer 'Come Lord Jesus' (*maranatha*) hastens the coming of Christ in glory.[56]

A Dominican Father who shared his experiences from participating in the Liturgy of Hours in a Charterhouse noted that the Carthusian prayers often ended with the word '*maranatha*'. The understanding of this Dominican was that this ancient expression had a dual temporal meaning: simultaneously referring to the coming of Christ into the present moment 'now' and the eschatological future 'then'.[57] The Aramaic word '*maranatha*' can indeed be interpreted in different temporalities with possible references to past (the Incarnation), present (experienced relationship), and future eschatology. According to Marian Vild, a scholar of Biblical Studies, the expression '*maranatha*' can be translated in three ways: (1) As an indicative: 'Our Lord has come!' or 'Our Lord is present!' In this case it works as a confession of faith and implies an already established eschatology. (2) 'Our Lord is coming'—the timing is shifting towards a future eschatology. And (3) as an imperative: 'Our Lord, come!' which preserves not only the future timing of eschatology but also echoes the tension of the expectation of the Early Church, which was awaiting an imminent *Parousia*. Vild's conclusion is that all these interpretations are possible and supported by the old manuscripts.[58]

5.3   Monastic Reflections of Eternal Life

A distinct temporal theme that emerged from the monastic sources indicates that, because God is understood to be dynamic, it is logical to assume that also eternity is dynamic. This means that the relationship established during the earthly life between the soul and God can continue to deepen into all eternity in heaven. Therefore, even if eternity may be perceived as stable, peaceful, atemporal, that does not exclude dynamic movement and expansion. Here, the challenge to define God and eternity in human 'dualistic' terms again requires acceptance of 'paradoxical realities' when attempting to explore divinity.

[56] André Louf, *The Cistercian Way* (Kalamazoo, MI: Cistercian Publications, 1989; trans. N. Kinsella), 95.

[57] Conversation with a Dominican Father on 27 August 2018.

[58] Marian Vild, 'The Aramaic *maranatha* in 1 Cor 16:22. Translation Queries and Their Theological Implication' in *Text și discurs religios* (Nr. 5 / 2013 Lucrările Conferinţei Naţionale conference publication), 97–108: 100–101.

5.3.1   The Dynamism of Eternity

The journey towards God can be perceived as timeless and dynamic. A Carthusian Novice Master suggests that the pilgrimage will continue for all eternity: 'When we love something, we are never weary of knowing it better … This impulse is without end, because the mystery of God is infinite. It will not cease even in heaven when we are face-to-face with God. We will move ever more deeply into the infinite abyss of his mystery for all eternity'.[59] Thus, the relationship that began on earth is not stagnant; it is expected to evolve and deepen further in heaven.

Kallistos Ware, summarising the Eastern monastic tradition, remarks that some Eastern authors such as Isaac the Syrian (Isaac of Nineveh, seventh century) considered the spiritual journey complete when we have reached love: then we have reached God and our journey is at an end. Ware argues, however, that another strain of Eastern spirituality holds that since God is infinite, the blessed even in heaven will never cease to grow in the knowledge and love of God. Thus 'the journey is *never* at an end'.[60] These traditions reconcile through another paradox: heavenly peaceful rest experienced as an infinite dynamic movement into the depths of the divine mystery. Kevin M. Clarke, in fact, interprets Gregory of Nyssa's theory of heavenly repose in which there is perpetual movement towards God as a paradox: 'God is the one who is the source of all motion, and there must be something active about the heavenly rest, especially because of the infinitude and incomprehensibility of the divine essence'.[61] John Polkinghorne, a physicist and theologian, writes about this kind of dynamic new creation as the realm of realised love. His view is that unending life will never become boring but will be endlessly enriching as the redeemed are led deeper and deeper into the inexhaustible life and energies of God, made available to us as we come to know the divine nature as it is progressively unveiled.[62]

---

[59] A Carthusian, *The Way of Silent Love*, 57. See also, for example, Bernard of Clairvaux, *Selected Works*, 84 in the treatise 'On Loving God' referring to the condition of those who deserve to be at the wedding feast of the Lord as: 'insatiable curiosity that is not restless, an eternal and endless desire that knows no lack'.

[60] Kallistos Ware, 'Ways of Prayer and Contemplation: Eastern' in Bernard McGinn, John Meyendorff and Jean Leclercq (eds.) *Christian Spirituality: Origins to the Twelfth Century* (London: SCM Press, 1996), 395–414: 402.

[61] Clarke, 'Moses's Dark Cloud, Teresa's Dark Night and the Soul's Entrance to the Divine Presence', 133–134.

[62] Polkinghorne, *Exploring Reality*, 125.

If, as Thomas Aquinas proposes, faith and hope will cease in heaven but charity will remain,[63] the idea of the dynamic deepening in the knowledge and love of God relates to the dynamism of the Trinitarian Love, which itself is eternal.[64] This relational aspect indicates that faith and hope will accompany the religious through the journey until the arrival at the final threshold. It is charity, the loving relationship with the Eternal that will endure beyond death. Jean-Philippe Houdret, OCD, connects these three theological virtues with the analogy of pilgrimage to heavenly Jerusalem:

> Faith and Hope are the theological virtues of pilgrims in time … *en route* to the Jerusalem above. Faith is called to disappear in eternity to give way to vision. Hope, too, is called to disappear to be replaced by possession. Charity, *agape*, is the theological virtue for time and eternity. In eternity, Charity does not pass, but remains forever.[65]

The two 'temporal' theological virtues, faith and hope, cultivated on earth, will be replaced in heaven by the vision and possession of God while charity will endure forever, both in time and eternity. Therefore, the question is: why would a relationship that is based on charity change as one passes the transparent veil between life and death? At the end of the transformative monastic journey, it may be possible to confess like Desert Father Anthony: 'Now I no longer fear God, I love him, for love casts out fear'.[66]

---

[63] Thomas Aquinas, *The Summa Theologica* 1 2 q 67 (Of the Duration of Virtues after This Life), Articles 3 5. Translated by Fathers of the English Dominican Province http://www. documentacatholicaomnia.eu/03d/1225-1274,_Thomas_Aquinas,_Summa_Theologiae_ %5B1%5D,_EN.pdf.

[64] A Carthusian author in *The Blessed Trinity and the Supernatural Life*, at http://transfiguration.chartreux.org (accessed 20 July 2019), describes the infinite dynamism of the Trinitarian love with a powerful image: 'When two opposing currents in an ocean meet and mix, the very violence of their embrace produces an immense wave, which seems to assault the sky. The Holy Spirit has been likened to such a wave. The Father and the Son, essentially united in the same love, form but one Source for the breathing forth of the Holy Spirit... The life of the Father and of the Son is thus the breathing forth of the Spirit in love, and the life of the Spirit is to proceed from the Father and the Son, and therein lies the eternal superabundance of charity without end'.

[65] Houdret, 'Le temps et l'éternité', 14. Translation mine.

[66] *Sayings*, 177.

5.3.2   The Patience of Waiting

How is monastic time related to waiting? According to Ogliari, 'waiting' carries an eschatological meaning, a goal which includes 'our nostalgia for God and the craving for him, ceaselessly sought in the folds and wrinkles of time and of history, while waiting to enter into Time without time'.[67] The monastic stability (place) and the lifelong waiting (time) are related to the virtue of patience, as described by Michael Downey:

> The monk waits for God even when prayers seem to go unheard and unanswered. He keeps standing in one place ... He answered God's call to be in this place simply because God is God, and this is God's place. The monk lives by the promise of presence. The presence is known deep inside him from time to time. But mostly he goes from hunch to hunch ... He has staked his life on it and continues to do so day by day in lifelong fidelity ... He waits to see. And he keeps walking, seeking the face of God, and counting on grace.[68]

From the perspective of the religious, the anticipated dynamism of eternity is, paradoxically, counterbalanced with patience and stability; humble and obedient waiting is required while still on the journey. The eschatological hope is present in the liminality of waiting. One can see how the programme in the monastic transformational 'school' aims at teaching patience that maintains the eschatological hope and develops endurance to persevere until the end of the journey.[69] This is expressed also in a poem (dedicated to a fello
w monk) by the Carthusian monk-poet:

---

[67] Ogliari, 'Tempus Monasticum', 52.

[68] Downey, Trappist, 163–164.

[69] See, for example, Thomas à Kempis, The Imitation of Christ, for the dialogue between The Disciple (in Chapter 48) who laments: 'I am left poor and exiled in a hostile land, where every day sees wars and very great misfortunes... Whatever this world offers is a burden to me. I desire to enjoy you intimately, but cannot attain to it... I have become a burden to myself, while my spirit seeks to rise upward and my flesh to sink downward'. The Voice of Christ (in Chapter 49) assures that 'patience will receive the consolations': 'I know your longings... Already you desire the delights of the eternal home, the heavenly land that is full of joy. But that hour is yet to come... You long to be filled with the highest good, but you cannot attain it now. I am that sovereign Good. Await Me, until the kingdom of God shall come'. The emphasis here is on patience.

5.3.3   The Iron Bow[70]

Here in this lonely outpost
(Silent beneath the silent stars),
On the edge of life,
(A muffled rumbling I sometimes hear)
I am at home.
Here are the stark frontiers:
Time and Eternity,
Life and Death,
Satan and my Saviour.
All is reduced to simple terms:
A vast choice, a vast rejection.
The choice involves ceaseless
Labour, the rejection ceaseless
Vigilance;
The victory is in my Saviour's hands.
He alone can bend the Bow
of Iron.
Hidden in his quiver I wait.
One day he'll bend the Bow,
Fire me beyond the frontiers of time,
Death and Satan's chasm.
In eager expectation
I wait
(Silent beneath the silent stars),
Here in this lonely outpost …

The Carthusian monk-poet describes here his liminal eschatological waiting 'on the edge of life' (at the margins of society) hidden 'in the lonely outpost' of the monastery. In this kind of life, solitary and silent, everything is reduced to simple terms. Three stark contrasts emerge: (1) Time and eternity; (2) Life and death; (3) Satan and 'my Saviour'. The monk knows the victory is in his Saviour's hands. But in the meantime, he occupies himself with two ceaseless tasks: (1) 'choice' which entails labour for his Saviour; (2) 'rejection' which involves vigilance against Satan. The monk waits with 'eager expectation' that his Saviour will release him 'beyond' the three frontiers: time, death, and Satan. As a metaphorical

[70] A Carthusian, *In Praise of Silence*, 20.

arrow, the monk hopes to cross the transcendent chasm and arrive at the other side for: eternity, life and his Saviour. The monk knows that his waiting will end only at the time chosen by his Saviour. The key monastic themes are summarised here in a few beautiful lines of poetry: temporality, mortality, and self-transcendence, liminality, eschatological hope, and relationship with God.

Nicholas Diat interviewed several members of religious orders for his book *A Time to Die: Monks on the Threshold of Eternal Life*. He asked Carthusian Dom Innocent: 'Does a hermit want to die?' Dom Innocent replied: 'God decides. Modern society presents death in an unappealing way. We must move away from this vision. We must accept the darkness of the earth and wait impatiently for heaven'.[71] On further reflection, he later reached out to Diat with a note: 'You had asked me if I were waiting for death... it is not the door that I am waiting for. I am not waiting for death, but for Life. This should go without saying, but curiously enough it is not so common'.[72] The door as metaphor for death indicates a liminal experience which is not a permanent, enduring state. The door (physical death) represents merely a passage, a threshold between two lives: the temporal and the eternal.

There appears to be paradoxical dynamism in the monastic waiting. It is not idle or directionless. There is a known goal but the ultimate timing depends entirely on God. In the meantime, the monks wait, more or less patiently. Teresa of Ávila once compared life to a night in a bad inn, while Carthusian Dom Innocent compares life to a night on a train.[73] He explains this analogy:

> The important thing is not the journey but the place of arrival. I spend half of my life thinking about eternal life. It is the constant backdrop that lines my whole existence. I am not afraid of the Grim Reaper. It makes me curious. Eternity passes through death. We must love this door that will allow us to know the Father. We are born for heaven.[74]

This reflection highlights several monastic insights. First to note is the importance of the destination (eternal) over the journey (short and temporal). Secondly, the monk estimates that he spends half of his life

[71] Diat, *A Time to Die*, 168.
[72] Diat, *A Time to Die*, 169.
[73] Diat, *A Time to Die*, 166.
[74] Diat, *A Time to Die*, 166.

thinking about eternal life. Such a statement carries rich temporal meanings: half of one's earthly lifetime is already devoted to and directed towards eternal life. This indicates the monastic time-space as a liminal stage between temporality and eternity, between world and heaven. The door as the symbol of death is a liminal passage that opens the entry to eternity. Finally, what is ultimately desired regarding eternal life is God: to know the Father. The metaphor of door is used also by William of Saint-Thierry, O.Cist. (d. 1143) in *Meditation VI* where he asks,

> what does it avail us earthbound folk to see an open door in heaven? The answer is found in Paul: he who ascends is also he who descended. And who is this? Love. Love in us, Lord, ascends to you on high, because love in you descended here to us. You loved us, therefore you came down to us; by loving you we shall climb where you are.[75]

This could relate to the descent/ascent pattern between the Incarnation and contemplation. At the end of *Meditation VI*, William of Saint-Thierry returns to the metaphor of door. Here, he asks for the favour to make occasional and fleeting visits to the heavenly land (through contemplation) with the hope that one day he might be allowed to stay there permanently (through death).[76]

Monastic waiting—realised eschatology (already here and now)—is liminal in the relational sense because it still awaits the full revelation that is reserved for future eschatology (there and then). This is evidenced in the way Carthusian Dom Dysmas reflects on his views on eternity[77]:

> If you look at it from the perspective of eternity, our life is only a brief instant. But that does not prevent us from feeling that it is long, especially if

---

[75] William of Saint-Thierry in Pauline Matarasso, ed., *The Cistercian World: Monastic Writings of the Twelfth Century* (London: Penguin Books, 1993; trans. P. Matarasso), 114–120: 115.

[76] William of Saint-Thierry in *The Cistercian World: Monastic Writings of the Twelfth Century*, 120: 'Open to me, Lord, so that I, a stranger in your land and not yet worthy of enrolment as its citizen, may be granted the favour of occasional and fleeting visits… If I am found worthy to ascend more often, to linger longer, to return again, your citizens will come to know me, they who, like all inhabitants of heaven, know no suffering… If only I may see, if only I may persevere, if only I may one day hear "Enter into the joy of your Lord", and may so enter that I never leave!' This relates to waiting, patience and the eschatological hope in the contemplative life.

[77] Sarah, *The Power of Silence*, 213.

one is suffering. Let us keep this difference in mind; it will help us to understand. When we have gone over to God's side, we will see things as he does ... On this earth we have the unique opportunity to love God while he is hidden from our eyes and ears. Faith is not granted in the light because that dazzling splendour is reserved for eternity. But when the time comes for him to reveal himself fully, our joy will be eternal for having loved him thus without seeing him.

Spiritual marriage in monasticism was previously indicated as a motivation to enter the monastery and as spousal relationship. The idea of waiting is analogous with lifelong engagement, a patient and chaste love experienced during the monastic lifetime. Here, 'engagement'—as a liminal state—refers to the period of preparation for the eschatological promise to be fulfilled. For the religious, the temporal engagement on earth leads to an eternal marriage in heaven. This loving relationship between God and a soul, according to John Climacus, is transformative: 'If the sight of the one we love clearly makes us change completely, so that we turn cheerful, glad and carefree, what will the face of the Lord Himself not do as He comes to dwell, invisibly, in a pure soul?'[78] The metaphors of engagement and marriage therefore indicate a deepening and dynamic relationship in love. But in order for the wedding feast to take place, the bride must die.[79] Death opens the door to a timeless honeymoon, in the words of a Carthusian monk:

> Death is a paradox: what follows on
> Is the honeymoon, a time with time to spend
> In Love: a time with time for nought by Love;
> A time extravagant with the gift of time,
> The act of Being held in timelessness.[80]

This poem presents a brief summary of the key categories of the current study. Death and what follows on (Eschatology) leads to a wedding feast

---

[78] Climacus, *The Ladder of Divine Ascent*, 287.

[79] John of the Cross in *A Spiritual Canticle of the Soul and the Bridegroom Christ* writes about the bride's (soul's) request in Stanza XI: 'let the vision and Thy beauty kill me'. He concludes that there is no bitterness in death to the soul that loves (Stanza XI, 14); and nothing strange for the soul to desire to die by beholding the beauty of God in order to enjoy Him forever (Stanza XI: 8).

[80] A Carthusian, *Death Is A Paradox*, lines 1–5 In *The Outlaw: Poems 2000–2002*, unpublished collection.

for the lovers, the soul and God (Relationship). The eternal honeymoon represents the passage over the threshold (Liminality) between a period of engagement on earth and the endless, timeless marriage of love in heaven. For the soul, this kind of enduring existence represents true 'Being'—as opposed to dying—because it is held eternally by God who himself *is* 'Being' and *is* 'Love'. But, paradoxically, the only way to attain this life is to die.

5.4   DEATH IN MONASTERY

What can be learned from the anticipation of death and moments of death in monasteries? While each departure from this life is unique and individual, there is also a communal perspective. The religious share their lives with their community; they likewise share their deaths with their community. Membership in the monastic order 'offers the potential of solidarity both in life and death'.[81] The communal ties and the mutual support endure and extend across the border of this life through prayers.[82] The enclosure of monastic life is mirrored in monastic death: once the monastic journey is completed, the monks' bodies will remain inside the walls of the monastery, in their own secluded burial grounds.[83]

5.4.1   Anticipation of Death

As argued previously, entry to the monastery could already be viewed as death to the world. In the final stage of the journey, in a certain way, the circle closes. The journey has begun with a symbolic death as the individual enters the monastery and renounces the world. This was viewed as a liminal stage where a threshold is crossed. As the physical death approaches another threshold, the final journey even deeper into the unknown, awaits.

For the early Desert Fathers the entire monastic life was characterised by the daily expectation of death and preparation to meet one's Maker. Anthony taught his fellow monks that life is naturally uncertain and

[81] Andrews, *The Other Friars*, 47–48.

[82] See, for example, Kerr, *Life in the Medieval Cloister*, 166. A monk remained a member of the community even after death, and monastic friendship persisted beyond the grave. As a sign of remembrance, a pittance meal was served in the refectory on the anniversary of the death and the religious was remembered by the brethren in their prayers.

[83] See, for example, Andrews, *The Other Friars*, 48: The Carmelite order was given the right to have separate cemeteries at their cloister grounds already in 1262 by Pope Urban IV.

Providence allots it to us daily. As a monk rises in the morning, he should think that he will not live until evening; and when he lies down to sleep, he should think that he will not rise up.[84] Anthony's own last words, as recounted by Athanasius, included the advice to breathe Christ, trust him and, again, to 'live as though dying daily'.[85] Augustine's concept of time and journey is no different. He wrote: 'From the moment we begin to exist in this body which is destined to die we are involved all the time in the process whose end is death... If a man passes through a more extended period of time on the road to death, he does not proceed more slowly; he merely has a longer journey'.[86] The association between movement and time, central in Augustine's thinking, is again identifiable here. Time is allotted from the start; the length of journey is a function of time. Accordingly, the following description of the Benedictine monastic journey speaks of such acceptance of one's allotment of time:

> To the monk heaven was next door; he formed no plans, he had no cares ... He 'went forth' in his youth 'to his work and to his labour' until the evening of life; if he lived a day longer, he did a day's work more; whether he lived many days or a few, he laboured on to the end of them. He had no wish to see further in advance of his journey than where he was to make his next stage. He ploughed and sowed, he prayed, he meditated, he studied, he wrote, he taught, and then he died and went to heaven.[87]

This quotation expresses the acceptance of death as part of life which has begun already here, in relationship with God, and simultaneously as a simple daily movement towards him who awaits 'beyond', at the end of the journey. The journey itself then can be understood as a purificatory passage. A contemporary Carthusian writer connects 'purification' and 'passage' to Passover.[88] He defines these terms in relation to death:

---

[84] Athanasius, *Life of Anthony*, 16–20.

[85] Athanasius, *Life of Anthony*, 91.

[86] Augustine, *De civitate Dei*, 13.10 quoted in Knuuttila, *'Time and Creation in Augustine'*, 115.

[87] Introduction of W.K. Lowether Clarke to Palladius, *The Lausiac History*, 11–12. This quotation is attributed to Cardinal Newman.

[88] A Carthusian, *The Wound of Love*, 143. The reference to Passover here can carry multiple meanings. It may refer to the eschatological fulfilment in the kingdom of God. Cf. Lk 22:15–16 (NRSV): 'I have eagerly desired to eat this Passover with you before I suffer; for I tell you, I will not eat it until it is fulfilled in the kingdom of God'. It may also refer to a metaphorical journey: liberation from slavery, return to home.

Purification: 'the difficult ascecis of living the present moment, accepting one's finitude and one's death'.[89]

Passage: 'abandonment of every possession in the movement towards the One who awaits us, there behind the scene'.[90]

Nicholas Diat describes the 'Carthusian way' that closely resembles the framework of monastic journeys in this book (with a beginning, middle, and end). According to Diat, the 'Carthusian way' is: 'A beginning full of enthusiasm, a middle of difficult and contrasted experiences, then a peace that announces eternity. When the Carthusians arrive at the end of their road, they are already detached from life'.[91] It is worth noting here the dynamic nature of human and monastic paths. A young person may begin the monastic journey with certain ideas of time, or they might not consider their monastic vocation very deeply from this perspective. Nevertheless, perceptions of time can also evolve over time. During the stay in the monastery, the original ideas may deepen, mature, or evolve, or they might even remain largely unchanged. And finally, at the end of the monastic journey, when approaching one's death, different perspectives of time might still develop.

Adalbert de Vogüé, looking back over his fifty years' life in a monastery, concludes that death is a great educator of the living. Revealing the 'nonsense of an existence which comes to an end', it obliges one to look beyond the present world. He identifies three stages of development in his own thinking about life after death[92]:

1. Before becoming a monk and in his first years of monastic life, the next world consisted chiefly in the immortal life of the soul, admitted to the vision of God.
2. He later discovered the Resurrection of Christ as 'the first fruits and pledge of our resurrection'; that the glorious Christ—conqueror of sin and death—is the substance of our hope.
3. In the measure that age brought him closer to the end of his life, the thought of eternity continued to dominate and illuminate him. Its 'liberating hold' even intensified. He spent each Sunday an hour

---

[89] A Carthusian, *The Wound of Love*, 143.
[90] A Carthusian, *The Wound of Love*, 143.
[91] Diat, *A Time to Die*, 158.
[92] de Vogüé, *To Desire Eternal Life*, 10–11.

meditating on these two words: 'eternal life'. He argued that it would indeed be 'stupid' to have such a hope and not to think of it.

5.4.2   Moments of Death

Another way to approach the question of eternity is to ask: after a lifetime in the monastery, how is death experienced? What has been documented about the last moments of the dying religious in monasteries?

When introducing the monastic themes, a quotation from John Binns was used to illustrate the monastic journey during which the monk becomes closer to God, with the result that the moment of death loses its abrupt quality of discontinuity and, instead becomes 'a deepening of an already achieved status'.[93] This implies that the final threshold between transitory and eternal is softened and lowered through the closeness to God as a result of a lifetime in the monastery. Similarly, a recent study by Durà-Vilà and Leavey found that having a gradually more intense and continuous experience of God resulted in a lack of fear of death among contemplative monks and nuns.[94] The explanations for this were the religious belief in an afterlife and their experiencing God in their solitude. Moreover, in the state of silence and solitude, the boundaries between the living and the dead members of the community were blurred, and the relationships with those who had died were maintained both spiritually and physically (the monks' graves were in the monastery garden).[95]

To the extent the daily expectation of death has been practised, there could be a degree of familiarity or anticipation when the moment of physical death finally arrives. With regard to Desert Fathers, this monastic approach to death was recognised by Archbishop Theophilus, who, when he was dying, said to monk Arsenius, 'Arsenius, you are blessed of God, because you have always kept this moment before your eyes'.[96] Yet, it would be too simplistic to assume that all monastic deaths are experienced as smooth transitions and lacking an experience of abrupt discontinuity. The infirmarians of the Benedictine Abbey of Solesmes, who have a long

---

[93] Binns, *Ascetics and Ambassadors of Christ*, 239.

[94] Glòria Durà-Vilà and Gerard Leavey, 'Solitude among contemplative cloistered nuns and monks: conceptualisation, coping and benefits of spiritually motivated solitude' in *Mental Health, Religion & Culture*, 2017, Vol. 20, No. 1, 45–60.

[95] Durà-Vilà and Leavey, 'Solitude among contemplative cloistered nuns and monks: conceptualisation, coping and benefits of spiritually motivated solitude', 57.

[96] *Sayings*, 13.

experience of witnessing final moments, provide anecdotal evidence of this:

> In a monastery, the monks are preparing all their lives to meet God. Death is a violent rupture. The body and the soul are made to be together. If we live our lives for ourselves, we are necessarily unhappy. If we live for Christ, we already have one foot in eternity. Some saints may have had bursts of fear at the last minute. The combat ceases only with the final heartbeat.[97]

Noting the observation of some saints having had bursts of fear at the last minute, Thérèse of Lisieux, experienced moments fear and uncertainty at her deathbed, as described in the Epilogue of her *Story of a Soul*:

> Thérèse reached the end of her way of the cross like a tired traveller at the end of a long journey: *"It is into God's arms that I am falling"*. She experienced moments of uncertainty as she faced death: *"I am afraid I have feared death. I am not afraid of what happens after death; that is certain! I don't regret giving up my life; but I ask myself: What is this mysterious separation of the soul from the body? It is the first time that I have experienced this, but I abandoned myself immediately to God."*[98]

Liminality, 'this mysterious separation of the soul from the body' at the moment of death, relates to a threshold experience, a moment of discontinuity between this life and afterlife, to the unknown that waits beyond. Death reveals this ultimate inflection point: mortality of body and immortality of soul. Like Christ, Thérèse suffered the physical agony of painful death but commended her soul in the hands of God.

The last moments of Cistercian Abbot Aelred of Rievaulx (1110–1167), recounted by Walter Daniel, feature the traditional monastic language, as Aelred addressed his monks on his deathbed:

> Now with your leave and accompanied by your prayers I am going home from exile, out of darkness into light, from this evil world to God, for the time is now come when he who redeemed me of himself without me, and

[97] Diat, *A Time to Die*, 75.
[98] Thérèse of Lisieux, *Story of a Soul*, 428.

deigned of his grace to bind me yet more closely to him by the bonds of a better life lived here among you, will take me to himself.[99]

In this passage, several familiar monastic themes can be identified:

1. Monastic journey from transitory to eternal: 'going home from exile, out of darkness into light, from this evil world to God'. Here, Aelred uses both spatial references (from exile to home) and references to God as Person (explicitly 'from world to God'; and implicitly 'from darkness into light').
2. Monastic life: 'a better life lived here among you' refers to God's grace which called Aelred to join the monastery and share his journey with the brothers. He credits this as 'a better life', one which allowed him to bind more closely to God. Following the Cistercian tradition, the religious dies surrounded by the community, 'accompanied by your prayers'.
3. Time: 'the time has now come …' can be understood as an acknowledgement of an anticipated 'time of death', which Aelred prepared for by calling his monks to share this moment with him.
4. Relationship: Here, in one sentence, Aelred reveals a threefold nature of his relationship with God. The dying Abbot first speaks of God as his redeemer, followed by acknowledgement of God's grace which bound Aelred more closely to God during his monastic life. He concludes with death already in sight that God 'will take me to himself', to an eternal union. God is his redeemer at the start, his close companion during monastic life, and his destination at the end of his journey.
5. Liminality: The reference to 'exile' as a previous state which is about to end as Aelred is now 'going home', which transforms the moment of death into a threshold experience.
6. Eschatology: Aelred speaks about going 'home' (heaven), 'to God' (Person) with the hope and eschatological anticipation that God is now taking the dying monk to 'himself'. This is a realised microcosmic moment.

[99] Walter Daniel, 'The Life of Aelred', in Pauline Matarasso, (ed.), *The Cistercian World: Monastic Writings of the Twelfth Century* (London: Penguin Books, 1993; trans. P. Matarasso), 152–168: 165.

The presence of the community around the dying is a notable recurring theme in the monastic sources. When death is foreseeable, the one who is about to leave this world is accompanied and supported by the brethren. The general idea is that nobody dies alone and unassisted. There are, however, different traditions among enclosed contemplatives. Carthusians prefer to die in the solitude of their cells. The other members of the community are notified about the imminent death so that they can pray simultaneously for the one who is dying. Dom Innocent sums it up: 'Dying alone is part of our charism. This death resembles us'.[100]

Nancy Maguire records the event of the death of Dom Hugo-Maria in the Carthusian Charterhouse of Parkminster following the procedure laid out in the statute on 'Dying Monks'. According to the statute, there would be a ceremony of plenary indulgence which takes away the entire temporal punishment due to sin. This ceremony would be followed by the rite of anointing. In the imminent danger of death, there should always be one or more brothers watching over the dying. At the critical moment, all are given a signal to pray for his holy death. The *Credo* is said to strengthen the dying man's faith and encourage his hope. Those present continue to pray after the moment of death and a vigil is held until the community can be summoned.[101] If the dead Carthusian is a choir monk, he is clothed in a habit and cowl, hair shirt, and cincture. This applies also to novices. All garments should be in good condition. The body is placed on a bier and covered with suitable cloth.[102]

As recounted by Maguire, in accordance with the Carthusian tradition, Dom Hugo-Maria's body stayed in the church throughout the night as the monks sang Night Office as well as a special Office of the Dead. Two monks alternated keeping vigil until the funeral mass in the morning. A simple requiem Mass was said and afterwards Dom Hugo-Maria's body was carried to the monastery graveyard in a procession of the community singing Psalms. The burial was simple with no coffin, or flowers. The grave would later be marked with a wooden cross without a name or date. Maguire writes that Dom Philip, whom she interviewed, a novice at the time, reflected upon the transformation of the humiliation of the old monk's worn-out body to the body conformed to the glory of Jesus Christ. He felt that there was nothing left of Dom Hugo-Maria—God had

---

[100] Diat, *A Time to Die*, 160.
[101] Maguire, *An Infinity of Little Hours*, 209.
[102] Maguire, *An Infinity of Little Hours*, 209–210.

consumed him. It was a quiet passing and Dom Philip thought it a natural process that monks should go out the same way they came in, without anything.[103]

In a recent study of contemplative Augustinian nuns in the Spanish Monastery of Santa Mónica, the researchers found that a recurring theme that came up in the interviews was monastic deaths witnessed by the nuns. The accounts of their deceased sisters dying surrounded by the care and support of the community in peace and with the security of their resurrection were cherished among the nuns. The real examples of nuns who belonged to their community dying well gave a sense of security to them, an assurance that they too would die with hope.[104] The role of community was especially relevant when coping with terminal illness. The nuns had a conviction that they were going to be looked after by their sisters until death. This would not only be in a physical sense, but also by being spiritually enveloped and sustained in their faith and hope of an eternal life.[105] Furthermore, as the researchers concluded, the conviction of being in the world temporarily helps the religious to see death as relative. Death becomes a transition to a much better existence, as illustrated by the quotations of the Augustinian Sisters[106]:

> Dying is nothing to be afraid of: you just leave a house to go to another one that is much more beautiful. (Sister Teresa)

> I am not afraid of dying. Dying is the final step to meet the Lord. When my time comes, it will be because He calls me, He will help me to be ready for meeting Him. (Sister Carmen)

Sister Angela Thérèse, a contemporary Carmelite nun, describes the moments of death she has witnessed in her community as positive, even beautiful, experiences:

---

[103] Maguire, *An Infinity of Little Hours*, 211–213.

[104] Durà-Vilà, Dein, Littlewood and Leavey, 'The *Dark Night of the Soul*: Causes and Resolutions of Emotional Distress Among Contemplative Nuns', 562.

[105] Durà-Vilà, Dein, Littlewood and Leavey, 'The *Dark Night of the Soul*: Causes and Resolutions of Emotional Distress Among Contemplative Nuns', 563.

[106] Durà-Vilà, Dein, Littlewood and Leavey, 'The *Dark Night of the Soul*: Causes and Resolutions of Emotional Distress Among Contemplative Nuns', 562.

There've been five old ones go since I've been here, and they've been really beautiful moments, with the whole community gathered around the person that's dying and the priest there as well. It really is lovely, and I don't think I've ever seen anybody shed a tear.[107]

Dom Pateau, OSB, in a recent interview, compares monastic deaths with those of modern individuals. In his view, the acceleration of technology overwhelms people until the final moments. They do not have time for themselves and for God. They do not have time to die because they do not have time to live. In contrast to the modern man, 'the monk agrees to lose all his time for God. Monastic life is happy; monastic death is, also'.[108] This statement seems to summarise the meaning of monastic time as realised eschatology. The enclosed contemplative way of life allows time for oneself and for God. It removes some of the modern technological distractions which may overwhelm people in the secular world. The monastics willingly 'lose all their time for God'. This idea of 'losing one's time for God', paradoxically, allows for a happy life and for a happy death. It has been suggested that for the religious, time wasted on God, is time well spent.[109]

The Carthusian Statutes speak of a long and arduous monastic journey. It is described as a profound transformational process which leads to discovering joy at the end of the long exodus towards the Father:

It takes time to grow to maturity, to arrive at the unshackled liberty to give oneself, to love as we are loved. This comes about little by little, learning to listen to the Spirit, to let his light and love penetrate our hearts, and reconcile us with God, with ourselves and with our neighbours.

Through the grace of the Holy Spirit a very profound transformation in Christ takes place in solitude. Leaving the world physically is only the first step of a long exodus towards the Father. The journey entails the crossing of one's desert and the progressive discovery of our misery and fundamental need of the Lord's mercy in everything. When the monk is established on this solid rock, there is no end to his joy; the joy to be child of God, sharing

---

[107] Loudon, *Unveiled*, 40.

[108] Diat, *A Time to Die*, 135.

[109] A Carthusian, *When I hear*, an unpublished poem: 'All my time / Wasted seeking to gaze God was time / Well spent' (lines 3–5). The poem is about the monk's anticipation of his death and it concludes: 'Love's / Our only ally with moments left to live. / God gave himself; forever he will give…' (lines 12–14).

intimately in Christ's sonship, and in his tenderness and compassion for the whole of creation.[110]

The road may seem long but the promise of joy experienced (already now), and anticipated (for all eternity) continues to attract pilgrims to a monastic journey. This is what contemporary Carthusians try to convey on their website today. Even if this road appears less travelled today, over 900 years' tradition and lived experiences do add certain depth to these claims.

5.5   Conclusions

We have considered here the matters of life and death from various angles. However, the main argument relates to how eschatology provides a conduit that carries the hope that, through resurrection, death can turn into life. This is experienced in the enjoyment of a loving relationship with God that allows for a happy monastic life and a happy monastic death. Faith and hope are the travel companions that take the pilgrims of heaven to the final threshold through which charity carries them over to eternal life. In the meantime, trust and patience of waiting is required. What waits on the other side is life and heaven but most importantly, eternal rest in the Personal God whom one can grow to know better for all eternity. It is a peaceful yet simultaneously dynamic eschatological view.

The three familiar categories of Liminality, Eschatology, and Relationship are all present at the end of the monastic journey in different ways. Here, waiting is associated with the eschatological hope of resurrection. Death represents a liminal threshold experience and life is identified with a relationship, a union with God. Figure 5.2 indicates the trajectory of the last stages until the final destination is reached.

The final subsection provides a 'case study' of Carmelite Sister Kinga of the Transfiguration whose story was introduced in Chap. 3. She was the young woman who had fallen in love with God and entered the Carmelite cloister to devote her life to this relationship. Here, we shall return to her story which expands further into a wider question about the monastery as a waiting room and as a journey.

---

[110] Carthusian Parkminster website, accessed 18 December 2021 at https://www.park-minster.org.uk/journey. The transformational trajectory from the difficult early stages to finding joy in the end is consistent with observations made by the early monastics.

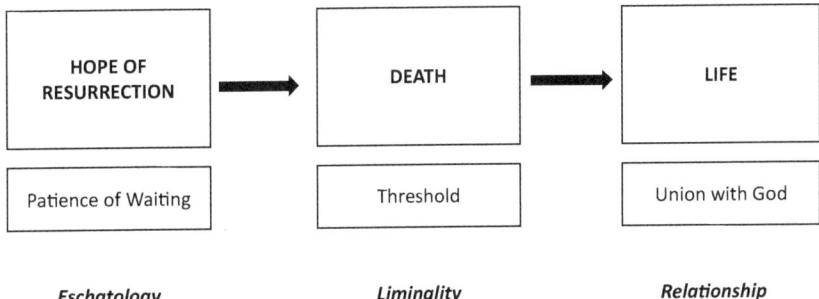

Fig. 5.2 Liminality, eschatology, and relationship at the end of the monastic journey

5.6   REFLECTIONS

'Is life a waiting room or a journey?' Katja Ritari uses this quotation from Margaret Atwood to reframe her research question about the medieval imaginations of the afterlife. Ritari's answer is that for the saints, this life is nothing but a waiting room, as they are already citizens of Heaven longing for their true home. For most other Christians, according to Ritari, life should be treated as a journey at the end of which awaits judgement.[111] This distinction could be understood in the context of Ritari's study which used Irish hagiographies as a source. In early Christian and medieval sources, members of religious orders were sometimes—using loose terminology—referred to as 'saints' or 'citizens of heaven', and monasteries were considered as intermediary places between the earthly life and the afterlife.

The experience of waiting at the crossroads of eternity is expressed in the diary of Sister Kinga of the Transfiguration, who entered a Carmelite convent in Hungary in 1998. In 2006, she was diagnosed with cancer followed by three years of various treatments. Nine months before her death (in 2009), Sister Kinga was asked by the Prioress of the convent to write about her life. In the final pages of her diary she describes her fight, the oscillations between life and death, and the waiting:

Time goes on, minute after minute, day after day. I'm not going anywhere. It's like I'm in an abandoned train station in the middle of the desert. I see

---

[111] Ritari, *Pilgrimage to Heaven*, 177.

the rails. But do trains pass on these rails? No soul on the horizon, to whom I could pose this question. I do not know what to do. I wait. I do not have the strength to get going. And I would not know where to go.

What to do? What does all this mean? What purpose?

A few days ago, a sentence came back to me: Live like someone who has seen the Resurrection of the Lord. Be a witness of the Resurrection of the Lord. What does this mean? A firm faith. To radiate hope in the most desperate situations. I do not feel the strength, but I do not see any other meaning or purpose to endure this ordeal.

How I wish for a train to take me away! It does not matter where, but let me leave this desert without horizon![112]

Is the monastery a waiting room or a journey? For Sister Kinga, it was perhaps both. She was on a journey, or rather wanted to be, but felt stuck in the waiting room of an abandoned railway station, at the crossroads of her cancer treatments, between life and death. There, her patience was tested but her 'greatest love-passion'[113] in God proved greater than fear.[114] She relied on faith and hope of resurrection. Sister Kinga writes that she was always touched by the phrases '*All things pass … God alone suffices*' in the prayer of Teresa of Ávila which her Carmelite community recited daily. The very last words at the end of Sister Kinga's diary reflect the changelessness of God as she faces the fear of the imminent moment of death. She writes:

> Therefore, despite all the fear:
> *Let nothing disturb thee;*
> *Let nothing dismay thee:*
> *All things pass;*
> *God never changes.*
> *Patience attains*
> *All that it strives for.*
> *He who has God*
> *Finds he lacks nothing: God alone suffices.*[115]

---

[112] Kinga de la Transfiguration, *Je ne me suis pas dérobée…*, 261–262. Translation mine.

[113] Cf. Kinga de la Transfiguration, *Je ne me suis pas dérobée…*, 17, 'le plus grand amour-passion' was the term Kinga used to describe her encounter with God which later led to her monastic calling.

[114] 1 Jn 4:18 (NRSV): 'There is no fear in love, but perfect love casts out fear'.

[115] Kinga de la Transfiguration, *Je ne me suis pas dérobée*, 263. Prayer translation: E. A. Peers.

For Sister Kinga, the train finally arrived and she completed her earthly journey at the age of thirty-six, losing the battle against cancer. During her time in the waiting room she discovered the transitory nature of this world—'All things pass'; and what is eternal—'God never changes'.

And how to conclude the question relating to monastic life: is it a journey or a waiting room? In the light of this study, the closest answer could be that monastic life is *a journey in a waiting room*. A journey takes place internally while, externally, only stability and lack of movement can be observed. Or, perhaps the 'journey' is the horizontal dimension which spans one's lifetime in the monastery. In the course of the earthly pilgrimage, timeless conversations with the eternal God are held in the verticality that opens up from the monastery, as the 'waiting room' of heaven.

CHAPTER 6

Conclusions: Monastic Perspectives on Temporality

The Christian eschatological hope constitutes the 'red thread' which motivates and carries through the monastic journeys from the transitory (temporal) world (spatial) to eternal (temporal) heaven (spatial). The hope of seeing God in heaven is the fundamental goal that is present in various degrees as motivation during the monastic journey.

Monastic time can be viewed through the categories of 'liminality', 'relationship', and 'eschatology'. Previous research on contemplative and monastic traditions has been published among others by Woolley (from the relational perspective) and by Ritari (from the eschatological perspective). It is therefore not surprising that these two categories— relationship and eschatology—emerged also through the lens of time in the current study. In contrast, liminality has not been previously identified in monastic studies as a distinct category by other scholars. Monasticism, however, has been explicitly mentioned as an 'example' of liminality by researchers in the fields of anthropology and social sciences.[1]

The question then arises: Looking through the lens of time, does 'liminality' hold a similar central motivation for monasticism, comparable to 'relationship' and 'eschatology' which have already been separately identified by other researchers? An affirmative answer to this is found in

[1] See, for example, Turner and Turner, *Image and Pilgrimage in Christian Culture*, 4; and Thomassen, *Liminality and the Modern*, 93.

R. Hujanen, *Monastic Perspectives on Temporality*,
https://doi.org/10.1007/978-3-031-34808-2_6

Chap. 3, where it was shown that early Christian monasticism was characterised by withdrawal to the desert, by leaving the secular society in order to be alone with God, and to form communities with like-minded renouncers. The Christian monastic tradition is defined by liminality from its very beginning.

Despite the different perspectives and stages of the journey, there is a distinct similarity across all three categories. This relates to the 'timelessness' of these themes. Liminality, Relationship and Eschatology are 'eternal questions', unrelated to a specific historical era. Monasticism, especially enclosed contemplative traditions, always seems to result in a fundamental liminal experience throughout centuries, even if the social or political environments vary. Likewise, the relationship with God is a 'timeless' consideration throughout human history. Finally, the eschatological perspective of monasticism and Christianity is unchanged, even if the emphasis on it may vary over time. Why is this? There are two observations to make.

The first is related to the inherent nature of these categories. They represent fundamental experiences that are deeply monastic. Nevertheless, one could argue that the category of 'seeking a relationship with God' applies to anyone. This is true. At the same time, monastic religious life can be seen as a *distinct form* of seeking that relationship. This has to do with the concept of time. One can seek such a relationship during a lifetime enclosed in the contemplative monastery, or equally outside of it. This represents a distinction of how one chooses (or, rather, is called) to spend their time in this life.

The second observation has to do with the self-referential nature of monasticism. The 'timelessness' of these categories is evident in both monastic literature and traditions. While admitting the risk of oversimplification, one could claim that 'all Christian monastic roads lead to Egyptian deserts'.[2] This is why it is possible to find a multitude of voices across centuries as a cloud of witnesses of similar ageless themes.

Looking at enclosed contemplative life through the lens of the concept of time a 'kaleidoscopic' view emerged (Fig. 6.1):

A central finding was that, instead of waiting until the eschatological end of the journey, a degree of divine presence can be enjoyed 'Already Here and How'. This enjoyment can be experienced through the lifelong development of a personal relationship with God in contemplative

---

[2] RB 73 refers to Cassian and *Lives of Desert Fathers* as well as to Basil.

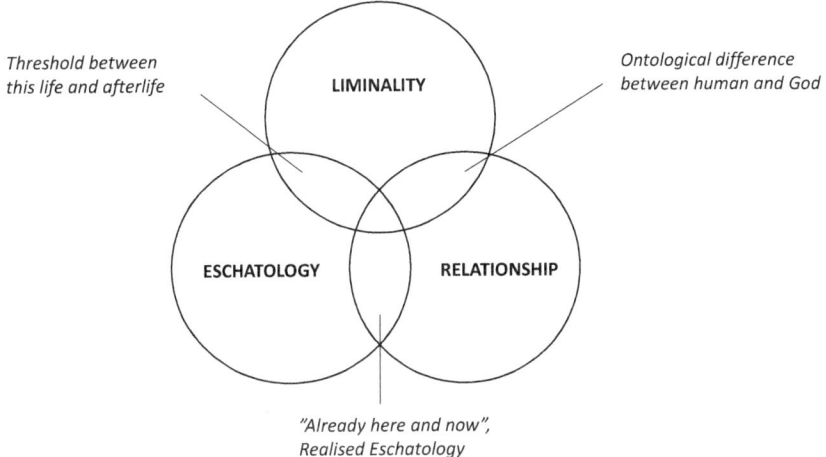

Fig. 6.1 Categories: liminality, relationship, and eschatology

monastic communities. The individual journeys find a parallel with the eschatological goal towards which humankind and the universe travel in accordance with God's eternal plan. Closing the circle from the initial withdrawal and renunciation, the lifelong monastic journey of 'dying to self' ends with physical death. And this marks the beginning of life in an uninterrupted union with God.

There can be a temptation to over-simplify the concept of time in the monastic context. There may be a risk of over-emphasising the present, the 'Already Here and Now' aspect. The other bias is to focus overly on the future destination, the 'There and Then' perspective. It would be possible to concentrate the attention mainly on the journey, with a preference for travelling over arriving. But one has to travel in order to arrive, and one is unlikely to take a journey without a destination in mind. Perhaps it is the dynamism of liminality—the internal tension between being a sinner and the hope of becoming a saint, the distinction between the mortality of the body and the immortality of the soul, the ontological difference between the human and the Divine, the distance between the heaven and the earth—that keeps the enclosed contemplatives moving forward and upward on their journeys.

6.1   THE MONASTIC WAYS

The conclusion from the three categories relates to the journey theme where the categories serve as conduits to connect concepts of faith along the way to God. The monastic ways, therefore, 'reconcile' what appears paradoxical. Despite the ontological difference between the Divine and human, the epistemological connection (knowledge, faith) can build a bridge over what seems like a nearly insurmountable gap.[3] The enclosed contemplative life is a 'paradoxical' journey, an ascent marked by descents and humility. Intellectual humility when encountering the Divine is required to acknowledge that God's thoughts are higher than human thoughts[4] and that 'God's foolishness is wiser than human wisdom'.[5] The monastic way of life facilitates the acceptance—if not full understanding—of fundamental Christian mysteries; the integration and reconciliation of what remains paradoxical in the ways of God. It is a way of humble ascents:

> The Lord makes poor and makes rich;
> he brings low, he also exalts.
> He raises up the poor from the dust;
> he lifts the needy from the ash heap,
> to make them sit with princes
> and inherit a seat of honor.[6]

The above applies to all Christians, but the enclosed contemplative monastic life makes an explicit effort to deal with some of the complex and paradoxical aspects of temporality through:

---

[3] Joseph Ratzinger, *Jeesuksen viimeiset päivät* (Kauniainen: Perussanoma, 2013, trans. J. Kiilunen from German *Jesus von Nazareth: Zweiter Teil: Vom Einzug in Jerusalem bis zur Auferstehung*, 96–97, argues that, in the biblical sense 'eternal life' can be found by 'knowing'. Knowing, which is provided by faith, creates unity between the object of knowing and the one who knows. The encounter with Christ leads the Christian to the knowing of God and the unity that leads to 'life'. Eternal life, therefore, is a *relational* concept. Human beings do not reach that life by their own power or only for themselves. They become 'living' in a relationship with him who is 'Life' himself. Translation from Finnish mine.

[4] Isa 55:8–9 (NRSV): 'For my thoughts are not your thoughts, nor are your ways my ways, says the Lord. For as the heavens are higher than the earth, so are my ways higher than your ways and my thoughts than your thoughts'.

[5] 1 Cor 1:25 (NRSV).

[6] 1 Sam 2: 7–8 (NRSV).

1. **Liminal** position between the ways of the world and divine ways, as intermediaries between the secular and divine. The withdrawal and separation from the world through physical enclosure creates a conduit, a 'consecrated bridge' that leads to contribution to the world. Liminality represents the 'Little Way' of those who make themselves strangers, marginalised, and the 'least in the world' to be called blessed in the kingdom of God.

2. **Relational** position that is personal and transformative. This is the salvific conduit that reconstructs the damaged relationship between the Divine and the world, God and the individual. In the context of monastic enclosure, it facilitates the vertical move from descent to ascent, from humility to glory.

3. **Eschatological** position as a waiting in hope that bridges the temporal virtue of faith with eternal virtue of charity. This is the conduit that leads from death to life, from microcosmic and macrocosmic destruction to resurrection. Enclosed contemplatives, in a dedicated way, accept the idea of 'dying' (to self, to the world) as a symbol of religious life, as a way to find the path to true Life.

From this follows that the monastic ways are situated between God's divine ways and the secular ways of the world, in a similar manner that the monastic time intersects between the divine time and secular time (Fig. 6.2).

This distinction aligns with the ideas of secularity and secular time proposed by Charles Taylor in *A Secular Age*. He argues that people who are in the *saeculum*, are embedded in ordinary time, they are living the life of ordinary time; as against those who have turned away from this in order to live closer to eternity. The word 'secular' is thus associated with 'ordinary' as against 'higher time'. A parallel distinction is temporal/spiritual. One is concerned with things in ordinary time, the other with the affairs of eternity.[7] '*Saeculum*', and the adjective 'secular', came to be used in Latin Christendom as several related contrasts. As a description of time, it came to mean ordinary time, the time which is measured in ages, over against higher time, God's time, or eternity. It can also mean the condition of living in this ordinary time, which in some respects differs

---

[7] Charles Taylor, *A Secular Age* (Cambridge, MA, and London: The Belknap Press of Harvard University Press, 2007), 55.

Fig. 6.2 Monastic ways in relation with God's divine ways and ways of the world

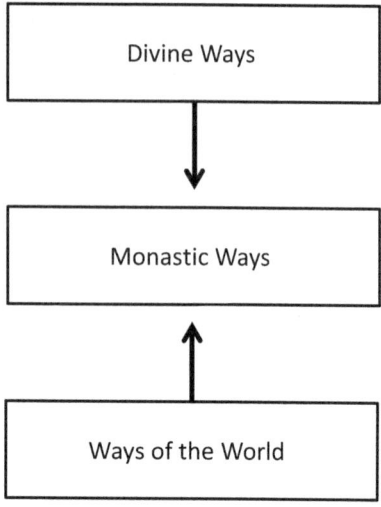

radically from those in eternity.[8] Or, by an extension, 'secular' can refer to the affairs of this world, 'temporal' affairs, and it contrasts with the affairs of the City of God, which are 'spiritual'. In general, clergy and monks belong to the 'spiritual' side, but there is an additional distinction between 'secular' and 'regular' clergy. The latter are monks, living separately from the 'world', under monastic rules; the former are parish clergy, ministering to their flocks, and so 'in the world'.[9]

Taylor further characterises secular time:

1. 'Secular' time is what to us is ordinary time, indeed, to us it's just time. One thing happens after another, and when something is past, it's past. Time placings are consistently transitive.[10]
2. As well as the 'horizontal' dimension of merely secular time, there is a 'vertical' dimension, also referred to as 'higher times' which gather and re-order secular time. An example of this would be seeing inconsistencies in profane time-ordering, for instance, the sacrifice of Isaac and the Crucifixion of Christ. These two events were linked through their immediate contiguous places in the divine plan. They

---

[8] Taylor, *A Secular Age*, 264–265.
[9] Taylor, *A Secular Age*, 265.
[10] Taylor, *A Secular Age*, 55.

are drawn close to identity in eternity, even though they are centuries apart. In God's time there is a sort of simultaneity of sacrifice and Crucifixion.[11] Unlike our ancestors, we tend to see our lives exclusively within the horizontal flow of secular time.[12]

3. As long as secular time is interwoven with various kinds of higher time, there is no guarantee that all events can be placed in unambiguous relations of simultaneity and succession. The high feast is in one way contemporaneous with my life and that of my fellow pilgrims, but in another way it is close to eternity, or the time of origins, or the events it prefigures.[13]

4. The dominance of instrumental rationality in our world, and the pervasiveness of secular time go together. So the 'buffered identity' of the disciplined individual moves in a constructed social space, where instrumental rationality is a key value, and time is pervasively secular. This is what Taylor calls 'the immanent frame'. This frame constitutes a 'natural' order, to be contrasted to a 'supernatural' one, an 'immanent' world, over against a possible 'transcendent' one.[14]

Hartmut Rosa, in a similar vein, suggests that in Christian life, the time of life and the time of the world are brought together in such a way that both aim towards the future end of the world in the final judgement. In contrast to the linear, quantitative profane time that belongs to the immanent world and everyday life, sacred time has a timeless, cyclical, qualitative character and belongs to another or higher world. With the help of sacred time, everyday time, the time of life, and the time of the world are bound together in a meaningful and congruent whole that orients culture and action.[15]

Therefore, positioned in the intersection between the horizontal (secular) and the vertical (higher) times and between the horizontal and the vertical journeys, enclosed contemplatives serve as intermediaries between the secular and the Divine. The monastics act as signposts from

[11] Taylor, *A Secular Age*, 55–57.
[12] Taylor, *A Secular Age*, 59.
[13] Taylor, *A Secular Age*, 209.
[14] Taylor, *A Secular Age*, 542.
[15] Hartmut Rosa, *Social Acceleration: A New Theory of Modernity* (New York, NY: Columbia University Press, 2013; trans. Jonathan Trejo-Mathys), 11.

the world to heaven, guiding those whose pilgrimage takes them through the secular ways.

A contemporary monastic perspective 'on the secular and the monastic' is expressed in the poem *In the Swing*. Here, a Carthusian monk realises that, having spent decades in the enclosure, he no longer is familiar with the famous names in sport and entertainment. He concludes:

> Enclosure circumscribes the glittering froth
> Of time, mankind's on-going story. I'm left
> With lighter baggage: God's holy presence, his love
> Radiating along my path, his call,
> "Sell the glittering froth and follow me!
> I walk in the rocky wilderness where beasts
> Roam and angels lend support, where death's
> The only event before me, a fearsome thought
> But God the Father could not withhold his grace."
> Simplicity! I am happier out of the swing…[16]

The poet-monk acknowledges monastic time in the enclosure has removed him from the 'glittering froth' of secular events and stories that continue to unfold. He does not mind. He is happier with the monastic path which has called him to follow Christ's earthly journey through the wilderness towards his death. The monk feels he travels with lighter baggage. God's holy presence and love radiate along his way. Like Christ, he trusts that God the Father would not withhold his grace at the moment of death. Therefore, monastic time is about simplicity and happiness. Monastic time is more about enjoying God's time and his presence and less about keeping up-to-date with current affairs and the 'glittering froth' of secular time.

This poem highlights how enclosure becomes a liminal place/space where God's vertical eternal time and horizontal temporal time can converge. By entering the monastery (place), one enters into monastic time which follows a rhythm and priorities that differ from secular priorities and preferences for the use of one's time. Further, by spending monastic time with God, temporal/eternal perspectives can lead to a convergence of times and assimilation of perspectives. Because God is eternal, as the religious spend time in a relationship with him, his temporality (or

---

[16] A Carthusian, '*In the Swing*', lines 7–16, an unpublished poem (2021).

atemporality) would likely have an influence and an impact on their perception of time as well.

This leads to the conclusion that, in some sense, monastic time is relative and relational time rather than linear and absolute.[17] Monastic time is relative because it belongs to God: time is not an independent factor. Monastic time is relational because it is lived in a relationship with the Divine. Relational and relative monastic time is derived from God's temporal and spatial omnipresence. This can be inferred from the paradoxical assumption that divine time is both temporal and eternal; it encompasses and contains two poles of time simultaneously. Therefore, on one hand, time matters because it is a gift of God: it is precious and full of meaning. On the other hand, there is a certain monastic detachment and indifference regarding time preferences. In the presence of God, all temporalities seem to converge.

The contemplatives live freely in a time that is not controlled by them but by God. Clocks can be used to denote daily schedules but, over longer periods, the linearity of time is simultaneously counterbalanced by the cyclicality of time. The human lifespan is associated with physical realities while at the same time the metaphysical salvific time runs its course towards eternity beyond pure physics. Monastic time, like God's eternity, therefore appears relative and dynamic rather than absolute and stale.

It could be argued that the monastic concept of time accommodates various temporalities but simultaneously goes beyond any human temporal terms with its perspective of eternity. In other words, rather than *being stuck in the past*, contemplative monastic orders are *living in the present time* while *anchored into eternity*. Here the difference between the horizontal and vertical becomes evident. In a similar way, it may be necessary for the active religious orders, with their more frequent and direct contacts with the contemporary secular world, to *keep up with times* while maintaining vertical access to *the eternal source* of their activity.

In summary, what was learned about monastic concepts of 'time' is:

---

[17] Cf. John Swinton in *Becoming Friends of Time: Disability, Timefullness and Gentle Discipleship*, (Waco, TX: Baylor University Press, 2017), 61, indeed argues that God's time is not linear in the way that we are used to understanding linearity. It rather contains linearity but is not defined or constrained by it. Swinton suggests that God's time is neither progressive nor static: 'Paradoxically, it is both. God's time mediates the fullness of God's kingdom in-the-now and yet contains within it the knowledge that the fullness of that kingdom is yet to come… God's time is uncontrollable; unmanageable; simultaneously past, present, transient, and in the future'.

1. Temporality itself is an enigma. It remains a mystery. Why did God create time? The monastic answer is: to have a relationship with humans who receive his loving-kindness, to share his perfect Being in the souls he created. The enclosed contemplative life is a way to respond to this mystery. A '*fiat*', a 'yes'.
2. In the hierarchy of priorities, time is subordinate to divine realities. Contemplative experience acknowledges that God is eternal and that in eternity only the present prevails. For the temporal human, the present has the capacity to create the instant in time and the place in space (in soul) for a momentary interaction with the Divine.
3. Time is relational. Temporality—the present—or atemporality (eternity) is valuable and valued only if it is lived in a relationship with God. Outside God, nothing else matters.
4. Time is relative. Time itself has no intrinsic value. God as the Creator alone determines the nature of time: whether it is temporal or atemporal (timeless), or both simultaneously. For him, a thousand years can be as one day.[18]
5. Time is creative. For every creature, time is received as a mouldable gift; material to transform creatively, for the greater glory of God. However, time also changes and transforms the religious. Time, therefore, has a dual and continuous creative function.
6. Time is dynamic. It is about growth, motion, movement, progress. Monastic time is filled and fulfilled by prayer and work in the omnipresence of God.
7. Time is temporary. It is transitory, a mirage, a dream. One day this temporal world will end. Temporality itself will end. What endures is charity and God's eternity.

[18] In Sarah, *The Power of Silence*, 215, Carthusian Dom Dysmas suggests that people lack the ability to imagine eternity: unending fullness granted through total communion with God. The worst sufferings experienced in this world will have an end which becomes evident 'when we have gone over to the side of the kingdom of God'. He concedes simply that God's time is different from ours: for him 'a thousand years [are] as one day'.

6.2   MONASTIC INSIGHTS AND CONTEMPORARY TRENDS

Looking—superficially—from outside in, enclosed contemplative life may appear grey and uneventful. No 'horizontal' travelling of the world but silent days lived in solitude. How does the world appear from inside the monastic walls, looking out to the secular world? The Carthusian poet-monk paints monastic life through colourful sceneries—Turner's expressive landscapes with vivid sunrises and sunsets, blazing of spectral light, rainbows—against the grey bleakness of secular life. In his poem *Colour Blind*, enclosed contemplatives feel compelled to enrich the hearths and complete the lives of people in the world, to show the vivid kaleidoscopic images that they see. They have been revealed insights and perspectives about life that the world would need to know. Yet, people in the world appear colour blind. They refuse to venture far from their homely darkness, capable of discerning only tints and shades of grey.

Colour Blind

By strange enabling we believe.
We see much more than sight reveals.
We see in colour, so to speak,
While others see but tints and shades.
This 'more' we must convey to them
Or live a lie to the truth. We must
Complete their lives, enrich their hearts.
Yet to express this 'colour' proves
Too much; people could never guess
Till shown: the rainbow is still grey
For them, its beauty has not flamed;
The sunset like a thunder storm
Sucked down the whirlpool of the West.
We speak that light splayed is hued
And men but smile. We self-exclude
Our lives from the stark grey world.
Our live's a blaze of spectral light.
Yet friends refuse to venture far
From homely things of grey. O cold,
Grey City, graveyard neat and clean!
May Turner's sun yet shine on you,
Spill its blood across your tombs,

Though men loved darkness more than light.[19]

It is a valid question to ask: what insights could Christian contemplative enclosed traditions provide for the perspective of contemporary secular life? Returning to the distinction between the secular and the monastic, three points emerge.

6.2.1   Mindfulness and Personal Relationship with Personal God

The recent rise in interest for purely secular 'mindfulness', if lacking a conscious reference to divinity or eternity, remains largely confined to the transitory world, or 'universe' as a general notion. This contrasts with the distinct 'personal relationship with personal God' aspect of Christian monasticism.

The idea of 'mindfulness', as an approach that focuses on the present moment, is indeed found in other religions and in secular meditative practices. As Gordon Bermant, an American scholar of Psychology, puts it: 'Old and new, East and West, religions celebrate the profound importance of the present moment. It is always in the present that one prays and calls out, and always in the present that one hears the response and call of the divine'.[20] This is noted also by Thomas Merton in the foreword of his translation of *Verba Seniorum* where he claims: 'In many respects... the Desert Fathers had much in common with Indian Yogis and with Zen Buddhist monks of India and Japan'.[21] There can be a certain inter-religious shared recognition of the spiritual dimension (acknowledging both things visible and invisible) as opposed to purely materialistic (things visible) approaches.

From the terminology perspective of this book, secular or God-less mindfulness practices propose to focus on the present moment within the

---

[19] A Carthusian, *Colour Blind* in Flames of Dust: poems 1964–1977, unpublished collection of poems.

[20] Gordon Bermant, 'Already but not Yet: Calling and Called in Religious Time' in David Yaden, Theo McCall, Harold Ellens, eds., *Being Called: Scientific, Secular and Sacred Perspectives* (Santa Barbara, CA: Praeger, 2015), 243–259: 251.

[21] See, for example, Thomas Merton, *The Wisdom of the Desert* (New York, NY: New Direction Publishing, 1970), 9. Peters in *The Story of Monasticism*, 29, suggests the possibility for indirect influences of Buddhism on Christian monasticism through Kerala region of India, although he names Jewish tradition as the most direct source of influence.

horizontal temporal axis while they exclude or ignore the intersecting vertical axis, the possibility of meeting with the Eternal, Personal God. This kind of mindfulness, which aims at arresting the restless movement between past—present—future (within the horizontal temporal sense of time), however, differs from the Trinitarian Christian approach that incorporates also the vertical axis which represents the relationship with the Eternal (Person) and the eternity (in the temporal sense). The concept of interpersonal connection is discussed, for example, by theologian Peter Tyler who, in his study of Teresa of Ávila, reflects on the relationship between mindfulness as understood in the Buddhist tradition and the process of contemplation in Teresa. He finds similarities in Teresa's 'deconstruction of self' and the Buddhist tradition of contemplation of self/non-self in mindfulness. Nevertheless, he argues that the two traditions differ notably in the importance given by Teresa to the personal 'Creative Deity' and in the importance of the role of desire as a *positive feature* in the search for the Beloved in the Spanish school, in Christianity.[22]

6.2.2   *Eschatological Hope and Time as a Gift of God*

The eschatological perspective that sets its sight towards the newness of the world to come seems to contrast with secular temporal views that cling to 'this-worldly', to what is 'tangible and visible'. A Carthusian's story about a woman standing at a wind-swept cliff top facing the sea instead displays a vision of detached freedom while the whole universe is breathlessly waiting at the edge of eternity:

> "I love it here," said Mamie, "on the edge of time. This moment is all there is, a kind of cliff top. The future is out there. To step into the next moment would be to step into non-existence. Our whole universe is here breathlessly awaiting the next second. Will it come? No one knows. What will it be like? No one knows. Will it bring pleasant things or disaster, fortune or misfortune? No one can be sure. We only guess. We assume nature's rhythm will continue; we assume the sun will rise again and the birds awake to sing; we assume the wheat will grow and be harvested; we assume friends will

---

[22] Peter Tyler, *Teresa of Avila: Doctor of the Soul.* (London: Bloomsbury Publishing, 2014), 201.

On comparison between Christian and Buddhist traditions regarding salvation and concept of time, see also Bermant, 'Already but not Yet: Calling and Called in Religious Time', 251–252.

return... But we control none of these: only our heart. And one day time will end: the cliff top will disappear. Oh living and true God, how vast you are! How incredible! You are bigger than past, present and future. And we, we hardly exist; we dangle on a silkworm strand. Our poverty is devastating. It is so great it makes us trust you... My littleness is what you love."[23]

In the face of a secular spatial-temporal perspective—that this is the only world there is and ever will be—the Carthusian text represents humble 'monastic realism' about the transitoriness of this world while clinging on to eternal God alone. This 'countercultural' humble monastic message means that life is accepted as a gift from God, the Creator. Life is precarious and precious, not a possession or a commodity. The monastic attitude to the gift of life is characterised by gratitude, not by a sense of entitlement. One's life from conception to death—and beyond—is simply left into the merciful hands of the Father. It is this hope and trust that will turn death into life.[24] Equally valuable monastic message to the busy modern world characterised by 'acceleration of time' is the realisation that 'all time belongs to God'.[25] As one freely gives up control and possession of one's 'own' time, one stops worrying about the pace or passage of time. This can turn the busy monastic *horarium* into a liberating freedom of 'being and becoming'. Time simply flows according to divine providence, *kairos*, and is therefore 'always right'. It can be argued that monastic death as a personal microcosmic event is characterised by the anticipation of meeting God and other lifetime friends in heaven. From this same

---

[23] A Carthusian, *The Dashing White Sergeant*, unpublished short story, 32–33.

[24] Cf. Taylor in *A Secular Age*, 725–726, argues that in Christian terms the locus of death, as the place where one has given everything, is the place of maximum union with God; and therefore, paradoxically, the source of most abundant life. This contrasts, in his view, with the modern secular perspective, where the locus of death takes on a new paradigm status. The Christian paradox drops away: death is no longer the source of life. But there is a new paradox: a renewed affirmation of transcendence, in the sense of a point to life beyond life. But at the same time, this is denied, because [in the secular paradigm] 'this point has absolutely no anchorage in the nature of reality'. To search for this point in reality is to encounter only *le Néant*, a void, a nothingness.

[25] Hartmut Rosa in *Social Acceleration* puts forward the theory of 'social acceleration', defined as changes of the tempo in modern social life, from the perspective of sociological-philosophical analysis. He arrives at the phrase 'frenetic standstill', characterised by the experience that 'on the one hand, the days and years seem to "fly" by, while on the other hand, looking back, we have the feeling that time literally slipped through our fingers', 307.

perspective, the apocalyptic eschatology, the end of times, would not cause fearsome anxiety; rather, it would be welcomed as an anticipated macro-cosmic moment when Christ will come in his glory to share endless time with his friends.

6.2.3   Attitude Towards Others

The third message, along the lines of 'what the world needs to hear', relates to the monastic experiences of communal life. Here, again, the phrase humble 'monastic realism' comes to mind. Happiness is found through humility. According to Evagrius Ponticus:

- Happy is the man who thinks himself no better than dirt.
- Happy is the monk who views the welfare and progress of all men with as much joy as if it were his own.[26]

With regard to our expectations and interaction with others, John Cassian (c.360–c.435) reminds us that much depends ultimately on our own conduct and attitude:

Do not hope to attain patience from the strength of others, meaning that you will achieve it only when no one irritates you – that can never happen, and is beyond your power – but rather from your own humility and perseverance, which does depend on your own will.[27]

Another monastic insight is one of self-knowledge and compassion.[28] It is said about the hermits of Scetis that 'their experience in conflict with themselves meant that they were able to help others along the way'.[29] This involves patient and painful transformation of self during the monastic

---

[26] Evagrius, The Praktikos & Chapters On Prayer, 75.

[27] Cassian, Institutes, Book 4, Ch. 42.

[28] Swinton in Becoming Friends of Time: Disability, Timefullness and Gentle Discipleship, 189–190, suggests that the idea of our identity being in Christ moves us beyond normal temporal logic and into a world of God's eternal simultaneity. We are alive in Christ but in a mysterious way, hidden from ourselves. Who we are is real and present but at the same time inaccessible to us. Only as we come to know Jesus do we learn to know ourselves. And even then the fullness of our selves will remain a mystery until the coming of God in glory.

[29] Sayings, 120.

journey, guided by God, in communion with others. John Chryssavgis writes about the compassion that the early ascetics learned in the 'school of the desert' amidst their own struggles through darkness; how the desert elders understood that 'they are not God' and knew that 'it is only through God that all things are possible'.[30] Therefore,

> In the struggle – in the very place where we meet God and are loved by God – we too discover how to love others… We understand that we are like others not primarily in our virtues and strengths, but especially in our faults and our flaws.[31]

Chryssavgis's modern expression, perhaps, underlines the timelessness of the desert dwellers' discovery:

> Their suggestion is not so much: "I'm OK and you're OK." On a much deeper level, it is their awareness and admission that "I'm not OK; and you are not OK." Yet, this recognition is also their reassurance; for they know that: "That's OK!"[32]

This reiterates the humble and realistic monastic message: not making oneself equal to God and not putting oneself above others. Enclosed contemplatives do not want to be put on a pedestal. They recognise their sinfulness and our shared weak human condition all too well. In comparison with the secular culture that appears increasingly preoccupied with hypocritical self-justification and indiscriminate judging of others, the monastic humble realism indeed seems to strike a countercultural contrast.

6.3   The Final Word

This book of enclosed contemplative journeys is a 'paradox of verbosity' itself. What sense does it make to write hundreds of pages about enclosed contemplative life, which is characterised by simplicity and silence? Let us leave the final word on this to 'Mel', a contemporary cloistered contemplative:

---

[30] John Chryssavgis, *In the Heart of the Desert: The Spirituality of the Desert Fathers and Mothers* (Bloomington, IN: World Wisdom, 2008), 105.
[31] Chryssavgis, *In the Heart of the Desert*, 106.
[32] Chryssavgis, *In the Heart of the Desert*, 106.

Sometimes no matter how many pages and words are written, it is almost impossible to encapsulate the eternal. Volumes upon volumes of books, treatises, essays, etc. have been written century after century not only on the topic of contemplative prayer and contemplative life, but upon the truths of the Faith and on God Himself. And still the world has not even begun to fathom the reality as it is! How can one explain the Infinite Being who is beyond all our imagining? That is why St. Thomas Aquinas, after he completed a good portion of his works said to burn everything, because after all the volumes of the Summa he wrote, it was just like a grain of sand compared to the Truth of things. He thought it was a big lie, since all those words did not even come close to explain the Truth as it really is.[33] We are not surprised then, that you feel so "powerless to express in human language all the beautiful material..." and that you keep on writing and still do not feel satisfied. And to be honest, you probably never will! These holy topics are too sublime for the human mind to comprehend and exhaust completely. Nevertheless, as many writers before you, they have at least tried to write on these subjects with the hope that one day someone will benefit from the holy words they try to express. And that is all we can do with our limited mind and understanding, leaving the rest to grace and the power of the Holy Spirit to inspire, to lift up, to bring closer to Himself. We will have all eternity to contemplate Truth, and even then, eternity will not be long enough for us to do so![34]

[33] 'Mel' possibly refers here to the reply of Thomas of Aquinas to his confessor on why he had abruptly ceased writing and dictating his *Summa Theologiae*: 'Everything that I have written seems to me chaffy in respect to those things that I have seen and have been revealed to me'. See, for example, Marjorie O'Rourke Boyle, 'Chaff: Thomas Aquinas's Repudiation of His Opera Omnia' in *New Literary History*, Spring, 1997, Vol. 28, No. 2, Medieval Studies, 383–399: 383. O'Rourke Boyle suggests that the metaphor of Aquinas hanging up his pens alluded to the exiled psalmist hanging up his lyre (Ps. 137:1–6), as if Aquinas were also estranged in a foreign land, his hand withered and his tongue stuck to the roof of his mouth (vv. 5–6), 393.

[34] Email from 'Mel', a cloistered contemplative on 27/04/2019.

Bibliography

Primary Sources

Arborelius, A. (2020). *Carmelite Spirituality: The Way of Carmelite Prayer and Contemplation*. EWTN Publishing.

Athanasius. (2014). *Life of Anthony*. Beloved Publishing.

Augustine. (1975). *Confessions* (R. S. Pine-Coffin, Trans.). Penguin Books.

Bernard of Clairvaux. (2005). *Selected Works* (E. Griffin, Ed., & G. R. Evans, Trans.). HarperCollins.

Bonaventure. (1978). *The Soul's Journey Into God* (E. Cousins, Trans.). SPCK.

Carthusian. (1993). *The Way of Silent Love: Carthusian Novice Conferences*. Darton, Longman and Todd.

Carthusian. (1994). *The Wound of Love*. Darton, Longman and Todd.

Carthusian. (1995). *The Call of Silent Love* (Anglican solitary, Trans.). Darton, Longman and Todd.

Carthusian. (1996). *Interior Prayer: Carthusian Novice Conferences*. Darton, Longman and Todd Ltd.

Carthusian. (1997). *Where Silence is Praise* (A Monk of Parkminster, Trans.).

Carthusian. (2000). *The Spirit of Place: Carthusian Reflections*. Darton, Longman and Todd.

Carthusian. (2001). *"O Bonitas!" Hushed to Silence* (R. B. Lockhart, Ed.). Gracewing.

Carthusian. (2006). *They Speak by Silences* (Monk of Parkminster, Trans.). Gracewing Publishing.

Carthusian. (2009). *In Praise of Silence: Poems and Images*. St Hugh's Press.

© The Author(s), under exclusive license to Springer Nature
Switzerland AG 2023
R. Hujanen, *Monastic Perspectives on Temporality*,
https://doi.org/10.1007/978-3-031-34808-2

Cassian, J. (1999). *The Monastic Institutes* (J. Bertram, Trans.). The Saint Austin Press.

Cassian, J. (2016). *Conferences*. First Rate Publishers.

Climacus, J. (1982). *The Ladder of Divine Ascent* (C. Luibheid, & N. Russell, Trans.). Paulist Press.

Colombas, G. M. (1961). *Paradis et Vie Angélique: Le Sens Eschatologique de la Vocation Chrétienne* (S. Caron, Trans.). Les Editions du CERF.

Daniel, W. (1993). The Life of Aelred. In P. Matarasso (Ed.), *The Cistercian World: Monastic Writings of the Twelfth Century* (P. Matarasso, Trans., pp. 152–168). Penguin Books.

de Cusa, N. (2007). *The Vision of God* (E. G. Salter, Trans.). Cosimo Classics.

de Vogüé, A. (1998). *To Desire Eternal Life: Hope Yesterday and Today* (J. B. Hasbrouck, Trans.). Saint Bede's Publications.

Evagrius Ponticus. (1972). *The Praktikos & Chapters on Prayer* (J. E. Bamberger, Trans.). Cistercian Publications.

Foster, D. (2015). *Contemplative Prayer: A New Framework*. Bloomsbury.

Freeman, B. (2010). *Come and See: The Monastic Way of Today*. Liturgical Press.

Gregory of Nyssa. (2006). *The Life of Moses* (A. J. Malherbe, & E. Ferguson, Trans.). HarperCollins Publishers.

Guigo I. (1997). In R. B. Lockhart (Ed.), *Listening to Silence: An Anthology of Carthusian Writings*. Darton, Longman and Todd.

Guigo II. (1997). In R. B. Lockhart (Ed.), *Listening to Silence: An Anthology of Carthusian Writings*. Darton, Longman and Todd.

Hilaire d'Arles. (1995). Sermon sur la Vie de Saint Honorat. In M. Labrousse, S. Honorat (M. Labrousse, Trans., pp. 101–140). Bégrolles-en-Mauges: Abbaye de Bellefontaine.

Hilton, W. (1901). *The Scale (or Ladder) of Perfection*. Great Britain.

Houdret, J.-P. (2000, December). Le temps et l'éternité. Carmel: Au seuil de l'éternité: Le temps et la vie spirituelle. *98*, 7–14.

John of the Cross. (reprint of 1889). *A Spiritual Canticle of the Soul and the Bridegroom Christ* (D. Lewis, Trans.). Great Britain.

John of the Cross. (2003). *Dark Night of the Soul* (E. A. Peers, Trans.). Dover Publications.

John of the Cross. (2010). *Ascent of Mount Carmel* (E. A. Peers, Trans.). Bottom of the Hill Publishing.

Kempis, T. (2003). *The Imitation of Christ* (A. Croft, & H. Bolton, Trans.). Dover Publications.

Kinga de la Transfiguration. (2017). Je ne me suis pas dérobée...: Journal. (Carmelites of Magyarszék, Trans.). Éditions du Carmel.

Kline, F. (2012). *Lovers of the Place: Monasticism Loose in the Church*. Liturgical Press.

Lawrence of the Resurrection. (2005). *The Practice of the Presence of God and the Spiritual Maxims*. Dover Publications.

Le Masson, I. (1997). *Listen to Silence: An Anthology of Carthusian Writings* (R. B. Lockhart, Ed.). Darton, Longman and Todd.

Louf, A. (1989). *The Cistercian Way* (N. Kinsella, Trans.) Cistercian Publications.

Louf, A. (2015). *In the School of Contemplation* (P. Rowe, Trans.) Liturgical Press.

Malone, M. (2014). *Living in the House of God: Monastic Essays*. Liturgical Press.

McGinn, B. (Ed.). (2006). *The Essential Writings of Christian Mysticism*. Modern Library.

Merton, T. (1951). *The Ascent to Truth*. Hollis & Carter.

Merton, T. (1961). *The Sign of Jonas*. Burns & Oates.

Merton, T. (1970). *The Wisdom of the Desert*. New Directions Publishing.

Merton, T. (1977). *The Monastic Journey* (P. Hart, Ed.). Sheldon Press.

Merton, T. (1999). *The Intimate Merton* (P. Hart, & J. Montaldo, Ed.). Lion Publishing.

Merton, T. (2005). *Contemplative Prayer*. Darton, Longman and Todd.

Merton, T. (2005). *The Pocket of Thomas Merton* (R. Inchausti, Ed.). New Seeds.

Merton, T. (2015). *The Seven Storey Mountain*. SPCK.

Miquel, P. (1986). *La voie monastique*. Abbaye de Bellefontaine.

Miquel, P. (1986). *Lexique du désert*. Abbaye de Bellefontaine.

Molinier, N. (1995). *Ascèse, contemplation et ministère*. Abbaye de Bellefontaine.

Monastère Demeure Notre Père. (1984). *Livre de vie monastique: Chemin d'Évangile*. Editions Saint-Paul.

Mother Thekla. (1997). *Eternity Now: An Introduction to Orthodox Spirituality*. Canterbury Press.

Nault, J.-C. (2015). *The Noonday Devil: Acedia, the Unnamed Evil of Our Times*. Ignatius Press.

Obbard, E. R. (1997). *To Live is to Pray: An Introduction to Carmelite Spirituality*. The Canterbury Press Norwich.

Ogliari, D. (2008). Tempus Monasticum: Reflections on the Architecture of Time in the Rule of Saint Benedict. *American Benedictine Review, 59*(1), 35–52.

Pachomius. (2014). *The Rules of Pachomius*. (G. H. Schodde, Trans.). Aeterna Press.

Palladius. (2014). *The Lausiac History* (W. L. Clarke, Trans.). Aeterna Press.

Philo of Alexandria. (1981). *The Contemplative Life, Giants and Selections* (D. Winston, Trans.). Paulist Press.

Piccardo, C. (2014). *Living Wisdom: The Mission and Transmission of Monasticism* (E. Varden, Trans.). Cistercian Publications.

Pseudo-Dionysius. (1987). *The Complete Works* (C. Luibheid, Trans.). Paulist Press.

Rafael de Pascual, F. (2015). "El hábito no hace al monje": formas y simbolismos de los hábitos monásticos. In J. Á. García de Cortázar & R. Teja (Eds.), *El ritmo cotidiano de la vida en el monasterio medieval* (pp. 11–31). Fundación Santa María la Real, Centro de Estudios del Románico.

Rivière, L. (2018). *Un temps supérieur à l'espace: La vie cloîtrée selon Thérèse d'Avila*. Éditions du Carmel.

Stinissen, W. (2013). *L'Éternité au cœur du temps* (M.-N. Talle, Trans.). Éditions du Carmel.

Teresa of Ávila. (1853). *Book of the Foundations* (J. Dalton, Trans.). T. Jones.

Teresa of Ávila. (2008). *Interior Castle* (E. A. Peers, Trans.). Dover Publications.

Teresa of Ávila. (2012). *The Way of Perfection* (E. A. Peers, Trans.). Dover Publications.

The Cloud of Unknowing and Other Works. (2001). (A. C. Spearing, Trans.). Penguin Books.

The Desert Fathers: Sayings of the Early Christian Monks. (2003). (B. Ward, Trans.). Penguin Books.

The Lives of the Desert Fathers: The Historia Monachorum in Aegypto. (1980). (N. Russell, Trans.). Cistercian Publications.

The Rule of St. Benedict in English. (1982). (T. Fry, Trans.). The Liturgical Press.

Thérèse of Lisieux. (1982). *Letters: General Correspondence 1877–1890* (J. Clarke, Trans.). ICS Publications.

Thérèse of Lisieux. (1997). *The Prayers of Saint Thérèse of Lisieux: The Act of Oblation* (A. Kane, Trans.). ICS Publications.

Thérèse of Lisieux. (2016). *Story of a Soul: The Autobiography* (J. Clarke, Trans.). ICS Publications.

Welch, J. (1996). *The Carmelite Way: An Ancient Path for Today's Pilgrim.* Paulist Press.

William of Saint-Thierry. (1993). Three Meditations. In P. Matarasso (Ed.), *The Cistercian World: Monastic Writings of the Twelfth Century* (P. Matarasso, Trans., pp. 110–124). Penguin Books.

SECONDARY SOURCES

Alighieri, D. (2009). *The Divine Comedy* (H. F. Cary, Trans.). Wordsworth Editions.

Allende, I. (2003). *Retrato en sepia.* Plaza & Janés Editores.

Amulf, I., Brion, A., Pottier, M., & Golmard, J.-L. (2011). Ring the Bell for Matins: Circadian Adaptation to Split Sleep by Cloistered Monks and Nuns. *Chronobiology International, 28*(10), 930–941.

Andrews, F. (2015). *The Other Friars: Carmelite, Augustinian, Sack and Pied Friars in the Middle Ages.* The Boydell Press.

Annuario Pontificio 2015: Pontifical Yearbook 2015 Catholic Church Directory. (2015). Vatican City: Libreria Editrice Vaticana.

Batson, C. D., Schoenrade, P., & Ventis, W. L. (1993). *Religion and the Individual. A Social-Psychological Perspective.* Oxford University Press.

Bermant, G. (2015). Already but Not Yet: Calling and Called in Religious Time. In D. B. Yaden, T. D. McCall, & J. H. Ellens (Eds.), *Being Called: Scientific, Secular, and Sacred Perspectives* (pp. 243–259). Praeger.

Bernstein, M. (1976). *Nuns*. Collins.

Binns, J. (1996). *Ascetics and Ambassadors of Christ: The Monasteries of Palestine* (pp. 314–631). Oxford University Press.

Brakke, D. (2006). *Demons and the Making of the Monk: Spiritual Combat in Early Christianity*. Harvard University Press.

Brotherton, J. R. (2017). Hope and Hell in Balthasar. *The Thomist, 81*(1), 75–105.

Burton, J., & Kerr, J. (2011). *The Cistercians in the Middle Ages*. The Boydell Press.

Canales, J. (2015). *The Physicist & the Philosopher: Einstein, Bergson, and the Debate that Changed Our Understanding of Time*. Princeton University Press.

Caner, D. (2002). *Wandering, Begging Monks: Spiritual Authority and the Promotion of Monasticism in Late Antiquity*. University of California Press.

Catechism of the Catholic Church. (1995). Doubleday.

Chadwick, H. (1993). *The Early Church* (revised ed.). Penguin Books.

Chadwick, H. (2010). *Augustine of Hippo: A Life*. Oxford University Press.

Chryssavgis, J. (2008). *In the Heart of the Desert: The Spirituality of the Desert Fathers and Mothers*. World Wisdom.

Clark, J. G. (2011). *The Benedictines in the Middle Ages*. The Boydell Press.

Clarke, K. M. (2019). Moses's Dark Cloud, Teresa's Dark Night, and the Soul's Entrance Into the Divine Presence. *Logos, 22*(1), 131–146.

Congregation for Institutes of Consecrated Life and Societies of Apostolic Life. (1999). *Verbi Sponsa: Instruction on the Contemplative Life and on the Enclosure of Nuns*. Libreria Editrice Vaticana.

Cottingham, J. (2005). *The Spiritual Dimension: Religion, Philosophy and Human Value*. Cambridge University Press.

Craig, W. L. (2002). The Elimination of Absolute Time by the Special Theory of Relativity. In G. E. Ganssle & D. M. Woodruff (Eds.), *God and Time: Essays on the Divine Nature* (pp. 129–152). Oxford University Press.

Cunningham, L. S. (1999). *Thomas Merton and the Monastic Vision*. William B. Eerdmans Publishing Company.

Cunningham, L. S., & Egan, K. J. (1996). *Christian Spirituality: Themes from the Tradition*. Paulist Press.

Davis, C. B. (2008). *Mysticism and Space: Space and Spatiality in the Works of Richard Rolle, The Cloud of Unknowing Author, and Julian of Norwich*. The Catholic University of America Press.

de Dreuille, M. (1999). *From East to West: A History of Monasticism*. Gracewing.

de Vogüé, A. (1998). *Le monachisme en occident avant saint Benoît*. Abbaye de Bellefontaine.

de Vogüé, A. (2014). *A Critical Study of the Rule of Benedict* (C. M. McGrane, Trans., Vol. 2). New City Press.

de Waal, E. (1998). *The Way of Simplicity: The Cistercian Tradition*. Darton, Longman and Todd.

Diat, N. (2019). *A Time to Die: Monks on the Threshold of Eternal Life* (D. le Merrer, Trans.). Ignatius Press.

Downey, M. (1997). *Trappist: Living in the Land of Desire*. Paulist Press.

Downey, M. (1997). *Understanding Christian Spirituality*. Paulist Press.

Duarte Rodrigues, A. (2015). Beyond contemplation, the real functions held at the cloisters. In A. Duarte Rodrigues (Ed.), *Cloister Gardens, Courtyards and Monastic Enclosures* (pp. 13–35). Centro de História da Arte e Investigação Artística da Universidade de Évora and Centro Interuniversitário de História das Ciências e da Tecnologia.

Dunn, M. (2007). *The Emergence of Monasticism: From the Desert Fathers to the Early Middle Ages*. Blackwell Publishing.

Durand, E. (2014). Prayer and Providence. *The Thomist, 78*(4), 519–536.

Durà-Vilà, G., Dein, S., Littlewood, R., & Leavey, G. (2010). The Dark Night of the Soul: Causes and Resolution of Emotional Distress Among Contemplative Nuns. *Transcultural Psychiatry, 47*(4), 548–570.

Durà-Vilà, G., & Leavey, G. (2017). Solitude Among Contemplative Cloistered Nuns and Monks: Conceptualisation, Coping and Benefits of Spiritually Motivated Solitude. *Mental Health, Religion & Culture, 20*(1), 45–60.

Eire, C. (2010). *A Very Brief History of Eternity*. Princeton University Press.

Eliade, M. (1987). *The Sacred and the Profane: The Nature of Religion* (W. R. Trask, Trans.). Harcourt.

Emelu, M. N. (2017). *Our Journey to God*. EWTN Publishing.

Fermor, P. L. (2004). *A Time to Keep Silence*. John Murray (Publishers).

Foulcher, J. (2015). *Reclaiming Humility: Four Studies in the Monastic Tradition*. Liturgical Press.

Frend, W. (1986). *The Rise of Christianity*. Darton, Longman & Todd Ltd.

Ganssle, G. E., & Woodruff, D. M. (Eds.). (2002). *God and Time: Essays on the Divine Nature*. Oxford University Press.

Golitzin, A. (2011). A Monastic Setting for the Syriac Apocalypse of Daniel. In R. Darling Young & M. J. Blanchard (Eds.), *To Train His Soul in Books: Syriac Asceticism in Early Christianity* (pp. 66–98). The Catholic University of America Press.

Gordon, J. R. (2018). Rethinking Divine Spatiality in Philosophical and Theological Perspective. *The Heythrop Journal, 59*(3), 534–543.

Görg, P. H. (2011). *The Desert Fathers: Saint Anthony and the Beginnings of Monasticism* (M. J. Miller, Trans.). Ignatius Press.

Gothóni, R. (1991). *Pilgrimage = Transformation Journey. The Problem of Ritual* (pp. 101–115). Symposium on Religious Rites.

Groeschel, B. J. (1983). *Spiritual Passages: The Psychology of Spiritual Development*. Crossroad.

Harmless, W. (2004). *Desert Christians: An Introduction to the Literature of Early Monasticism*. Oxford University Press.

Harmless, W. (2008). *Mystics*. Oxford University Press.

Hausherr, I. (1982). *Penthos: The Doctrine of Compunction in the Christian East* (A. Hufstader, Trans.). Cistercian Publications.

Heale, M. (2009). *Monasticism in Late Medieval England, c. 1300–1535*. Manchester University Press.

Holmes, A. (2000). *A Life Pleasing to God: The Spirituality of the Rules of St Basil*. Cistercian Publications.

Hood, R. W., Jr., Spilka, B., Hunsberger, B., & Gorsuch, R. (1996). *The Psychology of Religion: An Empirical Approach* (2nd ed.). The Guildford Press.

Howells, E. (2013). Understanding Augustine's On the Trinity as a Mystical Work. In L. Nelstrop & S. D. Podmore (Eds.), *Christian Mysticism and Incarnational Theology: Between Transcendence and Immanence* (pp. 155–164). Ashgate Publishing.

Huizing, R. L. (2013). *Benedictine Times: The Flow of Life in the Holy Rule: The Downside Review* (pp. 171–183).

Jamroziak, E. (2013). *The Cistercian Order in Medieval Europe 1090–1500*. Routledge.

John Paul II (1994). *Tertio millennio adveniente*. Libreria Editrice Vaticana.

Johnson, M., Wittberg, P., & Gautier, M. L. (2014). *New Generations of Catholic Sisters: The Challenge of Diversity*. Oxford University Press.

Kenney, J. P. (2013). *Contemplation and Classical Christianity: A Study in Augustine*. Oxford University Press.

Kerr, J. (2009). *Life in the Medieval Cloister*. Continuum.

King, P. (1999). *Western Monasticism: A History of the Monastic Movement in the Latin Church*. Cistercian Publications.

Knuuttila, S. (2006). Time and Creation in Augustine. In E. Stump & N. Kretzmann (Eds.), *The Cambridge Companion to Augustine* (pp. 103–115). Cambridge University Press.

Korpela, S. (2022). *God, Time, and the Concept of Potentiality in Quantum Physics*. Unigrafia.

Labrousse, M. (1995). *Saint Honorat*. Abbaye de Bellefontaine.

Lawrence, C. H. (2015). *Medieval Monasticism: Forms of religious life in Western Europe in the Middle Ages* (4th ed.). Routledge.

Layton, B. (2016). *The Canons of Our Fathers: Monastic Rules of Shenoute*. Oxford University Press.

Lekai, L. J. (1953). *The White Monks: A History of the Cistercian Order*. Monastery of Our Lady of Spring Bank.

Levoy, G. (2015). Sacrifice: The Shadow in the Calling. In D. B. Yaden, T. D. McCall, & J. H. Ellens (Eds.), *Being Called: Scientific, Secular, and Sacred Perspectives* (pp. 215–224). Praeger.

Lockhart, R. B. (1985). *Halfway to Heaven: The Hidden Life of the Sublime Carthusians*. Thames Methuen.

Lockhart, R. B. (1997). *Listening to Silence: An Anthology of Carthusian Writings*. Darton, Longman and Todd Ltd.

Loudon, M. (1992). *Unveiled: Nuns Talking*. Chatto & Windus.

Louth, A. (1981). *The Origins of the Christian Mystical Tradition: From Plato to Denys*. Oxford University Press.

MacCulloch, D. (2010). *A History of Christianity: The First Three Thousand Years*. Penguin Books.

MacCulloch, D. (2014). *Silence: A Christian History*. Penguin Books.

MacDonald, S. (2006). The Divine Nature. In E. Stump & N. Kretzmann (Eds.), *The Cambridge Companion to Augustine* (pp. 71–90). Cambridge University Press.

Maguire, N. K. (2006). *An Infinity of Little Hours: Five Young Men and their Trial of Faith in the Western World's Most Austere Monastic Order*. PublicAffairs.

Maksjan, A. (2007). *The Mystical Dimension of the Poetry of John Bradburne and the Carthusian*. Institut für Anglistik und Amerikanistik, Universität Salzburg.

Maloney, G. A. (1978). *La spiritualité de Nil Sorskij: L'hésychasme russe*. Abbaye de Bellefontaine.

Matteo, S. (2014). *Horizontal and Vertical Journeys in the Italian Imagination: Marco Polo and Garibaldi versus Dante and Victor Emanuel II*. MLN 129 Supplement, Johns Hopkins University Press, SS7-S20.

McCall, T. D. (2015). Hope and Eternity: God as Transcendent Presence in the Ordinary. In D. B. Yaden, T. D. McCall, & J. H. Ellens (Eds.), *Being Called: Scientific, Secular, and Sacred Perspectives* (pp. 193–202). Praeger.

McDannell, C., & Lang, B. (2001). *Heaven: A History* (2nd ed.). Yale University Press.

McGinn, B. (2006). In B. McGinn (Ed.), *The Essential Writings of Christian Mysticism*. Modern Library.

Michel, C.-M. (2017). *Le Ciel sur la Terre: Élisabeth de la Trinité et la spiritualité sacerdotale*. Éditions du Carmel.

Miller, C. L. (2013). Seeing and Being Seen in Nicholas Cusa's The Vision of God (1453). *The Downside Review, 131*(464), 147–155.

Mullins, R. T. (2016). *The End of the Timeless God*. Oxford University Press.

Nouwen, H. J. (1976). *The Genesee Diary: Report from a Trappist Monastery*. Darton, Longman and Todd Ltd.

O'Rourke Boyle, M. (1997). Chaff: Thomas Aquinas's Repudiation of His Opera Omnia. *New Literary History, 28*(2 Medieval Studies), 383–399.

Ouspensky, L. (1996). Icon and Art. In B. McGinn, J. Meyendorff, & J. Leclercq (Eds.), *Christian Spirituality: Origins to the Twelfth Century* (pp. 382–394). SCM Press.

Peat, A. (2003). Modern Pilgrimage and the Authority of Space in Forster's Room with a View and Woolf's The Voyage Out. *Mosaic: A Journal for the Interdisciplinary Study of Literature*, 139–153.

Peeters, T. (2015). *When Silence Speaks: The Spiritual Way of the Carthusian Order.* Darton, Longman and Todd.

Peters, G. (2015). *The Story of Monasticism: Retrieving an Ancient Tradition for Contemporary Spirituality.* Baker Academic.

Pilch, J. (2000). *Healing in the New Testament: Insights from Medical and Mediterranean Anthropology.* Fortress Press.

Podmore, S. D. (2013). Mysterium Horrendum: Mystical Theology and the Negative Numinous. In L. Nelstrop & S. D. Podmore (Eds.), *Exploring Lost Dimensions in Christian Mysticism: Opening to the Mystical* (pp. 93–116). Ashgate Publishing.

Polkinghorne, J. (2005). *Exploring Reality: The Intertwining of Science and Religion.* SPCK.

Priest. (2017). *Report from Calabria: A Season with the Carthusian Monks.* Ignatius.

Ratzinger, J. (2013). *Jeesuksen viimeiset päivät (Jesus von Nazareth: Zweiter Teil: Vom Einzug in Jerusalem bis zur Auferstehung)* (J. Kiilunen, Trans.). Perussanoma.

Ritari, K. (2010). "Pilgrims in the World": Monastic Life as a Quest for Heaven in Early Medieval Ireland. In R. Hämäläinen, H. Pesonen, M. Rahkala, & T. Sakaranaho (Eds.), *Pilgrimage of Life: studies in honour of Professor René Gothóni* (pp. 336–345). Finnish Society of Sciences and Letters, Study of Religions, University of Helsinki, Maahenki.

Ritari, K. (2011). Holy Souls and a Holy Community: The Meaning of Monastic Life in Adomnán's Vita Columbae. *Journal of Medieval Religious Cultures, 37*(2), 129–146.

Ritari, K. (2015). Librán as Monastic Archetype. In J. Carey, K. Murray, & C. Ó. Dochartaigh (Eds.), *Sacred Histories: A Festschrift for Máire Herbert.* Four Courts Press.

Ritari, K. (2016). *Pilgrimage to Heaven: Eschatology and Monastic Spirituality in Early Medieval Ireland.* Brepols Publishers.

Rosa, H. (2013). *Social Acceleration: A New Theory of Modernity* (J. Trejo-Mathys, Trans.). Columbia University Press.

Rousseau, P. (1999). *Pachomius: The Making of a Community in Fourth-Century Egypt.* University of California Press.

Rowe, E., & Neyrey, J. (2010). Christ and Time - Part Three: "Telling Time" in the Fourth Gospel. *Biblical Theology Bulletin, 40*(2), 79–92.

Rubenson, S. (1998). Christian Asceticism and the Emergence of the Monastic Tradition. In V. Wimbush & R. Valantasis (Eds.), *Asceticism* (pp. 49–57). Oxford University Press.

Rubenson, S. (2012). Monasticism and the Philosophical Heritage. In S. F. Johnson (Ed.), *The Oxford Handbook of Late Antiquity* (pp. 487–512). Oxford University Press.

Salenson, C. (2016). *L'échelle mystique du dialogue de Christian Chergé*. Bayard éditions.

Sarah, R. (2017). *The Power of Silence: Against the Dictatorship of Noise* (M. J. Miller, Trans.). Ignatius.

Sbalchiero, P. (2008). *Histoire de la vie monastique*. Desclée de Brouwer.

Schneiders, S. M. (2000). *Finding the Treasure: Locating Catholic Religious Life in a New Ecclesial and Cultural Context*. Paulist Press.

Schneiders, S. M. (2001). *Selling All: Commitment, Consecrated Celibacy, and Community in Catholic Religious Life*. Paulist Press.

Schnell, T., & Pali, S. (2013, December). Pilgrimage today: the meaning-making potential of ritual. *Mental Health, Religion & Culture*, 887–902.

Sheldrake, P. (1995). *Spirituality and History: Questions of Interpretation and Method* (Revised ed.). SPCK.

Skinner, J. (1985). *Hear Our Silence: A Portrait of the Carthusians*. HarperCollins Publishers.

Swinton, J. (2017). *Becoming Friends of Time: Disability, Timefullness and Gentle Discipleship*. Baylor University Press.

Taylor, C. (2007). *A Secular Age*. The Belknap Press of Harvard University Press.

Thomassen, B. (2018). *Liminality and the Modern: Living Through the In-Between*. Routledge.

Turner, D. (1999). *The Darkness of God: Negativity in Christian Mysticism*. Cambridge University Press.

Turner, V., & Turner, E. (2011). *Image and Pilgrimage in Christian Culture*. Columbia University Press.

Tyler, P. (2014). *Teresa of Avila: Doctor of the Soul*. Bloomsbury Publishing.

Underhill, E. (1930). *Mysticism: A Study in Nature and Development of Spiritual Consciousness* (12th Revised ed.).

van Nieuwenhove, R. (2017). Aquinas on Active and Contemplative Lives. *The Thomist, 80*(1), 1–30.

Vild, M. (2013). The Aramaic maranatha in 1 Cor 16:22. Translation Queries and Their Theological Implications. *Text și Discurs Religios, 5*, 97–108.

Ware, K. (1996). Ways of Prayer and Contemplation: Eastern. In B. McGinn, J. Meyendorff, & J. Leclercq (Eds.), *Christian Spirituality: Origins to the Twelfth Century* (pp. 395–414). SCM Press.

Ware, K. (1998). The Way of the Ascetics: Negative or Affirmative? In V. L. Winbush & R. Valantasis (Eds.), *Asceticism* (pp. 3–15). Oxford University Press.

Webb, D. (2002). *Medieval European Pilgrimage, c. 700–c. 1500*. Palgrave.

Wittberg, P. (1994). *The Rise and Fall of Catholic Religious Orders: A Social Movement Perspective*. State University of New York Press.

Woolley, A. (2019). *Women Choosing Silence: Relationality and Transformation in Spiritual Practice*. Routledge.

Yates, S. (2019). Does the New Testament Teach Resurrection in Death? In A. B. Morris (Ed.), *Aspects of Doctoral Research at the Maryvale International Catholic Institute (Volume One)* (pp. 16–49). Cambridge Scholars Publishing.

MOTION PICTURES

Gröning, P. (Director). (2005). *Into Great Silence* [Motion Picture].
Ordre de Chartreux. (2018). *Une vie en Chartreuse* [Motion Picture].
The Salt River Production Group. (Producer). The CatholicTV Network. (2018). *Hidden: A Life All for God*. Retrieved June 27, 2020, from https://www.youtube.com/watch?v=Ntt98rTky-g

WEBLIOGRAPHY

Aquinas, T. (n.d.). (Trans. Fathers of the English Dominican Province). *The Summa Theologica*. Retrieved from Documenta Catholica Omnia: http://www.documentacatholicaomnia.eu/03d/1225-1274,_Thomas_Aquinas,_Summa_Theologiae_%5B1%5D,_EN.pdf
Carthusian. (1928). *A Carthusian Speaks.*. Retrieved July 20, 2019, from The Carthusian Order: http://transfiguration.chartreux.org/
Carthusian. (1962). *The Blessed Trinity and the Supernatural Life*. Retrieved July 20, 2019, from The Carthusian Order: http://transfiguration.chartreux.org/
Carthusian Statutes. Retrieved December 14, 2021, from The Carthusian Order: http://transfiguration.chartreux.org/statuts-en-1.htm
Curia Generalizia dei Carmelitani. *Carmelite Charism*. Retrieved October 31, 2020, from http://ocarm.org/en/content/ocarm/charism
Douai Abbey. *Guesthouse*. Retrieved April 27, 2021, from Douai Abbey: https://douaiabbey.org.uk/guesthouse.php
John Paul II. (1996). *Post-Synodal Apostolic Exhortation Vita Consecrata*. Retrieved December 14, 2021, from https://www.vatican.va/roman_curia/congregations/ccscrlife/documents/hf_jp-ii_exh_25031996_vita-consecrata_en.html
Missionaries of Charity: Mother Teresa Center. *Missionaries of Charity*. Retrieved October 31, 2020., from https://www.motherteresa.org/missionaries-of-charity.html
Monastère de la Grande Chartreuse. *Carthusian Houses: Transfiguration*. Retrieved October 31, 2020., from http://www.chartreux.org/en/houses/transfiguration/cart-2.pdf
Parkminster Carthusian Monastery. (2021). Retrieved December 18, 2021, from Journey https://www.parkminster.org.uk/journey

Sisters of Carmel. *Carmelite Order History.* Retrieved June 26, 2020, from Sisters of Carmel: https://sistersofcarmel.org/carmelite-order-history

The British Province of Carmelites. *Carmelite Family: Sisters.* Retrieved November 3, 2020., from http://www.carmelite.org/family/sisters

The Rule of St. Augustine. Retrieved December 18, 2021., from https://www.op.org/wp-admin/admin-ajax.php?juwpfisadmin=false&action=wpfd&task=file.download&wpfd_category_id=860&wpfd_file_id=1sPj9wlxKCROJhtX86 GNEfTUUgLRFhok4&token=&preview=1

INDEX[1]

---

[1] Note: Page numbers followed by 'n' refer to notes.

© The Author(s), under exclusive license to Springer Nature   243
Switzerland AG 2023
R. Hujanen, *Monastic Perspectives on Temporality*,
https://doi.org/10.1007/978-3-031-34808-2

Augustine (*cont.*)
  on interiority, 163
  ladder construtions, 138
  on time, 33, 34, 145
Augustinian, 7, 14, 19, 206

B
Baptism, 115
Basil of Caesarea, 11, 24
Benedictine, 16, 65, 97, 98, 123, 190,
  200, 202
  Rule, 47, 50, 61, 152
  tradition, 53, 54, 64, 120, 190
Bernard of Clairvaux, 5, 11, 25,
  162n123, 179n13
Binns, John, 55, 202
Bonaventure, 26, 129, 139, 164,
  165, 165n130
Brakke, David, 137

C
Carmelite, 10, 15, 17, 23, 26, 27, 47,
  88, 110, 110n109, 121, 126,
  139, 143, 165, 167,
  206, 208–210
  habit, 108n99, 108n100
  tradition, 14, 15, 153, 154, 165
Carthusian, 10, 16, 39, 112
  on ascent, 154
  on contemplation, 155–157
  on death, 196, 198, 200, 205
  on eternity, 192, 197
  journey, 83, 201, 208
  on prayer, 169, 191
  profession, 115, 117, 149
  solitary, 15
  on time, 33, 44, 112
  tradition, 138, 205
  on transformation, 153

Carthusian Statutes, 57, 63, 65, 115,
  149, 190, 207
Cassian, 11, 23, 25, 83, 98, 106, 124,
  136, 136n27, 139, 227, 227n27
Cataphatic, 162
Catholic Church, 13, 19,
  175n4, 178n11
Cenobitic monasticism, 14, 105, 106
Chadwick, Henry, 102
Chain of Mysteries, 140–143, 170, 189
Charity, 72, 124n152, 136, 193,
  193n64, 208, 222
Charterhouse, 15, 153n88, 191, 205
Chastity, 94, 95, 97
Chronos, 27, 143
Cistercians, 16, 25, 124, 190
Clarke, Kevin, 161, 162n121, 192
Climacus, John, 63, 90, 138, 198
Cloud of Unknowing, 4, 18, 26,
  35n18, 139
Colombas, Garcia, OSB, 118, 147
Community, 90, 147
  Carmelite, 206, 207, 210
  Christian, 24, 74
  Church, 116n123
  duties for, 48
  monastic, 7, 39, 51, 52, 64, 71, 80,
    93, 95, 110, 113n118, 128n3,
    174, 199n82, 202, 204–206
  paramonastic penitential, 92
  in pilgrimage, 81n2
  relationship, 113n118
  religious, 6, 7, 65, 151, 199
  role of, 206
  society, 119, 121
Contemplation, 28, 34, 121, 136,
  137, 157, 168, 168n142, 170,
  181, 185–187, 197
  ascent, 18, 138, 139, 160
  definitions of, 6, 155–157,
    156n98, 164